# design
## in context

BLOOMSBURY

A QUARTO BOOK

Copyright © 1987 Quarto Publishing plc

'First published in paperback
in 1991 by Bloomsbury Publishing Ltd'
2 Soho Square
London W1F 5DE

A CIP Catalogue record
for this book is available
from the British Library

ISBN 0-7475-1094-6

This book was designed and produced by
Quarto Publishing plc
The Old Brewery, 6 Blundell Street
London N7 9BH

**SENIOR EDITOR** Helen Owen
**ART EDITOR** Vincent Murphy

**EDITORS** Lydia Darbyshire, Peter Dormer
**DESIGNERS** Michelle Stamp and Alun Jones
**PICTURE RESEARCHER** Anne Marie Ehrlich

**ART DIRECTOR** Moira Clinch
**EDITORIAL DIRECTOR** Carolyn King

Typeset by Text Filmsetters Ltd.
Manufactured in Hong Kong by Regent Publishing Services Ltd
Printed by Lee Fung Asco Printers Ltd, Hong Kong

# design
# in context

# CONTENTS

# INTRODUCTION

**T**he responsibility for the relationship between industry and culture falls, in the modern world, on the shoulders of design. The product is the mediator between manufacture and the consumer, and its design is the container of the message that is mediated.

To see design in this context, rather than simply as the bestower of instant social status and style—which is what the advertisements would like us to believe—we must place it in a much wider framework than the one the media normally present.

Design is a complex concept. It is both a process and the result of that process—the shape, style and meaning of artefacts that have been 'designed'. Many factors influence the process: the ideas of the designer (if one is involved); the technological determinants of the products' manufacture; the socio-economic constraints of the manufacturing process and the consumption of the final product; the cultural context that gave rise to the need for the object in the first place; and the conditions of its manufacture. The political situation in the country manufacturing the object may influence the way it is made and its final appearance.

We could go further. Design is also affected by, and in turn, influences, social ideology and change. Attitudes towards hygiene, the changing role of women, the move from home- to factory-based work—these and other social attitudes and changes have influenced the nature of the mass-produced artefacts with which we surround ourselves. Forces that encourage social cohesion are often felt through designed objects—as are, at times, those that suggest social change.

The designed artefact is on its simplest level, therefore, a form of communication and what it conveys depends on the framework within which it functions.

Since the eighteenth century the dominant framework for design has been the system of mass production and mass consumption, based on the joint forces of industry and commerce. It is that context that these chapters will highlight, demonstrating the way in which design and the designer have been increasingly entrenched within it.

There has, of course, been resistance to this model, and the changing nature of that resistance provides a sub-plot in the story. By turns a number of sub-themes emerge, among them the changing nature of the designer, the vexed question of mass culture and taste, developments in technology, and the influence of design reform.

*Design in Context*, then, has a wide brief. The picture of design that emerges from its pages will be a much-needed counterbalance to the one that strikes us continually from hoardings and Sunday newspaper supplements.

One of its main themes is design's inevitable link with the growth of the capitalist economy. As Adrian Forty has written in his book *Objects of Desire*: 'In capitalist societies, the primary purposes of the manufacture of artefacts, a process of which design is a part, has to be to make a profit for the manufacturer.' This is evident throughout design's evolution, as it is clearly an intrinsic part both of the developing division of labour and of the desire, on the part of manufacturers and entrepreneurs, to capture new markets. Fashion and design have always been inextricably linked in this process, and remain so up to the present day.

Yet design is more than this. In countries eager to communicate a strong national identity, it can become a tool of nationalism. In the hands of manufacturers keen to promote a life-style for women through their domestic appliances, it can be related to feminism. Design, as a means of communication, is capable of conveying as many meanings as we are capable of transmitting.

There is a danger, however, in emphasizing the social, economic, political, and ideological context at the expense of design's own influential role. In the hands of responsible manufacturers, designers, critics, and theorists, design can act as a powerful agent of change. This is the positive side of the story.

This book attempts to strike a balance between these two accounts of design— between the view that design grew out of changes in manufacturing and marketing from the eighteenth century onwards, and the view that it reflects a range of individual designers' interpretations of culture and their own differing visions. The latter story starts with the reform movements of the second half of the nineteenth century and moves through Modernism into the world of post-Modernism. Here design acted as an important touchstone as its values penetrated the mass arena and influenced the lives of many people.

Unlike so many other books on design, which focus exclusively on the objects designed, this study is about both design *and* its context. Design is here taken to include not only the traditional decorative arts (the subject of so many other books in this area) but the products of the new technologies as well. The structure of the book is chronological, as it traces the processes of change and evolution, and it sets out to provide readers with the information which will enable them to evaluate for themselves the importance of design in the contemporary world.

# PART ONE

# 1750
# 1914

The knobbliness of the 1765 Chelsea vase and the hand-made 1908 model T Ford look fussy to modern eyes. Early nineteenth-century American slaughterhouses provided the model for Ford's later assembly-line production methods. His vehicle was a response to a classless society. The pot pourri vase, like the Biedermeier furniture, 1820-40 **(above)**, was geared to a middle-class market.

In the period between 1750 and the outbreak of the First World War the foundations were laid on which modern industrial design was subsequently built. Indeed, the structure of modern industry was created and society reorganized around it. Huge transformations took place: factories were developed, and work moved away from the home. In turn, this created new roles for men and women and the modern concept of the nuclear family. Above all, mass consumption became a reality, making design a feature of everyday life.

This section focuses on the elements that made up the framework within which the modern concept of design was formulated. It begins with the change in the nature of British society and commercial life in the eighteenth century, and proceeds to look closely at the way in which three pioneering commercial men—Thomas Chippendale, Josiah Wedgwood and Matthew Boulton, all of them involved in the production of consumer goods in Britain in the eighteenth century—organized their systems of production and sales.

It then considers the role played by new technology in shaping modern industry. Its impact in Britain on traditional products, particularly textiles, is contrasted with its much more radical role in the USA, where new machinery transformed the production of goods such as textiles and furniture and made possible the manufacture of new products, from sewing-machines to automobiles. The final section of Chapter 2 focuses on the relationship between technology and design in this context and examines whether technology or the pressure of the market made the greater demand on the design of goods in the mid-nineteenth century.

The third chapter looks at some of the ideological influences on design in this period, focusing on the ideas of individuals concerned to improve design standards in Britain in the nineteenth century, in the face of what they saw as the malevolent force of commerce.

It was within this area that early thoughts about the ideal aesthetic for goods manufactured in the modern world were formulated. This chapter also examines the ideas of the British theorists—Augustus Pugin, John Ruskin, William Morris and the so-called 'Aesthetes'—before turning to the continental arena at the turn of the century, where proto-Modernism reached its apogee in the words and work of designers such as Henri Van de Velde and Josef Hoffmann. These developments are placed in the context of art nouveau, the fashionable design style of the turn of the century. By the end of the section most of the important formative influences upon modern design have been discussed and the scene set for a more detailed examination of its essential components—the subject of the second section.

Frank Lloyd Wright's oak furniture, 1902-4, dances to geometry and exaggerates its own modernity, whereas the glass by botanist-designer Dr Christopher Dresser (1824-1904) was tempered with nature.

12

# CHAPTER ONE

# DESIGN & COMMERCE IN THE EIGHTEENTH CENTURY

> **"THE EARLY BEGINNINGS OF THE INDUSTRIAL REVOLUTION AROSE FROM AN AFFLUENT SOCIETY WANTING MORE GOODS THAN THE LABOUR FORCES, AS THEN ORGANISED, COULD PRODUCE. AFTER ALL, THE NEW INDUSTRIAL METHODS BEGAN IN THE CONSUMER INDUSTRIES – TEXTILES, POTTERY, THE MANUFACTURE OF BUTTONS, BUCKLES AND PINS OF BOULTON AND WATT"**
>
> N. MCKENDRICK, J. BREWER AND J.H. PLUMB, THE BIRTH OF A CONSUMER SOCIETY (1982)

A history of design could begin with the first pot to store grain that was made on the river banks of Mesopotamia and go on to discuss the changing functions, styles and significance of the countless artefacts that have emerged since that time. However, if we accept that the main influences on the modern concept of design are the forces of mass production and mass consumption, the history of modern design need reach back only to the period during which these two phenomena began to have a significant impact on everyday life—the eighteenth century.

This account does just that, taking as its starting point commercialization in Britain in the eighteenth century. It was in this context that design began to accrue the significance that it bears today; it became a factor within the production, marketing and consumption of artefacts. As such it became a vehicle for aesthetic and social communication, and was defined as a *sine qua non* for the capitalist economic system. As the social historian Neil McKendrick has explained in *The Birth of a Consumer Society: The Commercialization of Eighteenth Century England*: 'Adjustments to design, like adjustments to price, were part of the successful business man's constant effort to trim his sails to meet the slightest variations in the winds of change.'

In the area of countless consumer goods—from Wedgwood ceramics to Chippendale furniture to clothing—novelty in design became a major means of selling.

The force behind those winds of change was fashion, a concept which in eighteenth-century England took on a new meaning across the whole spectrum of society. Again, McKendrick explains: 'Novelty, new fangledness, must be matters of excitement for an aggressive commercial and capitalist world: ever increasing profit is not made in a world of traditional crafts and stable fashions.'

These last two concepts—'traditional crafts' and 'stable fashions'—moved into a realm of their own, outside the dictates of fashion and taste.

Where the latter concepts were concerned, however, design became all important. The designer became, in this context, an important agent of change. While eighteenth-century designers essentially sustained the traditional role that had been defined for them several centuries earlier—ie, as the artists who created forms and surface patterns which were translated into and onto objects—within the context of changing production methods this role became increasingly isolated from the 'making' process, and, within the context of changing patterns of consumption, increasingly crucial as the source of 'artistic input'. Thus while the designer's function was not, in itself, radically redefined, its definition was hardened and its significance modified dramatically by the new context in which it found itself.

Architects led the way as designers in the eighteenth-century, creating goods which had previously been the preserve of the craftsman. Not only did they determine the appearance of a wide spectrum of goods, they also designed artefacts for social groups which had not previously been the customers of 'design'. Thus while the design process itself remained constant, its parameters, within manufacture, became clearer and, in social terms, its application more widespread.

As copying, or modifying, exisiting designs also became more common, many craftsmen joined the ranks of designers in the effort to provide increasing numbers of people with fashionable objects.

Robert Adam's neo-Classicism **(opposite)** spread to France and America. Styles spread more easily as communications improved.

# Expansion of the market

14

The eighteenth century, or at least the second half of it, was when the so-called Industrial Revolution took place in England. The roots of this phenomenon—most apparent in the new organization and manufacturing methods in the textile, metal and pottery industries—lay in the growing affluence of the emerging British middle classes and their increasing demand for new goods.

A sense of general affluence had, however, already been apparent by the closing years of the seventeenth century, as studies such as Margaret Spufford's *The Great Reclothing of Rural England* have indicated. In her book, which focuses on the role of the pedlar in the late seventeenth and early eighteenth centuries, Miss Spufford shows how even the humblest sectors of British society were able to afford small luxuries such as lace, ribbons, threads and buttons, and points to rising standards of general domestic comfort in, for instance, the consumption of fabrics used for curtains, napkins and tablecloths. Sheets and pillows (previously considered fit only for women giving birth) were replacing the straw and blankets used in the past by large sections of society. Textiles constituted between 10 and 15 per cent of expenditure on household goods at that time—a good measure of the level of domestic comfort.

The reasons for this increased general affluence were straightforward. The years up to the 1650s saw a population rise, and from that time onwards the same wages bought more goods. More items could be bought as imported goods such as tobacco and sugar and Indian textiles became available. There were growing signs therefore of what Miss Spufford calls 'a humble consumer society' in late seventeenth-century England.

England's transformation into a formidable power in Europe at the end of the seventeenth century (in spite of the fact that its population was only a third that of France) was based on such factors as its improved military and naval power, the development of its banking and credit systems and the progress made in agricultural methods. By the beginning of the eighteenth century England had achieved a degree of political stability; founded colonies and established overseas trade; and accrued capital from the profits of its wool trade.

## FROM AGRICULTURE TO INDUSTRY

With a growing demand for goods in the home market, England was ready for the transition from an agricultural to an industrial country in which the population changed

### TIMES PAST
Do these eighteenth-century paintings stimulate a sense of loss in us? Joseph Wright's heroic **The Iron Forge** radiates a belief in the goodness of technology. William William's painting of **Coalbrookdale** is poignantly romantic, while Stubbs' man occupies a landscape that has gone forever.

### COLLECTORS AND ECLECTICS

The eighteenth century practised various styles from baroque **(above)** to the classical **(left)**. Culture became a commodity as Johann Zoffany captures in his painting **Charles Towneley in his Gallery**. Young gentlemen did European tours and Venetian style was influential **(opposite above)**. Fashion-conscious amateurs like Sir John Vanbrugh created eclectic palaces such as Blenheim **(below right)** for the ruling class. Portentous Derby ware **(right)** fed the ambitions of bankers and traders.

from a rural one to an urbanized workforce. As manufacture became less reliant on a water supply and on home-based craft work, production began to be carried out in factories. As London became the centre of commerce, bankers, merchants and other people associated with the commercial world settled in the capital city.

Where culture was concerned, however, France was, in the early eighteenth century, still the home of taste. As J. Kenworthy-Browne explains in his book on the furniture-maker Thomas Chippendale: 'In sophistication of culture and intellect, France remained undeniably superior.' This was true for the first half of the century at least, with the dominance of the rococo style in many goods. Towards the end of the century Italy was also a source of inspiration when, as a result of the Grand Tour, neo-Classicism became the style of the day. The succession of fashionable styles in the eighteenth century—from baroque, to rococo, to chinoiserie, to Gothic, to neo-Classical—indicated the increasing need for novelty in the expanding market.

The aristocracy set the pace. Power in Britain from the early century onwards lay in its hands. It provided a model of taste which filtered through to the rest of the population. Architecture was the 'queen of the arts' and the architectural projects commissioned by the aristocracy set the style for many other applied arts. Furniture, for instance, followed the lead of architecture most of the time and the neo-Classical movement of the late eighteenth century was dominated by its architectural manifestations. In addition, it was the architects themselves, for the most part, who provided many of the designs that inspired the work of countless craftsmen in this period.

Taste in the eighteenth century was disseminated by 'upward emulation'. Whatever the aristocracy preferred was quickly copied by the middle classes—in particular by the new breed of bankers and merchants who were eager to express their new-found wealth through the consumption of the 'correct' goods. The humbler ranks of society followed their example. Manufacturers, keen to meet the needs of the new, expanded market, were careful to make sure that their goods met with aristocratic and fashionable approval before they aimed their goods at a wider section of society. Josiah Wedgwood was particularly aware of the need for such circumspection and his policy of making sure that his goods had an aristocratic seal of approval before he marketed them at an essentially middle-class audience—particularly in his Queen's ware range—was emulated by many.

The century saw the rise of marketing and advertising and a compression of the social spectrum, which meant that it became possible to speak about an increasingly homogeneous 'mass market', which it was therefore easier to supply with uniformly designed products.

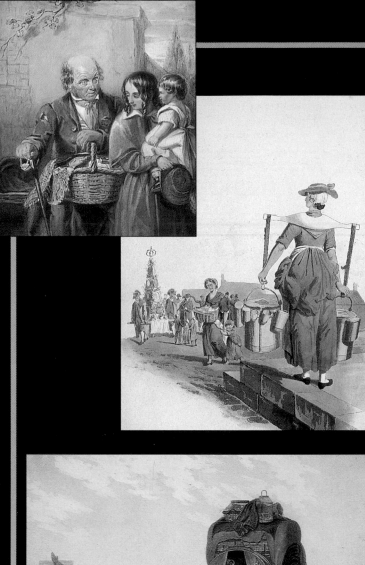

### NEW UNCERTAINTIES
For decades the isolation of rural communities was interrupted only by pedlars, but canals, railways and roads destroyed autonomy. Despite the new orthodoxy of factory production some crafts, like blacksmithing, continued on a local basis. **Blacksmith's Forge** by W.D. Sadler **(above)**; **The Pedlar** by A. Chisholm **(top left)**; **The Milkmaid** by W. Miller **(centre)**; and **Stage Wagon** (on a macadamized road) by J.J. Agasser.

# The division of labour

If the importance of 'fashion' and 'taste' was a vital factor in the evolution of modern design for an ever-widening sector of British society in the eighteenth century, the other side of the coin was the concept of the division of labour in the manufacture of goods. This rapidly developed into an intrinsic characteristic of the mass production of objects for the expanding market. Before the advent of modern industry and the transport system—roads, canals and rail—the production of most goods had occurred on a local basis with a community creating most of the products it needed for its own survival. In an eighteenth-century village, for instance, the population produced its own food and clothing in its own homes. The wheelwrights and blacksmiths produced wooden and iron implements and vessels to forms which had evolved through the centuries from technical and economic constraints alone. The potter made all the pottery that was needed; and the pedlar would bring such fancy goods as scissors, cheap jewellery and handkerchiefs, which were made elsewhere and which were more susceptible to fashion.

This craft activity was the norm until factory production and improved transport transformed it. It was sustained by the guild system, which had begun as associations of producers, representing the masters, journeymen and apprentices of the various crafts. The system remained strong in some trades throughout the century. The building trades, for instance—which included the work of the bricklayer, mason, carpenter, joiner and glazier, and of the decorative men, the plasterer, wood-carver and locksmith—retained their dependence on it during the building boom. All these skilled and semi-skilled tasks associated with building remained craft-based and, as a result, structured in the traditional way with, for example, an apprentice paying a premium to his master for board, lodging and teaching. In other areas, however, the role of the guild system diminished and there were clashes between guilds and the new structure of commerce. Increasingly, in many instances, the commercial capitalists weakened the power of the guilds and they lost their dominance. Though such bodies as the London Livery Companies were still being formed, the tight rules established by the guild system were abolished. (This did not happen in France, incidentally, where much stricter trade regulations prevented that country from experiencing the industrial and commercial changes that occurred in England.)

Within guild-controlled trades work remained craft-based and individuals continued to perform 'skilled' tasks, but in trades freed from guild restrictions specialization developed and the principle of the 'division of labour' soon became widespread. While the guilds were adapted to the needs of local commerce, the new commercial structure encouraged the development of specialized tasks. With the advent of the factory system this new development was consolidated and when, at the end of the century and the early years of the next century, mechanization came to a number of industries, many skilled jobs were replaced by a greater number of semi- and unskilled tasks. This applied to the design process as well and the work of the eighteenth-century designer was augmented, in the mechanized industries, by other more specialized activities, such as, in the potteries, mould-making and, in calico-printing, 'putting-on'. Sometimes, however, in products aimed at the lower end of the market, technological necessity was as much a determinant of the appearance of the final product as any preconceived design.

Seventeenth-century craft skills: a carved pear-wood mould for stamping cakes and a border of Argentelle needle lace.

# Eighteenth-century taste

The rule of aristocratic taste and the dominance of architecture in the eighteenth century meant, however, that there was still a place for the traditional crafts such as embroidery and handweaving, partly in order to meet the needs of the wealthy and their taste for the 'artistic', which implied exclusiveness rather than mass reproduction. The top end of the market was supplied, therefore, with buildings and artefacts which were 'made' by skilled individuals and which had strong stylistic affiliations with contemporary fashions in the fine arts. This mode of design and manufacture simply perpetuated the traditional role for the designer as the artistic conceptualizer. Often, however, in the case of furniture and the other applied arts, design and manufacture were not utterly distinct processes. While the year 1700 represented the culmination of the baroque style in Europe, this had little effect on British country houses of the eighteenth century, for which the more Classical style was preferred. This derived from the writings of Palladio who, where rules of taste were concerned, was taken as an authority. Ernst Gombrich explains in his book *The Story of Art*: 'The whole temper of the country was opposed to the flights of fancy of baroque designs and to an art that aimed at impressing and overwhelming the emotions.'

In line with the emphasis on 'reason' which dominated the cultural consciousness of the century, the architectural designs of men like Lord Burlington and William Kent conformed to the Classical ideal, as did the formal gardens that framed their houses. Chiswick House (c 1725), a Palladian villa designed by Lord Burlington and decorated by Kent, bears witness to their preoccupations. Taste, it was firmly believed, could be defined by a set of rules and therefore taught.

While the architecture of the early century was dominated by one 'correct' style, the later century saw, as in many other decorative arts, a move from 'style' to 'styles', and Palladian buildings were joined by products of a Gothic Revival and examples of 'Chinese' buildings as well as a reworking of the 'Greek Revival' at the end of the century, best demonstrated by the architecture of spa towns such as Cheltenham and Bath.

Eventually eighteenth-century educated taste favoured order not baroque fancy. The Royal Crescent, Bath.

# Thomas Chippendale and the eighteenth-century furniture trade

While Georgian architecture, built for the aristocracy and the new middle classes, tended towards the Classical style, furniture created for the same market in the eighteenth century was more eclectic. Like the building trades, furniture-making remained a traditional craft, but it neither continued to be local industry nor became completely commercialized. The freedom from guild restrictions in furniture-making in England in this period meant that free enterprise quickly came into operation. As a result, furniture-making was dramatically reorganized as a trade and its distribution system re-defined. The example of furniture emphasizes two of the eighteenth century's major characteristics: the increasingly important role played by entrepreneurs in reorganizing production and sales; and the significance of London as a commercial centre. Pioneers like Wedgwood, Chippendale and Boulton established bases in London, from which they began actively to market their products. They targeted their furniture and ceramics specifically towards the newly affluent middle classes, rather than working to private commissions from the aristocracy, as had been previous practice.

By 1700 the cabinet-maker had become a more important individual in the furniture hierarchy than the joiner, and chair-making had become a specialized trade. Carving had also become important and, in line with the other industries in that century, growing specialization gave birth to a host of other separate skills within the furniture trade, among them glassmakers and grinders (for mirrors), metalworkers and upholsterers. The growing market for fashionable furniture included the aristocracy, with its newly built country houses, and the merchants and bankers who, with their newly acquired wealth, emulated the aristocracy in wishing to furnish their houses tastefully. This expansion of demand caused furniture makers to reorganize their manufacture and teams of specialist craftsman emerged—often combining the functions, for example, of cabinet-making, chair-making and upholstery—who could take on the complete interior decoration of a country house.

The pioneering firm of Thomas Chippendale combined a number of specialized tasks and ran a decorating service in the second half of the century. Chippendale, son of a joiner, set up his business by opening a London showroom in 1753. In 1754 he published his pattern book, *The Gentleman and Cabinet-Maker's Director*, which served as an advertisement for his firm's services. The book was filled with illustrations of furniture in a range of styles from Classical to rococo to chinoiserie and

Gothic, demonstrating the firm's versatility and skills to a potential clientele. It also served as a source of inspiration for countless other

Ornament signifies wealth. Thomas Chippendale sold decorous ostentation and his pioneering firm offered the new merchant classes (ambitious but unsure of their aesthetic judgement) a complete decorative service, ranging from chairs to wallpaper.

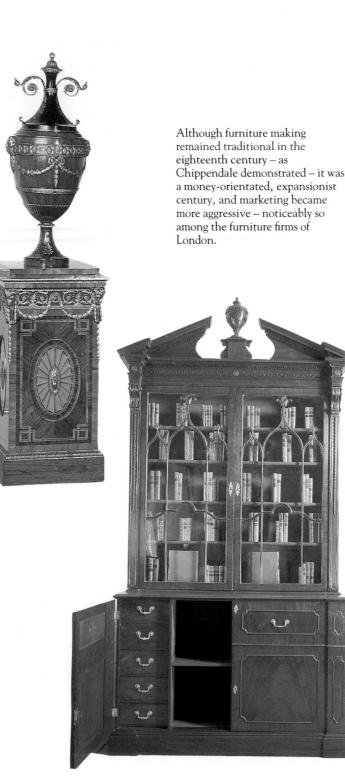

Although furniture making remained traditional in the eighteenth century – as Chippendale demonstrated – it was a money-orientated, expansionist century, and marketing became more aggressive – noticeably so among the furniture firms of London.

furniture craftsmen. Many of the subscribers to the *Director* were members of the aristocracy and Chippendale is known to have provided a number of country houses, including Harewood House (1770-5), with a complete decorating service down to the paper-hanging and curtaining.

Although the Palladian movement was in full swing when Chippendale first entered into business, he quickly abandoned it in favour of the much more decorated, expressive style known as rococo, which originated in France. St Martin's Lane became a centre for this anti-Palladian movement in the mid-century, as the furniture-makers William Vile and John Cobb, Chippendale's neighbours, also worked in the French style. It was a style with no architectural equivalent in England and remained the preserve of the decorative arts, in particular furniture and porcelain. It was especially well suited to the latter. From 1715 onwards, with the death of Louis XIV, it became widespread in France and the British porcelain manufacturers, among them Chelsea, Derby, Bow and Worcester, embraced it in the 1740s. With the passing of the fashion for rococo at the end of the century, and the enthusiasm for all things neo-Classical, the porcelain movement went into sharp decline.

Another of Chippendale's well-known styles was the one he borrowed from the Chinese which became known as 'chinoiserie', a movement inspired by the newly opened up trade with the Orient. It actually had little similarity to anything Chinese but became nonetheless a highly fashionable furniture style for ladies' boudoirs in the 1750s and 1760s.

On the heels of rococo, chinoiserie and a 'Gothic' style also favoured by Chippendale for a short period, came the neo-Classical style, which was made so popular by the Adam brothers. Overnight rococo vanished. Inspired by the interest in the excavations of Herculaneum and Pompeii, which unearthed a number of classical objects in the late 1730s, household decoration in England became dominated from the 1760s by the neo-Classical style. It was an elegant idiom characterized by careful proportions and visual restraint, and for all the smaller bankers and merchants who had developed ambitions to live like nobility it quickly came to represent 'good taste'.

Fashionable furniture of the eighteenth century was dominated by the use of mahogany. It replaced the traditional oak furniture made for centuries by country joiners and turners. Inevitably this new exotic material, imported from the Colonies to provide an alternative to the depleted stocks of home-grown oak (used up mostly by the ship-building industry), had an influence on design. Much richer in colour than its predecessor it also had a much closer grain. This made it easier to reproduce more flowing, sculpted forms, and eighteenth-century mahogany furniture quickly developed a highly refined aesthetic as a result. Mahogany also satisfied the growing need for novelty and exoticism expressed by the new clientele, a large proportion of whom travelled widely and saw it in use in its countries of origin.

The most significant aspect of fashionable furniture-making in the eighteenth century was the separation of design from making. Designing in this context meant drawing and presenting ideas in pattern books, a practice undertaken not only by Chippendale but also by Hepplewhite and Sheraton — the other major names in eighteenth-century furniture. The increasing specialization of labour, which reinforced the idea of planning before manufacture, brought engravers, designers and draughtsmen on to the staff of furniture workshops. Furniture firms or workshops were established that provided a total decoration service. An emphasis was placed upon increasingly aggressive marketing on a national scale rather than simply meeting the needs of the immediate community. Most of these workshops operated along with showrooms in fashionable areas of London, whether St Martins Lane or Soho, like the workshop of Seddon, or Berkeley Square, like that of William and John Linnell. Seddon's workshop was said to consist of about four hundred apprentices who included mirror workers, carpet fitters and locksmiths.

The manufacture of this kind of fashionable furniture remained traditional, however, in the sense that it continued to meet the requirements of a wealthy clientele and it operated primarily on the basis of commissioned work.

**TRADE WINDS**
Trade with the East encouraged Europeans to adopt the Oriental style (hence a pagoda in St James's Park). The rapidly industrializing pottery industry caught on fast to new fashions.

# Josiah Wedgwood and the pottery industry

The same cannot, however, be said of the pottery industry in the eighteenth century, which was reorganized in a much more radical way than furniture-making. The revolution affected both its commercial structure and its output, which had expanded by the second half of the century. The increase in production was a response to expanding demand, this time a result of more and more people participating in the social custom of tea (and coffee) drinking. By the end of the century these beverages had replaced beer and milk as working-class drinks. Another social change which helped swell the demand for more pottery was the increasing number of hot cooked meals consumed by the English population.

The man to respond most quickly to this changing picture was Josiah Wedgwood, born 1730, a potter's son from Staffordshire. Bevis Hillier has explained how, 'during the period 1760-1830, the Potteries changed from a haphazard collection of family businesses, conducted in rustic potworks, to an industry centralized in five towns'.

Wedgwood's role was central to that transition. It was he who saw the possibility of an industry, based in the Midlands, capable of supplying all the needs of the home market as well as that of the rest of the world.

From the beginnings of the century the area of Staffordshire that embraced the towns of Burslem, Tunstall, Hanley, Stoke, Fenton and Longton had the two natural advantages: the local availability of coal and clay. The peasant potters who had settled there in the seventeenth century had used primitive equipment—an oven, a few open sheds and an open tank for mixing the clay. Their ware was sold to travelling packmen, who transported it on horseback. This early industry was transformed in the eighteenth century by a series of technological improvements to the ware itself and in the methods of manufacture and distribution of both earthenware and china. The six towns took a lead in the production of the ware in the second half of the century, with the help of Josiah Wedgwood.

The first major change in manufacture was the transition from hand-making on the potter's wheel to, in 1730, the use of moulds made of porous clay from alabaster blocks. In turn, in about 1750, the clay was replaced by plaster of Paris, a development that gave rise to new classes of pottery workers—mould carvers, mould designers and the 'flat and hollow ware pressers' who forced the clay into the moulds. Smaller objects, such as handles, were shaped by children. Increased demand meant that clay from Devon and Cornwall was used, and the idea of the factory arose to replace the master potter with his small team of men and boys.

Among Wedgwood's chief contributions to the new industry was his initiation of a campaign for good roads and canals to help the easy distribution of the pottery. As a direct result of his pioneering efforts two turnpike roads were built and in 1777 the Potteries were linked with Liverpool and Hull by the Trent and Mersey Canal.

Wedgwood's main contribution to pottery itself, however, lay in his improvements in the body glazes, colours and forms of the pieces. Among his innovations were the development of a durable lead-glaze, resulting in cream-coloured utility pieces which became known as Queen's ware because of their popularity with British royalty; his black basalt ware; his green glazed ware; and his much-loved and more expensive jasper ware, in which he imitated models from Greece or Rome, pressing white ornaments or figures on a coloured ground. His reproduction of the Portland vase, in the fashionable neo-Classical style which he espoused so enthusiastically in the 1770s, was perhaps the best known example of his work in this area.

Wedgwood was not alone, however, in his grasp of new pottery manufacturing techniques at this time. Enamelling, for instance, previously a separate activity undertaken elsewhere, became a regular Staffordshire trade by 1750, and in 1755 Saddler and Green of Liverpool invented a method of printing the outlines of a design on ware that was already glazed, leaving only the colours to be filled in by hand. Another step forward was achieved by Turner of Worcester who, in 1780, found a more satisfactory process of printing by which a coloured pattern was printed on the biscuit ware before it was dipped into the glaze. 'Blue printing' was especially successful and the same Turner designed the famous willow pattern, a ubiquitous decoration by the end of the century. This printed ware became so cheap and popular, in fact, that it rapidly superseded all other forms of 'useful' earthenware. The potters most closely associated with these developments were the Spodes, who played an important role in the Staffordshire potteries in this period.

## WEDGWOOD: THE CREATOR OF POPULAR TASTE

While Wedgwood undoubtedly pioneered a number of improvements in the materials, techniques and forms of pottery, his lasting contribution to the manufacture of mass-produced goods was the way in which he commercialized his industry and

## BUILDING ON CLAY

Josiah Wedgwood **(below left)** transformed the pottery industry. As far as possible hand throwing gave way to production in moulds. Wedgwood, who wanted to reach big markets, campaigned for new canals and roads to improve the distribution system. As James Pollard's engraving **(below)** shows, the new post houses were lively affairs.

26

Wedgwood flattered *nouveau riche* conceit with reproduction Roman imagery as well as domestic grandeur, as is shown in this group of stoneware items **(right)**. Later, other potteries caught the public imagination with lyrical ornamentation such as the ubiquitous mid-nineteenth century Willow Pattern.

established sophisticated marketing techniques for selling 'taste' to the expanding middle-class market of the day. This aspect of Wedgwood's work has been excellently documented by the historian Neil McKendrick in his essay *Josiah Wedgwood and the Commercialization of the Potteries.*

Josiah Wedgwood set up in business as an independent master potter in 1759 but expanded rapidly, opening larger premises three years later. In 1773 he moved all his manufactory to a new factory, which in true neo-Classical fashion he named Etruria. The key to his success lay, as McKendrick explains, in his commercial skills. Central to Wedgwood's marketing policy lay the desire to exploit the late eighteenth-century's obsession with all things fashionable. Far from wanting to produce hundreds of designs as cheaply as possible for the new markets, Wedgwood remained committed to the idea of selling 'good quality' pottery to taste-conscious customers. This sector of the market was expanding rapidly and was prepared to spend more money than ever before in pursuit of taste and fashion. As McKendrick explains: 'By 1750 all Europe was already in the grip of a china fever. Royalty led the way. Augustus, King of Poland and Elector of Saxony, established Meissen in 1710; Louis XV of France sponsored the manufacture of china at Vincennes in 1747 and later in 1756 at Sèvres; the King of Naples set up a factory at Capo di Monte and later at Buen Retiro near Madrid.'

Wedgwood cleverly exploited the growing demand by capturing the world of fashion. This was achieved by acquiring royal patronage, thereby giving his goods social cachet. They were shown to the public at both his London and Staffordshire showrooms and, stylistically, slavishly followed the fashions of the day. His black teapots, for instance, were

produced to show off to better advantage the feminine vogue for bleached white hands, and he was quick to move away from the rococo and chinoiserie styles and adopt the neo-Classical idiom just as it became the style of the day, and collecting classical objects became all the rage.

### THE USE OF FINE ARTISTS

Wedgwood ensured that his wares would conform to the most artistic, fashionable tastes of the day by acting as a patron for fine artists—among them John Flaxman, Joseph Wright of Derby and George Stubbs.

Flaxman was a successful sculptor of the day in the neo-Classical style and maintained a strong relationship with Wedgwood. In 1775 he modelled some tablets for him and in 1788 he visited Italy, at Wedgwood's expense, where he made a study of classical sculpture and ceramics. Bevis Hillier has explained how Flaxman and Wedgwood worked closely together, the latter suggesting the kind of work he wanted, the former then submitting a drawing and preparing a wax model and sometimes a plaster mould (although this was usually left to the workmen at Etruria). A block mould, in biscuit ware, was made from the plaster mould and, after some modelling was done on it, this was used to make the final mould. Flaxman was responsible for the design of a number of Wedgwood plaques, in jasper ware, which depicted scenes from classical life.

Wedgwood's relationships with Joseph Wright and George Stubbs were rather different from the one with Flaxman. Both men were painters and Wedgwood admired their work and sought ways of associating himself with them as a means of raising the status of his products. He commissioned Wright to paint 'The Corinthian Maid' in 1782-4, and in 1780 Stubbs visited Etruria and painted a portrait of Josiah and Mrs

Wedgwood sitting on a bench in their park. Both painters undertook other commissions for Wedgwood as well and provided designs and models for his pottery. The task he set himself of both widening his market and retaining the 'social cachet' associated with his ware was a difficult one, but he fulfilled it nonetheless by aiming to reach a national market. This was achieved through advertising and by using travelling salesmen. He also succeeded in capturing markets in other countries, among them France, Poland, Spain, Denmark and Italy.

Wedgwood had to evolve different marketing techniques to reach different nations and the different classes at home, and he set about this in a highly sophisticated way, producing different styles for different markets. To America, for instance, he shipped mainly cheap goods, while wares destined for Turkey were much more exotic. McKendrick claims, in fact, that 'it was by such methods that a local craft became a national industry and served an international market'. He describes Wedgwood's strategies as including 'inertia-selling campaigns, product differentiation, market segmentation, detailed market research, and embryonic self-service schemes', thereby establishing him as a pioneer of modern marketing techniques.

**27**

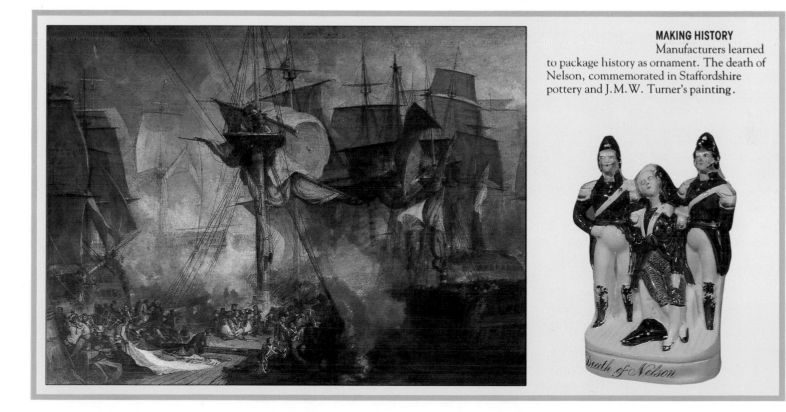

**MAKING HISTORY**
Manufacturers learned to package history as ornament. The death of Nelson, commemorated in Staffordshire pottery and J.M.W. Turner's painting.

These commercial methods helped make design a central element, not simply of production but of marketing itself. For Wedgwood, design became the conscious means by which different items were directed at different markets through the agency of 'taste-values' communicated. He was very clear about the way in which he defined the 'artistic' function of his pottery. It was, in essence, a means of establishing the social role for his wares, a policy that was essential to the financial success of his enterprise.

Another way in which Wedgwood influenced the evolution of design was by encouraging new systems of production. By reinforcing the notion of the division of labour he turned the specialized activity of 'designing' into an important and self-contained element in the production process.

The pottery industry was not, however, mechanized in this early period, as Maxine Berg explains in her book *The Age of Manufacture (1700-1820)*: 'In the cutlery trades, metal working and the potteries, the factory was only a building where skilled artisans carried on their separate crafts.' There were developments in the division of labour and in the use of a new power source, however. Steam replaced water power for the flint and glaze mills, for instance. Josiah Wedgwood installed a steam engine in Etruria in 1784. As a result the system of work there was completely transformed and the tasks of journeymen potters categorized, being undertaken by throwers, turners, oven men, flat pressers, hollow-ware pressers and dippers—to mention only a few.

In 1768 about six thousand people were employed in the potteries at Burslem. Subsidiary trades also developed in the district, such as those of the crate-makers, colour-makers and lathe-makers. When it was not in the hands of the fine artists he brought in, design was undertaken by Wedgwood himself, but the interpretation of his designs involved many different processes and contributions. Although it became easy to isolate design as a conceptual, visualizing process within manufacture, as a result of his initiatives, its interpretation was no longer the task of a single man. It inevitably involved numerous modifications and adaptations before manufacture and, to these ends, a number of individuals were employed to perform different tasks. We still live with the heritage of this development.

Wedgwood obtained his designs from a number of different sources. While those aimed at the top end of the market were often the results of commissions to fine artists of the day, others were ideas of his own. Either they were taken directly or in modified form from pattern books or, more frequently, from actual antiques such as the Portland vase. The designs were worked on by draughtsmen employed by Wedgwood at Etruria and then they were developed further by modellers. All the workmen had fairly low status and were not credited for their design input.

Wedgwood's chemists and technologists were, however, also important in determining the appearance of his more lowly ware, which made greater use of glazes for their visual effect than of 'design' in the traditional sense. All the design work undertaken at the Wedgwood factory resulted from his careful observation of market needs and of fashionable styles, although it is also true to say that he was as much in the business of creating popular taste as of fulfilling it.

A portrait of Josiah Wedgwood by George Stubbs R.A., created in paint on a ceramic plaque.

# Matthew Boulton: steam power and the metal 'toy' industry

The role of new technology was central to the transformation of British industry in the second half of the eighteenth century. The use of steam power, for instance, was the first step in mechanization. A central figure in developing the steam engine and adapting its function to manufacturing industry was Matthew Boulton. He was also the man responsible for commercializing the metal 'toy' industry in England.

The development of the iron industry in the eighteenth century was spurred on by England's military requirements and by the release from its dependence on charcoal. Shipbuilding was expanding and with it the manufacture of iron on a large scale. Because such a large quantity of fuel was needed to make iron, the search for cheap fuel was felt earlier in that industry than elsewhere. However, the use of mineral fuel in the blast furnace was not mastered until the first decade of the eighteenth century and that was by Abraham Darby of Coalbrookdale. The famous iron bridge built by his grandson (also named Abraham Darby) in 1779 stands as a testimony to the new technology. Constructed along the lines of a timber bridge—the material which iron most commonly replaced—the bridge was one of the first uses of new material in an engineered structure anywhere in the world.

Another aspect of the metal industry at this time was that of hardware and this also expanded, as a result of growing consumer demand. By the late seventeenth century the Birmingham-based button, buckle and 'toy' trades were already expanding as more people participated in the consumption of luxury and fashion items. Until 1786, when shoelaces were introduced, the shoe-buckle was a highly fashionable object and many stylistic variations were available to meet the needs of the new fashion-conscious markets. The designs were copies of aristocratic examples, executed by the manufacturer or his draughtsman.

## THE TOY MAKERS

The Birmingham manufacturers had decided that they were best fitted for concentrating on highly finished metal articles and the so-called 'toy' industry grew up, popularizing trinkets from a variety of design sources for the new market. A contemporary definition explained the meaning of that somewhat misleading term by describing 'the gold and silver toy makers who made Trinkets, Seals, Tweezers and Tooth Pick cases, Smelling Bottles, Snuff Boxes and Filligree work such as Toilets, Tea Chests, Inkstands etc etc.

The Tortoiseshell Toy maker makes a beautiful variety of the above and other articles; as does also the Steel: who make Cork Screws, Buckles, Draw and other Boxes; Snuffers, Watch Chains, Stay Hooks, Sugar Knippers and almost all these are likewise made in various metals'.

Like Wedgwood, Boulton (b 1728) was born into his business and set out to make superior goods at a time when other manufacturers were meeting the demands of an expanding market by simply lowering the quality of their wares. Also like Wedgwood, Boulton sought to integrate his business vertically by combining manufacturing and merchandising under the same roof. The main way open to Boulton of expanding his output (as it was to Wedgwood) was to reorganize the structure of manufacturing. To this end, he extended the principle of the sub-division of labour that already existed in the Birmingham trade. Boulton needed an ample space, supplied with water power, where he could bring together men from various hardware and 'toy' trades, and warehouse and merchandising facilities.

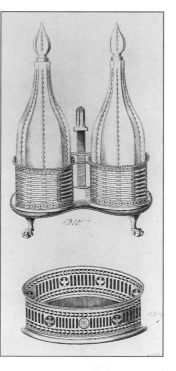

A design for a cruet set by Matthew Boulton. Boulton (1728-1809) was a pioneer British industrialist, a collaborator with James Watt on steam engines and a Fellow of the Royal Society.

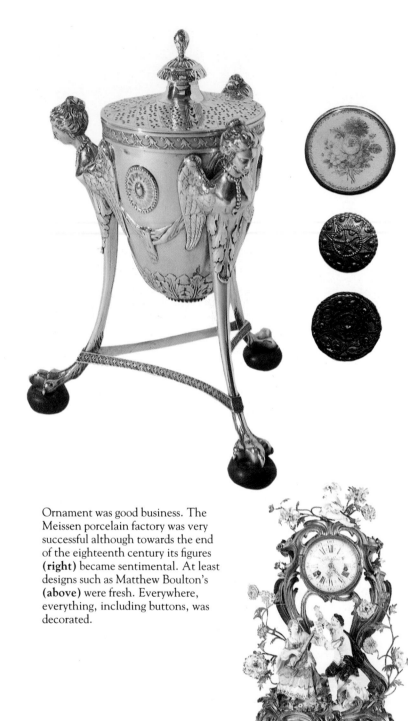

Ornament was good business. The Meissen porcelain factory was very successful although towards the end of the eighteenth century its figures (right) became sentimental. At least designs such as Matthew Boulton's (above) were fresh. Everywhere, everything, including buttons, was decorated.

In 1762 Boulton went into partnership with John Fothergill and together they opened the Soho factory in Birmingham, where production quickly expanded. Among their many products was jewellery made of highly burnished, faceted steel which remained highly popular fashion items until the end of the century. Designs were copied from pattern books, but modified according to the dictates of the manufacturing process. Wedgwood mounted cameos on cut-steel frames made by Boulton, thereby conforming to the neo-Classical taste of the day. Another of Boulton and Fothergill's new ventures, buttons, were items for which the fashion-conscious often paid vast sums. By 1765 the Soho factory employed six hundred people and was still expanding. Sheffield plate was among the new areas into which they soon ventured and this led to the manufacture of a range of silver-plated products, from candle-sticks to coffee-pots.

The ware for which Boulton was best known, however, was his ormolu, brass of high purity with a high content of zinc, a material which has first appeared in France in the reign of Louis XIV. Always ready to experiment with new products for the fashionable market, Boulton moved into the production of ormolu cast in ornamental forms such as candelabra, clocks and other decorative items. Once again the source for many of the designs lay in pattern books. Sometimes, however, original pieces of Classical art were used as stimuli.

Like Wedgwood, Boulton was aware that the current taste favoured the 'artistic', and according to his biographer, H. W. Dickenson: 'For the purpose of obtaining designs for his products Boulton sought the aid of his friends in order through them to borrow works of art to act as models. The friends in question were mostly fashionable fine artists of the day.' At the same time he sought to manufacture his art objects in a volume never before conceived of and continually to expand his market. Many of Boulton's ormolu pieces were influenced by the work of the Adam brothers and it appears that he cooperated with them in a number of instances. Boulton's financial successes apparently derived more from his buckles and buttons, which were purchased in vast numbers, than from his more explicitly artistic experiments.

### STEAM POWER FOR INDUSTRY

In addition to his acute sense of the need to reorganize and commercialize the hardware and 'toy' trades, Boulton was also instrumental in bringing steam power into the metal industry.

The supply of power had always been a difficulty at Soho: the grinding mill was driven by a waterwheel but, with the water frequently running dry, horses were also used. Solving this problem obsessed Boulton and he corresponded with Benjamin Franklin about the idea of using a fire engine

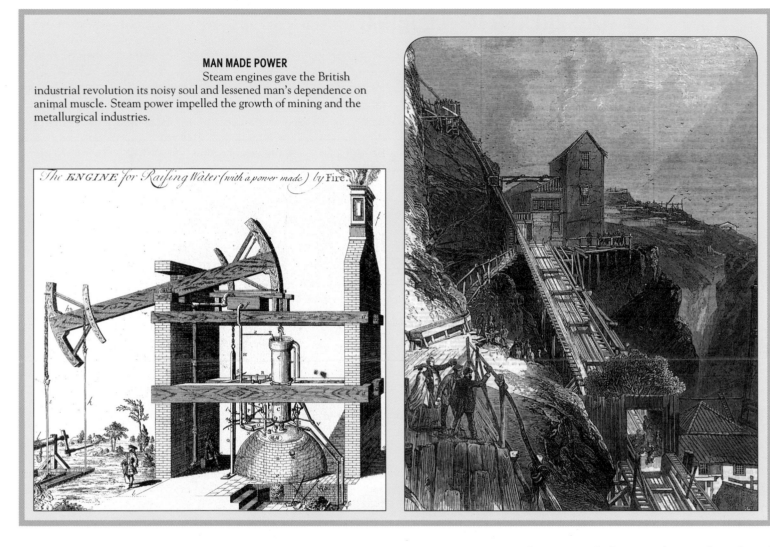

**MAN MADE POWER**
Steam engines gave the British industrial revolution its noisy soul and lessened man's dependence on animal muscle. Steam power impelled the growth of mining and the metallurgical industries.

*The ENGINE for Raiſing Water (with a power made) by Fire.*

to pump back the water. Boulton became acquainted with James Watt, who had been experimenting with steam power, and quickly invested money in the project. Boulton installed a trial engine at Soho in 1773 and Watt spent a couple of years testing it there. From 1776 Boulton and Watt supplied steam engines to a number of industries—most of their custom was in the Cornish tin and copper mines.

Steam power was used in the iron industry in three ways: for the bellows, for the hammers and for rolling and slitting. In 1776 John Wilkinson used one of James Watt's steam engines for blowing blast furnaces directly, and after Watt's invention of rotary action in 1781 the steam engine was used to work forge hammers in 1782. By 1784 it was used for rolling and slitting. These uses made the iron industry independent of water power, a fact that had immediate geographical implications.

It was, however, the application of steam power in spinning mills that was to have the greatest impact. The machinery previously used was worked by water power, so factories had to be built on streams. The substitution of steam power for water made it possible to set up factories wherever the general conditions were most advantageous—particularly the cheap supply of adequate coal. The significance of this innovation was enormous, enabling new forms of mass manufacturing to be developed.

# Design in a new context

Although the growth of demand through the eighteenth century meant that new consumer products were needed, the acceleration in manufacture took place mainly on the level of reorganization rather than through the influence of new technology. This meant, in essence, an intensification of the division of labour and a greater emphasis on marketing. Although Chippendale still worked to commissions, Wedgwood and Boulton were creating markets for the unsolicited goods that they produced in ever increasing numbers. This new relationship between supply and demand meant a closer link between design and marketing and an increasing emphasis on the roles of taste and fashion in the distribution of goods.

Along with manufacturing, retailing grew apace in the eighteenth century as, indeed, did advertising, and London became increasingly important as a fashionable, commercial centre. According to McKendrick, the capital became the undisputed leader in the commercialization of fashion, which helped to bring about unprecedentedly high levels of spending. Many of the famous names of retailers emerged in London during the century, among them Fortnum and Mason in Piccadilly; Flint and Clark (later Clark and Debenham) in 1778; Dickens and Smith (later Dickens and Jones) in 1790; and Heals in 1810. The rest of the country was served by travelling salesmen and provincial shopkeepers, and more goods were distributed than ever before through this network of outlets.

All the tradesmen discussed in this section had showrooms in London, and it became common practice—though the rest of Europe and America did not 'centralize' similarly until almost a century later—for increasing numbers of middle-class customers to travel to London to see what was available and to make purchases. Catalogues showed them the whole range of available items and, in this way, choices were made.

The question of design in this process of commercialization was clearly of fundamental importance. As the rule of fashion affected increasing numbers of consumers, it was taste, rather than utility, that guided the public in purchasing all but its most basic requirements. As Clive Bell notes in his essay, *Civilization*: 'The eighteenth century understood the importance of art; and its taste, though limited, was pure enough. In the minor and domestic arts it could discriminate finely; and the rich were willing to pay for beauty not in cash only but in time and trouble.'

Discrimination became, increasingly, the order of the day, not only for those who had always been able to afford to indulge in it, but also for those new classes of consumers who emulated their social betters. For them it was even more important that they made no mistakes and it was at them that far-sighted entrepreneurs like Josiah Wedgwood and Matthew Boulton aimed their goods, combining 'artistic quality' with bulk production and therefore guaranteeing their customers the right amount of social cachet at a price they could just afford and were more than willing to pay.

## PATTERN BOOKS

Fashionable style was, throughout the century, both easily discernible and readily available. This stemmed from the well-established tradition of 'artists' or 'designers' working on patterns and forms which were then published as pattern books and made available to workshops and factories wishing to produce objects in the style of the day. While this had been the norm for several centuries where workshops supplying objects for the court and church were concerned, the practice spread in the eighteenth century.

In his book *Industrial Design* John Heskett explains that it was in Italy and Germany in the sixteenth century that 'nascent designers began to cater for the need with pattern books'. He described these publications as 'collections of engravings produced in quantity by new mechanical printing methods, illustrating decorative forms, patterns and motifs, and generally intended for such textile trades as ribbon-making, or for cabinet-making'. The separation of the artist or designer from the

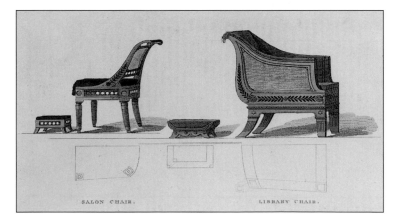

SALON CHAIR.　　　　　LIBRARY CHAIR.

**33**

Although the late eighteenth century saw the growth of a retail market for which goods could be designed and made in bulk, the wealthy could still commission items from pattern books **(opposite)**. By the early nineteenth century, as Thomas Shotter's lithograph shows, London was a lively shopping centre, living off an expanding manufacturing base.

34

subsequent manufacture of goods, with the help of pattern books, was the first step in the division of labour process which increased through the seventeenth, eighteenth and nineteenth centuries. In its early stages, however, this separation affected only the objects destined for the court and members of the nobility. Where the production of goods for the rest of the population was concerned, design and making were usually integrated in the work of the craftsman, who supplied local needs.

With the advent of commercialization and the early stages of centralized mass production the eighteenth century saw the widespread collapse of the craft system. As a result the pattern book principle affected a wider spectrum of production as more people sought to consume fashionable goods. The notion of royal patronage, for example, which had been a feature of the production of porcelain (a product initially produced as an adjunct to court life), was applied by Wedgwood to the humbler pottery. Until then this had been associated more with the concept of utility than with that of luxury.

The fashionable styles—whether baroque, rococo, chinoiserie or neo-Classical—which turned these items into luxury objects, were available to manufacturers in pattern books and it was to them that they inevitably turned. With the French Revolution of 1789 designers

previously employed by the court had to make a living as independent employees working within the commercial system. British designers had, however, experienced this independence much longer, as the principle of 'free enterprise' had, in the absence of the Continental form of absolute monarchy, evolved much earlier.

In the eighteenth century the word 'design' still carried the idea of a close association between planning on paper and the complete work. This definition of the concept was inherited from the Renaissance. It applied as much to the images in pattern books as to the objects themselves. The early pattern books may also, like Chippendale's *Director*, have served to advertise wares as much as to disseminate their appearance to other workshops and craftsmen. They certainly served as a means of spreading knowledge about styles and of influencing taste. Throughout the century pattern books served, therefore, as major ways of communicating fashionable styles and of allowing manufacturers to conform to prevailing tastes.

Wedgwood produced pattern books of his own as he took a positive role in creating styles as well as copying what was 'in the air', while Boulton, whose goods were more overtly fashionable and ephemeral than Wedgwood's utility ware, depended strongly on pattern books to provide

Companies began advertising themselves with fancy trade cards. The printing trade was one of many services to benefit as a consumer society took shape (**above** and **opposite**).

his workmen with models. Standard models could function only at a time when fashionable taste was fairly uniform and when designers and makers could be sure that what the aristocracy desired one day, the middle-class would demand the next.

Such was the fixed nature of early eighteenth-century society and so entrenched was the principle of social emulation that producers of multiple goods could be sure of a market for their wares, provided they were in the correct style of the moment. An acceleration of stylistic expendability came about, however, in the second half of the century. Examples of eighteenth-century pattern books include a set of engravings by Matthew Darly which is described as 'A New Book of Chinese Designs Calculated to improve the present Taste, consisting of Figures, Buildings and Furniture, Landskips, Birds, Beasts, Flowrs (sic) and Ornaments & c'. It undoubtedly had a strong influence on many of the objects in the 'Chinese' style which emerged at the time. Darly was, in fact, as *Pattern and Design*, the catalogue to an exhibition at the Victoria & Albert Museum in 1983, explained, 'a manufacturer of paper hangings, an engraver and designer who engraved many of the plates in Chippendale's *Director*, and also published ornamental borders for print rooms'. He was also a well-known caricaturist.

In the 1770s the illustrated trade catalogue, as distinct from the pattern book proper, emerged, and it was particularly associated with the manufacturers of metal plate in Sheffield. Catalogues were probably used to promote sales abroad and it is certain that the manufacturers allowed copies of the original to be made in great numbers. Boulton's two catalogues for silver plate were engraved anonymously, the first in the 1770s and the second in the 1780s.

## THE MANUFACTURING STRUCTURES

Although factories emerged in England in the eighteenth century, especially in the consumer product industries, many variations of manufacturing structures existed alongside each other. As Maxine Berg explains: 'Eighteenth-century manufacture was practised in all manner of different settings; it was organized along many different lines, each of which was "rational" or legitimate in its own environment. Cutting-out systems co-existed with artisan and cooperative forms of production, and all of these styles frequently interacted with some type of manufacture or protofactory.'

This was the case both within any one region and within any one industry. While Boulton created a factory, many artisans in the hardware trades in Birmingham 'put out' the production of parts and pieces. Whatever system proved economically viable survived, and design and fashion played an equally important role in each. In the end, it was the nature of the market, rather than the changes in the production system,

that necessitated a much more style-conscious approach to manufacture and sales. Aggressive marketing was a natural corollary of volume production, but this did not mean that manufacturers on a smaller scale were gearing their products to a less fashion-conscious market—simply a smaller one.

The search for larger markets led, nevertheless, to increased production and to greater division of labour, which in turn affected the appearance and nature of the objects made. It was not until the following century, however, that the rule of mechanized production began to have a direct influence on design. Design in the eighteenth century was still applied to production; it was not a result of it, even in the volume production of men such as Wedgwood and Boulton. Their stylistic ideals were preconceived and their designs drawn before production took place. They were determined absolutely by the fashionable tastes of the market. Only in products for the rural areas where, in a few cases, the craftsman still held sway producing goods of an essentially utilitarian nature, did the old values remain.

The division of labour accelerated production but did not significantly alter the nature of it. The increased numbers of hands involved did not, on the scale experienced by the eighteenth century, fundamentally alter the appearance of the product. It was not until the following century, when mechanization became, in a number of manufacturing industries, a force to be reckoned with, that new production techniques and accompanying concepts such as standardization began to affect the appearance of products. As a result, design and mechanization began in certain instances to move closer together.

# CHAPTER TWO

# MECHANIZATION & DESIGN 1830-1914

**"MECHANICAL CONTRIVANCES OF EVERY SORT ARE PRODUCED TO SUPPLY THE WANT OF HUMAN HANDS. THUS WE FIND AMERICA PRODUCING A MACHINE EVEN TO PEEL APPLES; ANOTHER TO BEAT EGGS; A THIRD TO CLEAN KNIVES; A FOURTH TO WRING CLOTHES—IN FACT HUMAN HANDS HAVE SCARCELY BEEN ENGAGED IN ANY EMPLOYMENT IN WHICH SOME CHEAP AND EFFICIENT LABOUR-SAVING MACHINE DOES NOT NOW TO SOME EXTENT REPLACE THEM "**

*WRITTEN IN 1865 AND QUOTED IN H. J. HABAKKUK, AMERICAN AND BRITISH TECHNOLOGY IN THE NINETEENTH CENTURY (1967)*

The question of mechanization dominated nearly all the discussions about the theory and practice of design in the nineteenth century. People were either for it or against it, and endless debates took place concerning the role of the machine, in terms of both a search for an appropriate aesthetic for its products and its beneficial and detrimental effects on society as a whole. The latter discussion took place, for the most part, in Britain and the Continent, where labour was widely available. In the US, however, the machine was given a much more enthusiastic reception as labour was both in short supply and costly; the idea of the machine as a means of saving labour seemed to be the answer to all the problems of the US.

The relationship between the machine and the design of manufactured artefacts was highly complex. It was not the machine's taking over from hand-work that altered the state of play so much as the changes within the organization of production brought about by mechanization that proved significant. The increased use of specialized machines and the intensified development of the division of labour within production meant, for instance, that design was irrevocably separated from the making activity. The craftsman's role was inevitably diminished and the designer became a link in an ever-complex chain of events.

Where the volume of production was increased, however, and manufacturers sought an expanded market across a wider social spectrum, the tendency was to dispense with the skills of a designer and to produce goods either inspired by pattern books or copied from other manufacturers. These sold by virtue of their low price and wide availability. This was particularly true in the US where the market was more homogeneous than in Britain and where the 'artistic' quality of the product was less crucial. In this context, product design became determined almost entirely by technology and it was seen as a matter of decorating the surface of the product—more an afterthought than a planned project. With the advent of standardization and interchangeability of component parts in the US, the design process was separated from manufacture once and for all.

The rapid construction of the railroads helped the twentieth century to be America's.

# The British textile industry

While it was undoubtedly in the US that mechanization had its greatest impact in the middle of the nineteenth century, it was in England that the first steps towards mechanized production had taken place. This occurred within textiles, in particular the cotton industry. As Maxine Berg explains, the effects were quite dramatic: 'The textile industries form a fascinating terrain for the acting out of the human drama of technological change. The technologies fundamental to any production process interacted in a fatal way with the lives of men and women at work, and the community around them. New technologies meant the pinnacles of wealth and success to some; destitution to others. The social divisions they created might appear within one small community or provoke a great regional split. New technologies were resisted or welcomed; they were stamped with age and gender as were the older methods which had gone before. They created some new jobs, but they also meant unemployment in a whole

new way to many others. New methods, new machines, did not just mean temporary bad times; they could eradicate a trade and with it the assumption of work for the rest of a person's lifetime.'

While the social effects of mechanization were widely felt, its influence on the objects of mass manufacture was no less dramatic. Spinning was the first area of work in textile production to be mechanized: it was revolutionized by Arkwright's water frame, patented in 1769, Hargreaves' 'spinning-jenny' (named after his wife) of 1770, and Crompton's 'mule' which altered production in the 1780s. The major effect of these inventions was to change the scale of production so that making textiles in domestic and workshop settings gave way, gradually, to centralized factory production. The jenny, which could be, and was, used in workshops, increased the number of spindles used at any one time in such a way that the number of spinners was reduced. Later, so-called 'jenny factories' were introduced. The application of water power, and later steam power, in the 1790s encouraged centralization, although

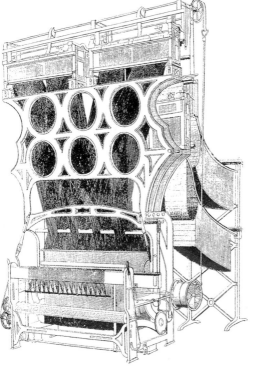

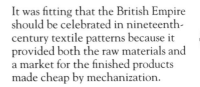

It was fitting that the British Empire should be celebrated in nineteenth-century textile patterns because it provided both the raw materials and a market for the finished products made cheap by mechanization.

Calico printing, c.1835. The mass
production of complex decorated
textiles gave the working classes an
opportunity to buy cheap ornament
– hitherto, ornament was the
property of the well-off.

much hand work still went on. Where the design process was concerned,
the increased complexity of the mechanical means of production meant
that either a design had to be thought out very clearly before manufacture
began, or technological determinism became the norm.

The second process in textile manufacture to be mechanized was
weaving where, first, the flying shuttle and later, in the early to
mid-nineteenth century, power looms were introduced to increase
production. The invention that had the greatest influence on the design
activity was, however, the Jacquard loom, introduced from France by the
1820s. This machine made it necessary for plans concerning the final
appearance of the textile to precede manufacture. The new loom was
based on a programmed system: a card was punched with holes, the
positions of which determined the nature of the pattern to be woven. This
system necessitated the inclusion in the work process of an employee who
could translate a designer's idea onto a card. It meant, also, that designers
had to acquaint themselves with the production machinery in order to be
able to design appropriately for it.

The introduction of powered weaving took place fairly slowly,
however. Despite being patented in 1789, the Jacquard loom was not
perfected or used effectively until the middle of the following century.
Even then its impact was only in the production of goods for low-income,
low-quality markets.

## MECHANIZATION AND
## THE MARKET

While all these new machines had
radical implications for the way in which design was or was not integrated
into the manufacturing process and they all tended to replace skilled
craftsmanship by unskilled labour, it was essentially the nature of the
market that had the strongest influence on the appearance of textiles.

Mechanization answered the desire for volume production, and this in turn implied an expanding market which extended further into the low income end of the social spectrum. As a result of this orientation, price increasingly took over from quality as a determining factor in the majority of sales. The design input in the goods involved therefore diminished. The ruling taste of the day was simply translated into what it was possible to produce, given the restrictions of mechanized production and price and pattern books. Rather than depending upon original designs, aids such as bird and flower books were turned to as the main source of inspiration.

At this level of the market availability became more important than taste. At the aristocractic and upper middle-class end of the market, however, few changes were made to the existing system of design and production, and hand-made woollens and silks continued to fulfil needs.

The calico-printing industry provides an interesting case-study of the way mechanization and design related to each other. In the hands of men like Robert Peel, who established new centres of calico printing in Lancashire, the trade became highly mechanized. Although the roller-printing machine was introduced in 1783, its full effects were not felt until after 1830. With mechanization designers were first joined by, and subsequently replaced by, a team of anonymous individuals whose specialized tasks included 'pattern-drawing', 'engraving' and 'putting-on'. In the 1830s the designs were still influenced by French taste, but a disparity began to emerge between the 'tasteful' objects aimed at the top end of the market and the more market-oriented goods aimed at lower income groups. In the words of the Lancashire calico printer, Edmund Potter: 'Taste in a print can only be estimated or defined by reference to the consumer for whom it is intended.' To provide the necessary designs, as Hazel Clark writes: 'The Lancashire printer did not need to employ designers to produce imitative or copied patterns when an art workman who could draw could reproduce whatever was required.' In addition to the use of such anonymous individuals in the trade, the roller-printing machines themselves dictated to some extent the nature of many of the small repeat patterns evolved for calico at this time.

England's first forays into mechanization took place therefore within the realm of a traditional industry. Although now manufactured in new ways, textiles had been used for centuries, and, as a result, traditional designs continued to appear—modified, however, whenever necessary for mechanical reproduction. New markets joined the existing ones, as custom for the new mass-produced textiles and consumer choices were primarily based on the well-known principle of 'upward emulation'.

## CHANGE PROVOKES CONFLICT

John Kay (1704-64) experiments with the flying shuttle **(above).** The British textile industry industrialized quickly, and much money was made. The impact of new manufacturing methods on weavers, used to working at home, was painful. Workers formed friendly societies which later, as trades unions, became the engine of the Labour movement. But reforms as well as penalties accompanied new technology and old grievances were attacked.

# The American system

In the US mechanization had, in contrast to the situation in Britain, an enormous influence upon the manufacture and design of both traditional products and the new consumer goods being invented and developed in that country. Their design was largely dependent on the level of mechanization and standardization employed by the industry in question.

In the eighteenth century the US was still predominantly an essentially agricultural country, but by the end of the nineteenth century it had overtaken both England and Europe to become the largest manufacturing force in the world. The reasons for this rapid development were complex. Strongest among them was the incentive provided by the lack of a cheap, available labour force and the presence of a very large, increasingly affluent, highly homogeneous mass market. England had never had a labour shortage, so mechanization took longer to develop there. In the US agriculture remained a viable and lucrative alternative to industrial labour. The search for 'labour-saving' machines to produce the mass of goods demanded by the ever-expanding market in the nineteenth century was therefore born out of necessity rather than mere curiosity. While the US was not responsible for the invention of many machines, its manufacturers were undoubtedly quicker to introduce their use into industry than their English counterparts. Where the US did take the lead (with some help from the French), however, was in the development of the concepts of interchangeability and standardization within industrial mass production. This meant that from an early date in the nineteenth century both manufacturing and consumer machines consisted of a number of identical component parts designed by anonymous engineers working within the production process. This provided a model of manufacture which stood in direct opposition to the craft process in which a single individual was involved in producing unique objects.

The American method meant not only that machines could be used to produce uniform parts, and hence speed up production, but also repairs could take place by the simple substitution of one part for another. In his book *American and British Technology in the Nineteenth Century*, H.J. Habakku writes that 'by the 1850s the Americans produced by highly mechanized and standardized methods, a wide range of products including doors, furniture and other woodworks; boots and shoes; ploughs and moving machines; wood screws, files and nails; biscuits; locks, clothes, small arms, nuts and bolts'.

As is so often the case, military events encouraged the acceleration of standardized production. In the US the small arms industry made huge advances in production organization and mechanization from the War of Independence at the end of the eighteenth century to the American Civil War in the second half of the nineteenth century. The names associated with the revolution of the American small arms industry are Eli Whitney, Simeon North and Samuel Colt.

As Sigfried Giedion has observed, America began by mechanizing the complex craft—that is, gun-making—rather than, as in England, the simple craft, textiles. This difference had significant implications, as the ideas about interchangeability and standardization that Whitney first developed were quick to influence the production of a number of other machines, among them the sewing-machine, the typewriter, the bicycle and, most importantly, the automobile. What came to be called the 'American system of manufacture' also helped, both practically and intellectually, the development of a particular aesthetic for the new,

Immigrants and Bellaire **(above and right)** helped the US to become the leading manufacturing nation of the world.

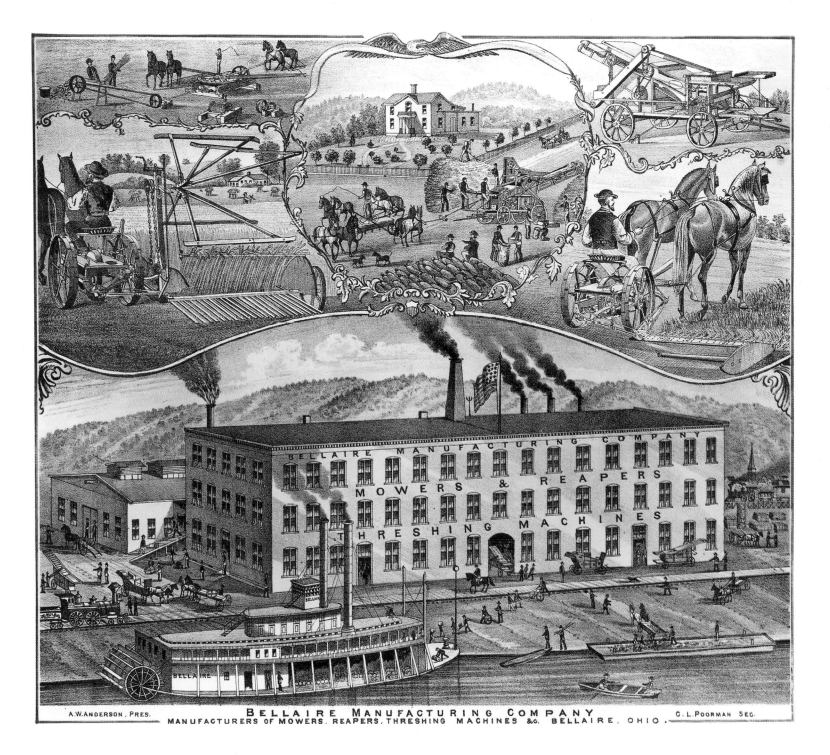

**BELLAIRE MANUFACTURING COMPANY**

A.W.ANDERSON, PRES.        C.L.POORMAN SEC.

MANUFACTURERS OF MOWERS, REAPERS, THRESHING MACHINES &c. BELLAIRE, OHIO.

## NEW CIVILITIES

All societies are terrified of civil war but the US emerged stronger in 1865. Belief in hard work, religion and a fierce patriotism provided Americans with a framework of self-confidence.

THE RE-UNITED STATES.

high-technology products destined for the office and home as well as for the factory. Whether or not these products were embellished with surface patterns aimed to fulfil the requirements of what were thought to be 'women's tastes', they brought the image of the machine into the domestic context, thereby providing some of the earliest examples of 'product design'. These were goods that had no traditions to follow and that had to create new identities for themselves.

The small arms industry was not important simply as an abstract model of manufacture, however. It also provided a direct line of entry into other areas. Many firms, including the Singer Sewing Machine Company and the Ford Automobile Company, employed engineers with a background in small arms machine tooling with the specific intention of developing a system of interchangeability. Many of the same machines were in fact re-used in new contexts, given that so many of the products under discussion were made out of metal. The Remingtons, for instance, began as small arms manufacturers before they moved into typewriter production, and many of the early electrical appliances were manufactured by fabricators with experience in other areas of metal production.

**45**

## THE AMERICAN MARKET

The concept of a homogeneous market was central to the idea of American mass production at this time.

US small arms-manufacturers improved their production systems, thereby influencing the manufacture of sewing-machines, typewriters and automobile components.

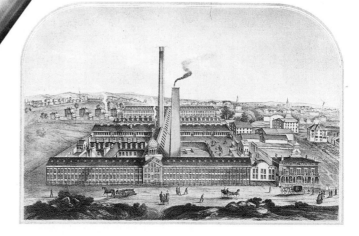

46

Writing in his book *America Comes of Age,* Sigfried maintains that in 1927: 'The 100,000,000 individuals in the US are astonishingly alike. They all speak the same language, with fewer different accents than are to be found in England; they all live in exactly the same way and are little influenced by the differences in their climate. The immigrants at first keep a little of their own originality; but owing to the sharp rupture with their traditions, their children fall into line without resistance. With such a stereo-typed clientele, industry is not obliged to prepare an infinite number of complicated products. A limited number of models suffice, repeated indefinitely and varying only according to certain fixed principles.'

However exaggerated this view, it contained a large element of truth. In the nineteenth century this kind of society greatly facilitated the standardization of products.

Following the adoption of English machinery by the American textiles industry, shoe-making was another of the industries to mechanize production in the US. In England this remained a craft-based activity right up to the end of the nineteenth century. It was one of the first handicrafts to develop in the American colonies and a number of shoe-makers' shops gradually emerged, some small, others quite large. Until the middle of the nineteenth century, hand-making was still the

norm. In 1845, however, a simple rolling machine was developed which saved much labour and time in preparing the leather for the soles, and in 1858 John McKay succeeded in making a practicable shoe-sewing machine which sewed the upper part of the shoes to the lower and stitched on the soles. Following these inventions, scores of other new machines took the making of shoes out of the hands of the old-fashioned cobbler and shoe-making became a mechanized, factory-based activity.

One implication of this growing dependence on the machine was less emphasis on quality in American goods. An American friend of de Tocqueville observed in 1832 that 'there is a feeling among us about everything which prevents us aiming at permanence'. Contemporaries

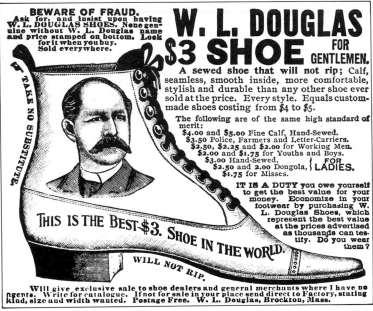

The early nineteenth-century attempts at advertising seem wordy to modern eyes – although Remington show here that they had learned the copywriter's art that less says more.

noticed a certain flimsiness in many of the machines. The reason was the readiness of Americans to scrap machines in favour of newly invented ones in their constant search for increased output. This led to an interest on the part of consumers in novelty rather than quality, a characteristic of nineteenth-century American life frequently remarked on by contemporary commentators.

# The American sewing-machine industry

The first domestic machine to follow the example of small arms, watches, locks and shoes into mass production was the sewing-machine. Although Whitney had applied the system of interchangeable parts to the firearms industry in 1798 it was not until the 1850s that it was used in the manufacture of the sewing-machine. The company that led the way in that decade was Wheeler & Wilson, set up in 1848 to manufacture small metal articles. In 1851 Wilson patented a design for a sewing-machine with a rotary hook and bobbin mechanism. William H. Perry joined the firm in 1855 and it was he who introduced New England armory practice, learnt at Samuel Colt's armory in Hartford, Connecticut, into the factory.

Wheeler & Wilson moved in 1857 into what had been a clock factory. There manufacturing followed a system, according to David Hounshell in his book *From the American System to Mass Production*, that included 'major running components initially drop-forged and then machined; machining work performed by numerous specialized machine tools operated sequentially; uniformity of parts controlled by a model-based gauging system along with a rational jig and fixture system'. The Wheeler & Wilson manufacturing company expanded enormously from the 1850s so that by 1872 its annual production was up to 174,088 machines. The machines themselves were a visual result of their standardized production. Their assembly procedure was visible in the

The US in the late nineteenth century led the way in making reliable domestic sewing machines. In this picture we see a well regulated factory, not yet organized on the mass production basis, but showing clearly the roots of modern organization.

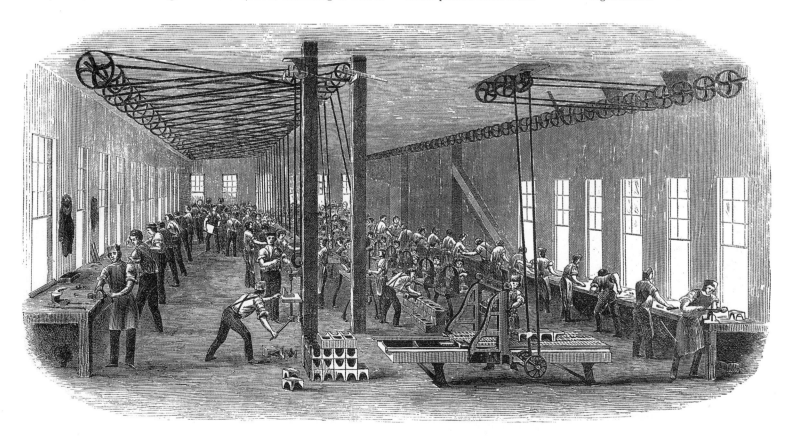

Isaac Singer and his first sewing machine (**below**). Manufacturers fancied up their products into elaborate furnishings to make them look domestic and thereby attract sales.

final object and there was little attempt to disguise its basic mechanisms.

The Singer Sewing Machine Company was slower to adopt the American system, however. Its innovation lay in the efforts it made to market its product, and to this end it used extensive advertising and demonstrations as the means of persuading the market of the necessity of owning a sewing-machine at home. Singer machines were more expensive than those of competitors, being more sophisticated in design and of a higher quality in manufacture. Hounshell writes: 'I.M. Singer & Co took a European view of the matter, believing that hand finishing by many skilled workmen provided the best means to achieve and maintain product quality. It sought to build its fortune by emphasizing advertising and marketing rather than by refining methods of manufacture.'

Instalment paying was also introduced as a means of expanding sales. The first home model was introduced in 1856 and it was designed with an attention to ornamental detail, both of form and surface. It had a japanned surface on its cast-iron body, covered in gold, flower-patterned ornamental scrollwork—modified from motifs obtained in a pattern book and applied to the surface by female painters. This decoration allowed it to blend into the living area of the domestic environment.

By the 1860s the company was forced to mechanize its production process because of the pressure of volume production, and in 1865 the New Family Sewing Machine was introduced. It became a staple product of the Singer factory into the twentieth century. Although other sewing-machine companies spent more time inventing new manufacturing techniques and tools for their machines than Singer, the latter company outlived them because of its emphasis on perfecting a worldwide marketing strategy and a domestic image for its machine.

# The American furniture industry

It is revealing to compare the American sewing-machine industry with the American furniture industry of the same period. Specialized woodworking tools were developed more quickly in the US than in England, although early advances in wood technology had been developed in the latter country through the work of Isambard Kingdom Brunel, Henry Maudslay and Joseph Bramah. After 1815 the emphasis turned to the US where specialized machines were made, first in wood and later in cast iron. These were taken around wood workshops on wagons by firms such as Page & Company and J.A. Fay. The Midwest workshops, based in Chicago and Grand Rapids, expanded in the 1850s and '60s as a result of the new tools, and furniture production began to be reorganized. By the 1870s many machines were steam-driven.

It would be false to suggest, however, that furniture production developed in the same way as the metal industries, for furniture workshops, however mechanized, did not expand beyond a certain size. Where design and taste were concerned, the new machines simply served to reproduce more quickly than by hand the fashionable styles of the day—most of which were European in origin—and to make them widely available for the growing mass market. Homogeneity was less in evidence where the market for mass-produced furniture was concerned. It seems, therefore, that where traditional items were concerned, there was a relative plurality of tastes in the American market.

J. H. Belter (1804-63), a German immigrant to the US, invented a means of perforating and curving rosewood into intricate forms.

# The American automobile industry

In the case of the automobile, the most highly standardized American consumer machine, it seems that, if the success of the Ford Motor Company is any indication, there was for a time a total uniformity of demand.

Although the automobile was not invented in the US it was there that it was developed as an object for everyday life. This was a result of Henry Ford's ability to combine three factors: the inclusion of armory practice in his manufacturing; the use of sheet-metal stamping; and the use of line assembly. He evolved a system of manufacture that perfected the concept of standardization, expressed in his belief that all his cars should look identical. This approach came to be known as Fordism. Ford was convinced that the American market wanted one automobile that everybody could afford and his model T provided an efficient replacement for the farm buggy, enabling the rural population of the US to go into town whenever it needed to.

Manufacturers soon learned to create a demand for novelties: a US egg whisk, 1873, and an English pea-sheller, 1901.

The Ford factory at River Rouge, 1923, and the model T **(right)** helped to develop the twentieth-century family leisure industry.

The manufacture of the model T was a completely centralized activity, beginning with the unloading of iron ore—the Ford Motor Company made its own steel—and finishing with the emergence of a completed car. Ford perfected this process in 1913 and 1914 at the Highland Park factory, which he had opened in 1910, and the model T Ford reflected his idea of simplified design, mass-produced at a price most people could afford. Many of the tools were purpose-built for the job having been prototyped at Highland Park. Because Ford was committed to a single design, the engineers installed many single-purpose machine tools.

The Ford experiment brought together all the innovations, both mechanical and organizational, developed in American industry over the preceding 150 years. While interchangeability and standardization had come out of small arms manufacture, the idea of the assembly line had originated in meat-packing and canning. Ford amalgamated all these production innovations into the manufacture of new, high-technology products and, happily, a large market existed for this highly standardized product.

# Technology and design

The relationship between mechanization and design is clearly a highly complex one. When a homogeneous market and a clear demand co-exist, mechanization often leads to product standardization and to products that are little more than the visual result of their production and assembly processes. Where pluralism of tastes and/or the need to create a market or markets are in evidence, the mechanical factor is less relevant; instead, some kind of product elaboration is required. The design variation in the cases of the automobile, the sewing-machine and furniture, while all the results of highly mechanized production systems in the US during the latter half of the nineteenth and the early years of the twentieth century, shows that design is as much a question of consumer acceptance and symbolic appropriateness as one of technology and production. In the first decades of this century the automobile could get away with an appearance that reflected its means of production, because it was both a new product and one that did not infiltrate the home and its conventional values. The

Electricity: the first commercial light bulb is on the left of Edison's original. Unlike **Iron and Coal** portrayed (**right**) by W. Bell Scott, electricity was not rooted in rural industry.

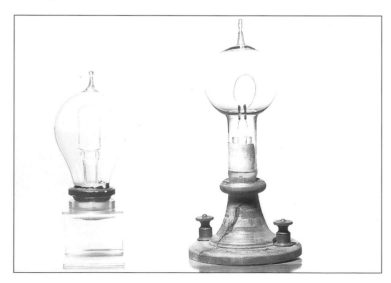

**ON THE MOVE**
In the late nineteenth
century, Americans became well used to travelling for
business and pleasure. The railroad and steamship
companies could sell travellers 'mighty fine' comfort.

Steam engines remain the natural symbol of nineteenth-century industry: the great Corliss steam engine at the Centennial Exhibition, Philadelphia, in 1876.

sewing-machine, however, had to become 'domesticized', and furniture had to sustain its traditional role as a symbol of affluence and social status.

The changing patterns of consumption in the US and in England in the nineteenth century are, of course, the other side of the story. Mechanized production emerged only as a response to an increased demand for goods on the part of the mass market, a fact that was evident on both sides of the Atlantic. In the US, however, the increase was more extreme. As Habakkuk explains: 'The major part of the demand for American manufactures came from the rise in agricultural incomes as cotton exports from the southern states rose and as the country was opened up and the population increased.'

This, he says, represented a larger demand than its equivalent in England. The crucial difference lay in the timing of the increased demand in relation to changes in technology. While England made its technological breakthroughs before the expansion of its market, the phenomena coincided in the US. This meant that America was able to build on British advances and meet the demands of its market. Thus, while England mechanized the production of textiles, the US mechanized the manufacture of sewing-machines, typewriters and cars and, as a result, went into the lead in levels of world manufacturing by the turn of the century. Habakkuk explains that: 'England had her period of labour scarcity while the techniques of the classical Industrial Revolution were being invented. America had hers when these techniques were being widely adopted.' The final contrast between England and the US as far as mechanization and design were concerned lay in their respective reactions to the machine. In general the US witnessed little antagonism to the use of the machine. It was seen as an aid to manual labour and not as a threat to existing jobs. This gave the US a pro-mechanistic flavour in the mid-nineteenth century and a sense of optimism about the mechanized future. It also tended to equate design ability with engineering skills and to undermine the 'artistic' association with the concept that had developed in Europe in earlier centuries. In England, in sharp contrast, there was much opposition to the use of the machine in factory manufacture, mainly as a result of the unemployment it frequently produced. This reaction was best expressed in the protests of the Luddites in the early part of the century in the textile industry. There was a continual sense also, in England, that mechanization had led to the loss of aesthetic standards in objects aimed at the mass market. Continued debate on this subject from the 1830s onwards focused on the equation between the demise of craftsmanship and the loss of the high aesthetic standards that had been widespread in the preceding century.

In the US one of the few fears about such 'tastelessness' was expressed by the sculptor Horatio Greenough in his book *Form and Function*. Here he reiterated his warning that standards of taste would be eroded in the US if it neglected its engineering and technological strengths and adopted instead the commercialism evident in the British goods made for export to the US. Greenough proposed a proto-Functionalist approach to design which maintained that designing for function rather than for sales led to pure form. He cited the works of the American ship- and bridge-builders as examplars.

American ideas about mechanization gradually filtered into England, but not until the boom years of the 1890s, when English industry had a renewed bout of energy. In general, however, England developed more slowly at this time than both the US and Germany. These countries were soon far ahead in the production of iron and steel and in the manufacture of cars and electrical equipment. Where consumption was concerned there was a dramatic swing in the US in the 1860s away from furniture to appliances and automobiles, and it was already clear that that country would lead the world in those areas. At the 1876 Centennial Exhibition in Philadelphia the emphasis was on technological progress. In it there was a large machinery hall in which the Corliss steam engine—the largest of its kind in the world—was displayed, while the Singer sewing-machine had a pavilion to itself. Metal- and wood-working machinery also had pride of place and it was obvious to all who visited the exhibition that it was in these areas that America's strength lay.

### THE ATLANTIC DIVIDE

The design emphases on each side of the Atlantic were clearly different ones. In the US design was becoming an increasingly intrinsic element within the production and consumption of mass-produced goods. 'Taste' was simply a European concept which could be applied to whichever goods needed it, particularly traditional goods and those aimed at the top end of the market. The market could, however, accept a high degree of visual and technical standardization in the goods it consumed so voraciously, particularly where new technology was concerned.

In Britain the concept of taste remained a live issue, with the exception only of the goods aimed at the poorest end of the market. The advent of mechanization, such as it was, was received with great ambivalence and was accompanied by countless fears that 'taste' was in jeopardy. Numerous books were written, reports made and steps taken to guard against the 'tastelessness' of machine-produced goods. Although these worries had been in the air for a while, it was in the decades after the Great Exhibition of 1851 that they were fully articulated.

Some people relish the present, as did Jean
Beraud in his photograph-like painting, 1880
**(above).** Others, like William Morris, yearned
for the past, and Philip Webb's Red House, 1859
**(right)** suited him. Josef Hoffman, Palais Stoclet,
Brussels, 1905 **(far right).** Like Morris, Hoffman
used ornament in a highly stylized way.

# CHAPTER THREE

# DESIGN REFORM 1830-1914

> **"IN EFFECT THE REVOLUTION IN TASTE BROUGHT ABOUT BY THE INDIVIDUAL PIONEERS WAS AS PROFOUND AS THE REVOLUTION THEY WROUGHT IN THE ORGANISATION AND TECHNIQUE OF PRODUCTION"**
>
> *F. D. KLINGENDER, ART AND THE INDUSTRIAL REVOLUTION (1947)*

While in the second half of the nineteenth century the US leapt ahead in the mass manufacture of mechanical, and later, electrical goods for the home, office and the street, Britain remained committed to elaborating the products of the more traditonal 'art' industries that it had reorganized and, to some extent, mechanized, in the second half of the eighteenth and the early years of the nineteenth century.

As a result, very different attitudes developed towards the concept of mechanized production and the question of design in these countries.

In the US, for instance, there was a clear break between the European-inspired goods aimed at the wealthy end of the market and the mass-produced objects which catered for the rest. Very often the former decorative items were imported from Europe for these customers or, at the very least, were made to order, reproducing European taste as closely as possible. The mass-produced objects—shoes, sewing-machines, type-writers, bicycles and, a little later, automobiles and the products of the electrical appliance industry—were in the early stages determined as much by their means of production as by the social milieu for which they were destined. The appliances were often sold to the general public on their technological novelty value, rather than any obvious functional benefit, and when the market became yet more competitive, designers sought to give them 'added value' by various means.

In England the preoccupation with the products of the traditional art industries led to a concern with what was considered to be declining standards of taste. As a result, a major theme in the second half of the nineteenth century was that of reform in the applied arts. Responding to the growing participation of the new mass market in the consumption of goods, the British reform movement of the nineteenth century sought to re-establish the standards of taste of a previous age and to eradicate what it saw to be the destructive effects of the expansion of the means of production.

# Design and taste

Writing in *Art and the Industrial Revolution*, Francis D. Klingender suggests that: 'In effect the revolution in taste brought about by the individual pioneers was as profound as the revolution they wrought in the organization and technique of production.'

While the evolution of modern design was dependent upon the changes in such abstract forces as the prevailing methods of manufacture, the nature of society, the economic and political framework and the technological status quo, a number of individuals were also important in formulating the ideas that underpinned the Modern Movement. In the early nineteenth century the designer became less significant as a force within manufacturing, as he was rapidly replaced by the team of both skilled and unskilled workmen, who set about translating designs into

Wall and portcullis wallpaper designed by A.W.N. Pugin for the Houses of Parliament.

mass-manufactured objects for the new middle classes. At the same time, individuals from the neighbouring areas—architecture and fine art— were keen to articulate their ideas about the ideal aesthetic of these products and the tastes of their customers.

There was a consensus among those individuals who sought to reform the design standards of the mid-nineteenth century that, as a result of both the increased level of production and the emergence of new classes of consumers, the taste of the nation as a whole was in a state of decline. In these years a strong reforming zeal inspired both the words and work of a number of architects and fine artists, who pinpointed the problem of taste as the key issue. They set about articulating theories of design which they hoped would change the course of events and bring about what would be, to their eyes at least, a more satisfactory relationship between design and modern society.

Much blame for the lowering of design standards was laid at the feet of mass manufacturing and technological progress in these years. A few decades later, William Morris was to widen the debate, examing the social ills and sense of alienation associated with industrialization. In the 1830s attempts were made to get away from the continual preoccupation with the future in order to reassess the contribution of the past. For A.W. Pugin and John Ruskin, for instance, the medieval world, with its strong rapport between art and Christianity, represented a peak of perfection, and they devoted much of their energies to re-creating its delights and singing its praises. Although predominantly an architectural movement, the Gothic Revival of the 1830s also influenced design and the decorative arts and became one of the most influential stylistic alternatives of the mid-century. It reached its apogee in Barry and Pugin's Houses of Parliament (built 1840-60) and was developed, by the latter architect among others, to a high level of sophistication.

## A. W. PUGIN

In 1812 Pugin published his book *Contrasts*, in which he demonstrated what he felt to be the dignity and superiority of the Gothic to the Classical style. In 1841 it was followed by *The Principles of Pointed or Christian Architecture* which argued that 'all beautiful forms in architecture are based on the soundest principles of utility', and demonstrated Pugin's belief that the Gothic style was a way out of the use of indiscriminate ornament, rife in the mass-manufactured products of early Victorian England. For Pugin, the Gothic Revival represented a design movement with a spiritual base—a necessary factor

### ESTABLISHMENT MANNERS

A.W.N. Pugin was commissioned by Sir Charles Barry, designer of the Houses of Parliament, to assist with the decorative details of the 'greatest modern gothic building in the world'. Gothic, the quintessential north European Christian architecture, provided the perfect imagery for an institution in which the right to govern and the Church of England were considered congruent. F. Winterhalter painted the portrait of Queen Victoria in 1851.

Pugin's ornamental designs were structured by the reason and necessity that, like John Ruskin, he saw in the Gothic style. But Pugin's style as seen at Eastnor Castle, England **(right)** was hardly domestic, whereas the European Biedermeier style **(below)** fitted graciously into the homes of the middle class.

in a world characterized by rapidly shifting values and a delight in style merely as a symbol of social status.

### JOHN RUSKIN

For John Ruskin the medieval world and nature provided the necessary unifying forces for the design that he felt to be appropriate in the mid-nineteenth century. Like Pugin, Ruskin published his thoughts in a series of texts, among them *The Seven Lamps of Architecture* (1849) and *The Stones of Venice* (1851-3). He too set out to dispel what he felt to be the growing confusion of ornament with design, as well as the false notion of disguising instead of beautifying articles of utility. As many design and architectural historians have been at great pains to point out, the ideas of Pugin and Ruskin, while still supporting ornament as a basic requirement of design, had within them countless proto-Functionalist tenets which were to be recalled in the early years of the following century. Ruskin was, however, adamant that 'the highest nobility of a building does not consist of its being well built, but in its being nobly sculptured or painted' and he maintained that ornament should, at all times, be 'visible, natural and thoughtful'.

The essentially moral base to the writings of both Pugin and Ruskin on the subject of architecture and design provided a strong contrast to the commercial framework which dominated most design practice at that time. It was a stance which encompassed the world of fine art as well, and Ruskin devoted much energy to the support of the painter William Turner and to the work of the Pre-Raphaelite group. He felt that both exhibited the same sense of honesty, whether to the world of the senses or to that of nature. If mid-nineteenth-century design reform had a spiritual base then it would extend its influence across the whole of visual culture.

As a keen champion of medievalism, Ruskin was, perhaps, most influential in his attacks on what he felt to be the evils of mechanized mass production and the use of new materials. It is as a supporter of the country rather than the city, a defender of craft rather than machine production, that he is best remembered. Ruskin was unremitting in his views and made fierce attacks on what he felt to be the overt commercialism espoused by the other major reforming group of the time attached to the civil servant Henry Cole. He was strongly opposed to the Crystal Palace, made of iron and glass—which he described, disparagingly, as a 'greenhouse larger than greenhouse was ever built before'.

What Pugin and Ruskin had in common with the Cole group, however, was their loathing of the use of indiscriminate ornamentation and the ever-decreasing standards of public taste.

Individuals associated with Cole made this clear on numerous occasions. Owen Jones, for instance, writing in his *Grammar of Ornament* of 1856, stressed in his 'Proposition 13' that: 'Flowers or natural objects should not be used as ornaments, but conventional representations founded upon them sufficiently suggestive to convey the intended image to the mind, without destroying the unity of the object they are employed to decorate.' Ralph Wornum, the keeper of the National Gallery, maintained that: 'Ornament is essentially the accessory to, and not the substitute of, the useful.'

## HENRY COLE AND HIS GROUP

Henry Cole, the man responsible for the Penny Black in 1839 and the invention of the Christmas card in 1845, was at the centre of a group of individuals who were committed to the idea of reforming design as part of the mass manufacture of products. Moves had already been made in the 1830s to improve public taste on the recommendation of a Select Committee which had been set up to look into the area. Robert Peel opened the National Gallery in 1832, the year of the Reform Bill, in an attempt to counter the fact that, in the words of Francis D. Klingender, 'already in the second half of the eighteenth century the real arbiter of taste was no longer the designer or even the manufacturer but the salesman'. Peel's aim was 'to instil a sense of design in the manufacturer and of elevating taste in the consumer'. In 1837 the

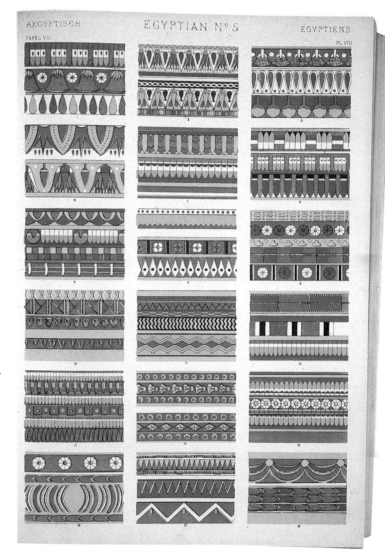

**61**

The design of ornament demands coherence and order. Since the eighteenth century designers have found that Egyptian imagery provides inspiration.

first government school of design was opened in South Kensington, and in subsequent years many other such schools were opened in the main industrial centres in England and Scotland in an effort to supply manufacturing industry with trained, sensitive designers. The scheme backfired somewhat as the curriculum of these institutions was dominated by fine art activities, and industry did not feel that its real needs were being adequately met.

The next official step in this programme of reform was the appointment of Prince Albert, in 1843, as the President of the Society of Arts. Then in 1847, Henry Cole, Owen Jones, Richard Redgrave and Matthew Digby Wyatt joined together to form 'Summerlys Art Manufacturers' in an attempt 'to put the fine arts at the service of manufactured objects'. In 1849 that same group was responsible for the publication of the first edition of the *Journal of Art and Manufactures*, which became very influential in improving the standards of British industry in the second half of the nineteenth century. Britain was alone at this time in organizing such an active, official design reform movement, although it was to inspire similar efforts elsewhere in subsequent years. The reforms

have, of course, been criticized many times subsequently, mainly for their rather abstract high-mindedness and their lack of real communication with, or understanding of, what went on inside the factories. In the 1930s, for instance, Herbert Read was to write that 'their minds and imaginations moved in an unreal world of taste, divorced from any direct connection with the tools, the processes and the materials of manufacture'. This is undeniably true, and in many ways these reforming activities operated on a level which was separated both from the real world of industry and from that of the new consumers, for whom status and comfort were the only qualities they sought in the goods with which they surrounded themselves. Taste implied fashion, which in turn implied social status for the vast majority of the population.

Cole focused on the question of taste, however, as if there were the possibility of establishing an absolute set of criteria for it. He abhorred the fact that: 'There is no general agreement in principles of taste. Everyone elects his own style of art . . . some take refuge in a liking for "pure Greek", others believe only in Pugin, others lean upon imitations of modern Germans.'

This is what shopping for home furnishings looked like in Leicester, England, in 1900. Yet our perceptions change constantly and our post-Modernist eyes can tolerate those styles that, 40 years ago, Modernists mocked.

# The Great Exhibition of 1851

The stylistic anarchy which provided the point of departure for so many design reformers in these years was nowhere more apparent than at the Great Exhibition of 1851, which was held in the Crystal Palace in Hyde Park, London. The manufactured objects exhibited at the Great Exhibition displayed a general enthusiasm for ornament for ornament's sake and an overall neglect of any fixed principle of design, other than those motivated by the market-place. The exhibition provided an opportunity for manufacturers to show off their goods to a huge audience and to display the way in which they could turn their products into highly desirable status objects through the application of 'art'.

The exhibition was backed by Prince Albert, who had been persuaded by Henry Cole that such an event was a necessary step in the attempt to improve public taste and to stop the acceptance of the haphazard imitation of past styles. Its lasting significance lies, however, in the way that it succeeded in bringing together historical streams. The building itself, designed by Joseph Paxton, was part of the tradition of engineering which used new materials in an utterly functional, undecorated manner, while the consumer objects it contained had no such restraining influences upon them. The Palace was completely constructed in iron and glass and was made of prefabricated standardized units, but its contents demonstrated the Victorian commitment to ornamentation as status symbolism. John Gloag has explained that: 'A philosophy of comfort, developed by the plutocracy and adopted by the middle classes, replaced educated taste. Comfort was respectable and, like ornament, had become an end in itself.' This was nowhere more apparent than in the rooms of sofas stuffed with horsehair and with heavily carved legs, and in all the other highly elaborate household objects visible to the crowds that thronged enthusiastically into the Palace in 1851. The decoration on most of the objects had an explicitly narrative content which complied with the mid-Victorian taste for naturalistic painting, epitomized in the work of artists such as Frith and Waterhouse. The quasi-scientific delight in detail which was evident in so many areas of Victorian life was also visible here in the myriads of flowers, leaves and other natural motifs on the objects exhibited. It was all part of the mid-Victorian faith in facts which permeated contemporary cultural life. The exhibition was, in many ways 'the true test of the point of development at which the whole of mankind has arrived', which Prince Albert and Cole had anticipated.

The Great Exhibition, 1851. Some visitors were shocked at the crudeness and inappropriateness of the decoration that was being applied indiscriminately to all artefacts, regardless of their function. Many people felt too much design looked absurd. Thus the Exhibition stimulated a long-lasting debate about good and bad in taste and design.

International
exhibitions, like the Great Exhibition, Paris,
1852 **(left)** became important and established
themselves as vehicles of trade and nationalism.
They fed the idea of consumerism as a leisure
activity. Crystal Palace, the home of the 1851
Exhibition, **(far left and bottom)** thrilled
visitors, but Henry Cole **(below)**, shown in
H.W. Phillips' portrait of the Royal
Commissioners, was disenchanted with what
he saw.

One of the problems about
ornament is knowing when not to
apply it. Furniture such as this chair
**(above)**, one of the 1851 Great
Exhibition wares, struck some
contemporary aesthetes as over-
elaborate. Ornament was thought to
indicate wealth, but the *nouveaux
riches* made the easy mistake of
sinking into excess.

One of the reasons for staging the Great Exhibition was the problem
of foreign, and especially French, competition, which was an increasing
threat by the middle of the century. Cole had visited the French
exhibition of 1849, and he conceived the 1851 exhibition as England's
answer. It was envisaged from the beginning as a display of industry and
art, and people travelled from all over the country to see it. Nikolaus
Pevsner explained, rather patronizingly, why he thought 1851 was such a
success. 'This admiration of the *trompe-l'oeil*, the cute disguise, the
surprising gadget, is as old as art, and will always remain the privilege of

Although the machinery of the nineteenth century that produced the goods was simple, the goods themselves were elaborated to flatter popular taste.

66

the naive, and the naivety of the visitors to the 1851 exhibition was beyond our conception.' He saw the period between 1840 and 1870 as one of 'assured possession between two phases of restlessness and revolt' and claimed that in 1851 'impressiveness was more important than edification'.

The Cole group's reactions to 1851 were utterly predictable. While *The Times* talked about 'sins committed against good taste', Ralph Wornum, Richard Redgrave and Gottfried Semper (a German who lived in London in 1851-5) deplored the arbitrariness of the ornament displayed there. In response, they set out to find ways of evolving 'appropriate' motifs which were taken from nature and elsewhere and then stylized and applied to an object in the light of its function and construction. This led to the development of such works as Wornum's *Analysis of Ornament* of 1856, Owen Jones' *Grammar of Ornament* of the same year and Semper's writings about the classification of objects, which were attempts to remove the arbitrariness of so much applied decoration by developing sets of rules for guidance. The Cole group obtained more pleasure from the machinery section of 1851 than from the array of manufactures, as they felt the former showed more understanding of the concept of 'fitness for purpose'.

# William Morris and the Arts and Crafts Movement

While the practical results of these reforming themes are rather hard to trace, the idea of linking ornament to utility certainly became important for design theory and practice in the second half of the nineteenth century. From the 1860s onwards the idea was to find its greatest champion in William Morris, whose writings and work testified to the need to provide controls for ornament at all times. What is even more significant about Morris' contribution to modern design, however, is, as Nikolaus Pevsner has pointed out, his preoccupation not with taste but with design as part of a much larger social problem. By moving beyond the sphere of the mere 'aesthetic' he was able to confront issues which were more profound and long lasting in their significance.

Like so many of the individuals associated with Henry Cole, William Morris was forced to clarify his thoughts about design in reaction to the 1851 exhibition. The later exhibition of 1862, at which Morris had a stand, got no nearer to solving the problem of arbitrary ornamentation and, like Ruskin before him, Morris saw the problem as being linked inextricably with the question of machine production. He was not a Luddite, explaining that: 'It is not this or that tangible steel or brass machine which we want to get rid of, but the great intangible machine of commercial tyranny which oppresses the lives of all of us.' He felt, nonetheless, that the division of labour had led to alienation in work, and hence to carelessly thought-out ornament. It was this lack of unity between ornament, form and function in the objects he saw around him, as well as an obsession with historicism, that made Morris decide to experiment with alternative ways forward. These feelings were reinforced after his marriage by his need to furnish a house for himself and his disappointment at finding nothing in the shops that he could use.

Red House in Bexleyheath, designed by Philip Webb, provided the perfect excuse for Morris and his immediate colleagues to go to work designing objects according to their own criteria. The furniture, wallpaper, textiles and other decorative items that they created for it were among the first experiments in the application of a new approach to design. Following Ruskin closely, Morris advocated the principle of truth to nature and felt very close to the medieval world, both aesthetically and spiritually. In his designs he combined natural imagery (albeit in a stylized form), handwork, recognition of the moral and social implications of medievalism and, most importantly, a visual simplicity which extended Pugin's idea of relating form, or ornament, to function. Morris explains his use of decoration: 'What we call decoration is, in many cases, but a way we have learned for making necessary things reasonable as well as pleasant to use. The pattern becomes part of the thing we make, its exponent, a mode of expressing itself to us, and by it we often form our own opinions not only of the shape, but of the strength and uses of a thing.' Decoration should, according to Morris, enhance objects' forms and functions rather than disguise them.

After coming down from Oxford, Morris trained as an architect. Red House was built in 1860, and immediately afterwards Morris formed a company with, among others, Dante Gabriel Rossetti, Ford Madox Brown, Edward Burne-Jones and Philip Webb. It was the first of many Arts and Crafts workshops that were to emerge in England in the second half of the nineteenth century. Although he worked with others on designs for furniture, Morris was, in the end, a designer of surfaces, and his

**William Morris** (attributed to C. Fairfax-Murray).

68

textiles, wallpapers and carpets testify to his skill as a pattern-maker. At first the company was involved mostly with commissions for stained glass, which suited the Pre-Raphaelite element of the group ideally, as it combined medieval subject-matter, a stylized flat treatment of the imagery selected and, above all, an emphasis on light. In 1871 Morris left London for Kelmscott Manor in the Cotswolds, and in 1875 the company was dissolved. It was in that same year that the first designs for machine-made carpets were executed, and embroidery and tapestry work became important means of expression for Morris.

## MORRIS THE SOCIALIST

The 1880s were dominated for Morris by more direct political activity. At the root of all his beliefs lay a fundamental concern with the concept of work and with Ruskin's idea that joy should be evident in every product. He wrote: 'Nothing should be made by man's labour which is not worth making or which must be made by labour degrading to the makers.' This concern with the nature of labour led Morris, in the 1880s, to become a committed and active Socialist and his ideas changed in the light of this. His famous statement, 'I don't want art for a few, any more than education for a few, or freedom for a few', united his dual interests in artistic production and social theory. In 1878 he expressed a great hope in the power of art to transform the everyday environment when he wrote that: 'Art will make our streets as beautiful as the woods, as elevating as the mountain-side: it will be a pleasure and a rest, and not a weight upon the spirits to come from the open country into a town. Every man's house will be fair and decent, soothing to his mind and helpful to his work.'

Paradoxically, however, in the last years of Morris' life, at the same time as his Socialist ideas developed, his designs became increasingly complex and expensive, and the commissions he received were to decorate the interiors of such exclusive buildings as St James's Palace and Balmoral. To understand Morris one has to separate his theory and his practical work, as the former functioned within the framework of a Utopian future while the latter had to grapple with the realities of industrialized Britain. Towards the end of his life Morris became increasingly interested in printing, and he set up the Kelmscott Press in order to pursue this interest. Once again medieval subject-matter predominated, but the form of the typography was unmistakably clear and modern.

Morris is a complex, ambiguous figure, combining radicalism—politically and in terms of design—with a deep-seated respect for tradition and a strong streak of romanticism. He wrote that: 'My work is the embodiment of dreams in one form or another.'

The strong link between ethics and design which had been established earlier in the century by Pugin and Ruskin continued to underpin

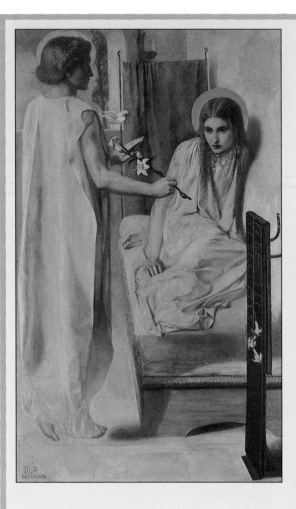

### MORAL YEARNINGS
*The Annunciation* (**top left**) by Dante Gabriel Rossetti. Rossetti was a founder member of the Pre-Raphaelite Brotherhood, which included the painters William Holman Hunt and Sir John Everett Millais. Their work was heavy with symbolism. Like William Morris, they were moralists and concerned with the apparent lack of values in their contemporary Victorian industrial society. But Morris, regardless of his utopianism, had a genius for ornament, as seen in the drawing-room (**right**), that remains influential.

the work of Morris and the many protagonists of the Arts and Crafts Movement, which took his cause on board and pushed it several stages further. Kenneth Clark has written that 'whenever aesthetic standards are lost, ethical standards rush to fill the vacuum', an observation which rings true in the context of British late nineteenth-century design.

**69**

## THE ARTS AND CRAFTS MOVEMENT

In her book on the Arts and Crafts Movement, Gillian Naylor writes that it grew out of a 'crisis of conscience'. The Movement was in fact an umbrella one, covering the formation of a number of guilds between the years 1880 and 1890, among them MackMurdo's Century Guild formed in 1882; Lethaby and Crane's Art Workers' Guild created in 1884; the Arts and Crafts Exhibition Society formed in 1885; and C.R. Ashbee's Guild and School of Handicraft established in 1888. The 'crisis of conscience' was focused on doubts about machine production and the nature of the environment. As

English architect William Burges, relished the medieval and pushed Gothic design into the theatrical. His washstand, 1880 **(above)**, is carved, painted and gilded.

The design of the title page of A.H. Mackmurdo's book **Wren's City Churches**, 1883, was considered revolutionary. C.R. Ashbee, who designed the glass vase, was another Arts and Crafts designer. Art nouveau revitalized organic decoration.

Ashbee explained in 1908: 'The Arts and Crafts Movement means standards, whether of work or life; the protection of standards whether in the product or the producer; and it means that these things must be taken together.'

The main protagonists of the Movement were MackMurdo, Voysey, C.R. Ashbee and Walter Crane. Most of them were trained as architects but, following Morris' example, they moved into the areas of interiors, furniture, textiles and small decorative objects. MackMurdo's Century Guild united designers, decorators and sculptors—among them Selwyn Image, Clement Heaton and Heywood Sumner. MackMurdo strove through his association with men like Whistler and Yeats to eliminate the barriers erected between art and craft; in his own words, 'to render all branches of art the sphere no longer of tradesman, but of the artist', in order to lift design out of the commercial abyss into which it had fallen.

Once again, attitudes towards the machine were ambiguous. 'Craft' came to be associated less with 'hand-made' than with a new aesthetic based on the craft process. Machine production, the guilds mostly agreed, was inevitable—as Ashbee explained: 'Modern civilization rests on machinery and no system for the endowment or encouragement of the teaching of art can be sound that does not recognize this.' But the results of machine production were in need of substantial reform, and this reform was seen as having to take place on a social as well as an aesthetic front.

Although he did not belong to any of the guilds, Voysey was a central figure within the Arts and Crafts Movement, contributing numerous textile and wallpaper designs through the 1870s, 1880s and 1890s. However closely his patterns resembled those which were emerging on the Continent under the banner of the new architectural and decorative art movement named art nouveau, Voysey was suspicious about what he felt to be the decadence of that particular aesthetic manifestation. He clung instead to the spiritual base that Ruskin had defined for English architects. 'The new architecture cannot last,' maintained Voysey. 'The architects have no religion. They are like designers who draw flowers and trees without remembering and honouring Him who created them.'

C.R. Ashbee's way of solving his particular 'crisis of conscience' was to reject in its entirety modern city life and to take his craft workshop to a small village in the Cotswolds. It was in Chipping Campden that he created his guild, on the medieval model, where not only the jewellery and metalwork produced but the entire life-style of the community bore witness to the ideals outlined earlier by William Morris. Ashbee explained: 'So it comes that when a little group of men learn to pull together in a workshop, to trust each other, to play with each other's hands and understand each other's limitations, their combination becomes creative.' The Chipping Campden experiment took the spirit of medievalism further than any other British example, and it provided a model for several other reforming bodies to emulate in a number of different countries.

Among the other individuals working in the guilds as designers and spokesmen for the cause were those who first formed the Art Workers' Guild and who later moved into the Arts and Crafts Exhibition Society, the most active and influential organization of all. They included Walter Crane, an ardent Socialist; W.A.S. Benson, a metal-worker; William Lethaby, later to become the principal of the Central School of Arts and Crafts, and Lewis F. Day. Morris, however, was sceptical about the guild's work and wrote that: 'It was not by printing lists of names in a catalogue that the status of the workman could be raised, or the system of capitalistic commerce altered in the slightest degree.' Morris was, perhaps, less optimistic than his colleagues about the power of design to transform society. Indeed, it did not take long for the Arts and Crafts style to become commercialized and to be transformed into mere aestheticism.

# Aestheticism and symbolism

The so-called 'aesthetic movement' existed simultaneously with the Arts and Crafts Movement and, to some extent, shared its reforming idealism. Its theories were, however, less social than aesthetic. Although its origins were highly élitist, it provided a model for a fashionable way of life which was enjoyed by a large sector of the new middle-class consumers of the 1880s. Its fountainhead was fine art and literature, and it strove to 'aestheticize' the environment as a response to what it saw as the declining standards of contemporary taste.

William Gaunt in his book *The Aesthetic Adventure* described the Bohemians in France, who embodied the attitudes that moved into English aestheticism. He explained that: 'Bohemians had one law, one morality, one devotion, and that was—Art. It had to be so, for it was their sole justification.' His idea of the artists becoming the sole guardians and apologists for art to the exclusion of everything else was, in England, closely related to the emergence of machine production. Isolated from his intrinsic role in the production system, the artist needed to reassert his position. The social theories of William Morris and the craft guilds were rejected as being more concerned with society than with art, which had to be its own justification and *raison d'être*. Gautier's *l'art pour l'art* became the English 'art for art's sake', and as Oscar Wilde, the spokesman for the movement, stated, there need be no barrier between the fine and applied arts. 'Love art for its own sake and then all things that you need will be added to you . . . nor in its primary aspect has painting any more spiritual message for us than a blue tile for the wall of Damascus or a vase.'

This appreciation of art for its own intrinsic qualities led towards 'aesthetic' pleasure, ie, pleasure in beauty in the absolute Platonic sense of the word, which led eventually to the decadence associated with the 1890s. In the 1870s and 1880s there was, however, a high-minded reforming zeal which wanted to bring beauty back to the world, and amongst the initiates of the movement high standards of taste prevailed. Whistler, for instance, cried out against the fact that: 'Art has of late become . . . a sort of common topic for the tea table. Art is upon the Town—to be chucked under the chin by the passing gallant.'

In total contrast to the Arts and Crafts Movement, which wanted objects to be manifestations of hand production, the aesthetes wanted to disguise the work of the hand, allowing only the work of the eye to be evident. A vogue for painted furniture and interiors emerged as a result.

The first examples of painted furniture had been produced by Morris

Aubrey Beardsley's line illustrations tantalized the Victorians by hinting at the pleasure rather than the sinfulness of a little light naughtiness.

and the Pre-Raphaelites. In his late paintings, Rossetti moved away from the early 'truth to nature' dictum towards a use of symbolism—his model Lizzy Siddal became the archetypal 'aesthetic' woman. The use of the lily motif also became an aesthetic movement trademark.

Caricatures in *Punch* showed long, languid men draped on sofas and gazing at bunches of lilies, and Oscar Wilde claimed that the lily and the sunflower, which by the 1880s had become ornamental clichés, were 'the two most perfect models of design, the most naturally adapted for decorative art—the gaudy leonine beauty of the one, and the precious loveliness of the other giving to the artist the most entire and perfect joy',

**A QUICKENING OF WITS**
'Work is the curse of
the drinking classes' said playwright Oscar
Wilde **(right)** who persistently teased the
Victorians away from their hypocrisies. The
English lapped up light satires like **Patience**
by Gilbert and Sullivan and performed by the
D'Oyly Carte Opera Company. The
Worcester teapot **(far left)** was inspired by
**Patience**.

# PATIENCE
## D'OYLY CARTE OPERA COMPANY

The opening of Japan to the West in the 1860s caused Europe to import a flood of wood block prints and other objets d'art. Much of the 'traditional' work was designed by the Japanese especially for export. European painters and designers followed Japanese style and found ways of assimilating it with western style as in **The Japanese Scroll** by James Tissot, 1873 **(left)**.

thus justifying the emblems as decoration. This was characteristic of aestheticism at its high point. The love of art for its own sake developed into a self-contained world of feelings and symbols, in which the artist communicated by means of a set of artistic triggers. This was best seen in the world of poetry and printing, where the well-known motifs—the beautiful woman, the pomegranate, the lily, the sunflower and the peacock—became more than the sum of their parts. The motifs remained within the sphere of natural images but, as Whistler pointed out, the real artist *never* copied nature as Ruskin would have him do. 'The artist is born to pick, and choose, and group with science, these elements, that the result may be beautiful—as the musician gathers his notes, and forms his chords, until he bring forth from chaos glorious harmony.' An element of synaesthesia, which Baudelaire portrayed in his poem *Correspondances* and which later aesthetes like Marcel Proust were to develop, was evident too in Whistler's early paintings.

## THE JAPANESE INFLUENCE

Whistler was perhaps the most important artist of this period. His work showed all the obsessions of the time. Born in America, he came to Europe to live first in Paris and then in England, and he demonstrated one of the major features of the aesthetic movement—the impact of Japan. There was a Japanese stand at the 1862 exhibition at the Victoria and Albert Museum in London, but even before that date William Burges had begun his own collection of Oriental porcelain and *objets d'art*. The influence of Japanese prints on western aesthetics focused on the ideas of asymmetry, delicacy of line and fine decoration.

After a number of private commissions, among them a parasol and a trellis for friends, Whistler continued his adaptation of Japanese proportions and motifs with his work on the Peacock Room. This was designed by Thomas Jeckyll for his wealthy patron F. R. Leyland, in a house in Queen's Gate, London. It was Japanese in its structure and decorated with a frieze of peacocks. In the end, the peacock, another Japanese image, became the characteristic symbol of aestheticism and was used as a recurrent motif on fabrics and wallpapers. Rossetti himself had kept peacocks at Cheyne Walk in Chelsea. Elizabeth Aslin described the atmosphere of the time when she wrote that, '"Art" could be bought for the price of a sunflower or a peacock's feather'.

The Japanese influence led to a new sense of simple structure in furniture, and to a new form of pictorial decoration on furniture like that designed by E. W. Godwin. (Godwin was a close friend of Whistler, and he designed the White House in Tite Street, London, which was Whistler's home for some years.) This desire to 'aestheticize' the whole environment was characteristic of an age in which, said a periodical of the time: 'There has assuredly never been since the world began an age in which people thought, talked, wrote and spent such inordinate sums of money and hours of time in cultivating and indulging their tastes.'

The painted decoration deriving from Japanese art also influenced pottery in this period. By the 1880s every big pottery manufacturing firm—among them Doulton, Minton and Coalport—had registered a patent for a Japanese-style design.

The symbolic crisis of the period came in the 1870s, when Whistler sued Ruskin for libel over a review of an exhibition at the Royal Academy, in which Ruskin wrote that Whistler had 'flung a pot of paint in the face of the public'. The question of 'truth' was thus raised—is true art that which is copied religiously from life, or that which can create its own reality? Whistler lost his case and was fined a farthing's costs. The conflict was significant, as it showed how little the public had moved away from the idea of naturalism which had underpinned the art and design of the mid-century. Whistler's was a cult of the human and, usually, female form as 'ultimate beauty'.

The other major developments in these years were the increased ease with which goods could be transported by sea and by rail, the growth of advertising and, finally, the expansion of communication channels with other countries, particularly on the Continent. It was, for instance, through the many design periodicals of the day that the first international style of the mass age—art nouveau—had such dramatic effect on the decorative objects of so many different countries at the turn of the century. The area of economic and political nationalism became vitally important in these years as the British Empire dwindled and the newly industrialized powers competed for trade overseas. Art nouveau, and its national variants, represented one of the ways in which countries competed openly in the international market-place.

**The Peacock Room** by J.M.
Whistler, 1876. Whistler rivalled
his friend Wilde in barbed
witticisms, and his painting
generally upset Ruskin, whom
Whistler sued when accused by
Ruskin of 'flinging a pot of paint in
the public's face'.

# Art nouveau

The architectural and decorative arts style known as art nouveau (or *Jugendstil* as it was called in the countries where it took a hold) was a manifestation of many factors—political, social, cultural and technological.

Politically, for instance, it represented the efforts of a number of newly independent and unified countries—among them Germany, Italy and Finland—to assert themselves in the international arena and to enter into increasingly intensive international trading. Socially, it was an attempt on the part of architects and designers to penetrate the modern mass environment by influencing the appearance of underground stations, Socialist Party headquarters, restaurants and department stores. Culturally, it reflected a new sense of unity across the visual arts, from painting and sculpture through to graphics, glass, silver and furniture; and technologically it showed a willingness to exploit the new structural materials such as wrought iron and glass.

While the art nouveau architects and designers cherished these highly democratic aims, it cannot be said that it was a style that affected great numbers of people. It remained for the most part allied to craft production and was available only in rather expensive, exclusive objects. The main impetus behind the emergence of art nouveau was a dissatisfaction with historicism and a feeling that the new century needed a new style to accompany it.

Many of the preparatory steps for the emergence of art nouveau had already been taken earlier in the century. These included an emphasis on natural imagery, the influence of the asymmetrical aesthetic of Japan and an interest in symbolism. Art nouveau's origins lay in the work of the Arts and Crafts Movement in England, particularly in the graphic images of MackMurdo and Walter Crane. It spread rapidly across natural boundaries into Belgium, France, Spain, Germany, Austria, Finland and the US, covering a wide range of work within the areas of the fine and applied arts and architecture in the period 1890-1910. It concerned itself with

Nineteenth-century art nouveau could be extremely curvilinear and the twentieth-century reaction against it was inevitable. Later, Henri Van de Velde rejected in embarrassment the style of his hanging **(above)**. French art nouveau c.1900 **(left)**.

decoration and with structure, and established many ideas about the relationship between these two concepts which were to underpin the theories of the Modern Movement. In Belgium, for instance, Henry van de Velde wrote that: 'Ornament and the form should appear so intimate that the ornament seems to have determined the form.'

The early manifestations of art nouveau were characterized by the ubiquitous use of a curved line, often with a whiplash end, inspired by plant stems, swans' necks, the flowing lines of women's hair and other such essentially organic symbols. It was used graphically and structurally, and had a strong element of implied dynamism within it. One aim was the visual unification of the environment—the *Gesamtkunstwerk*—which preoccupied so many artists at that time.

What mass dissemination of the style there was was made possible by the fact that, by the 1880s, Europe had become both socially and economically stabilized. There was an increase in the number of exhibitions and periodicals which placed art and design in an international context. In Great Britain *Studio* magazine was the major voice, while in France this role was played by *L'Art Décoratif* and in Germany by *Pan*.

It was in Belgium that the style was first translated into three dimensions in the work of the architect Victor Horta. He used it both as

**77**

Art nouveau seems fresh after 80 years in which figurative ornament has been displaced by geometry and abstraction. Our modern world is more artificial than the world of the early 1900s. A lizard-shaped doorhandle and the gracious melody of the stone doorway provide a feast for one's eye and hand; both handle and doorway are to a house in the Avenue Rapp, Paris, 1901. Tiffany glass **(left)**, and more French art nouveau **(above)**.

### SOCIETIES IN FLUX

Café society flourished in Europe but not in England. However, the rail link across the Channel began the still-continuing process of bringing England closer to Europe. Meanwhile the process of improving the links between the old world and the new was eased once steamships became common. Transport in the cities was changing, with first London's Underground railways and then the Paris Metro. More people at more levels of society now travelled.

surface decoration and a structural aesthetic for interior details such as door handles and the curve of the banisters for example, in his Hotel Solvay. Willi Sypher in has book *Rococo to Symbolism* has, in fact, described art nouveau as a 'mode of decoration that makes possible a return to architecture'. Henry van de Velde represented the rational end of the art nouveau spectrum: he stressed the necessity of abstracting nature in order to produce a rational, intellectual form of design which linked decoration with structure.

**79**

## ART NOUVEAU IN FRANCE

In Paris art nouveau flourished between the years 1895 and 1900, exhibiting itself in that city in a highly decorative form. The architect Hector Guimard, for instance, wanted to add artistic beauty to banal objects such as gates, the façades of buildings and underground stations. Sometimes this meant adding sculptural detail, sometimes modifying the actual structure of the architecture concerned. Guimard's most impressive work was for the Paris Métro, in which the lights to the entrances rose up like buds on a stem. Iron became an essential material, enabling Guimard to fuse decoration and structure as absolutely as he did in the Castel Béranger of 1897.

Paris also boasted restaurant interiors decorated entirely in the art nouveau idiom, amongst them Maxims and the Restaurant Julien. Here too, the poster, covered with images of Sarah Bernhardt and the veil dancer Loie Fuller, took on its new role as an environmental force. Through its applied arts—the glass, furniture, ceramics and jewellery of men like Emile Gallé, based in Nancy, Eugène Gaillard and René Lalique—France contributed to the art nouveau movement in a major way, and played an important role in the transition from the nineteenth to the twentieth century. French art nouveau linked with the nineteenth century in its stress on individualism rather than collectivity. In many ways it represented a final nineteenth-century outburst of subjectivity and craftsmanship. This was also true of much art nouveau in other countries, for example in the work of Gaudi in Spain, of Tiffany in the US and of Endell in Germany. Yet within this essentially backward-looking stance there were many seeds of a foray into the future. As Maurice Rheims has written in his book *Art Nouveau*: 'On the one hand there was bourgeois Mannerism, the final expression of an aesthetic already on its deathbed; on the other, a bold, prophetic, revolutionary impulse.'

# Proto-Modernism at the turn of the century

While art nouveau looked both backwards and forwards at the same time, from within its ranks came the individuals who were going to take design reform into the twentieth century. Among them were men like Henry van de Velde, Peter Behrens, C.R. Mackintosh and Josef Hoffmann. The movement provided a necessary breathing space within which nineteenth-century historicism was finally shaken off and, perhaps more importantly, the influence of the modern age in the fullest sense could be absorbed. Proto-Modernism was a transitional phase—a step towards an understanding of the changes that had taken place in the mass environment. Mechanization, mass production and mass consumption dictated new sets of rules for the designer, and the nineteenth-century preoccupations with individualism and symbolism seemed less and less appropriate to a world which was increasingly dominated by the machine. Walter Crane had already seen the danger of letting decoration become an end in itself when he described art nouveau, the movement upon which he was, ironically, so influential, as a 'strange decorative disease', and this argument was taken up much more forcibly by the Viennese critic and architect Adolf Loos, in his famous essay of 1908, *Ornament and Crime*.

Ideas about collectivism, democracy and the machine were stimulated by the tremendous social and economic forces in play at the time—industrial modernization, market competition and inter-imperialist rivalry. Before these ideas could take hold, however, there was a need for an interval during which a number of individuals could clarify their implications and work out ways in which they could be expressed. This was clearly seen in Germany. Hermann Muthesius came to England to study domestic architecture and published his conclusions in his book *The English House* in 1904. Early German Modernism cannot be separated from the economic and political position of the country, which was rapidly increasing its power in Europe and building up its industries. The AEG electric company employed the architect Peter Behrens to design its buildings and its products, and the very first examples of industrial design were thus developed. This industrial emphasis was consolidated by the formation in 1907 of a group of manufacturers, retailers, architects and designers working together called the *Deutscher Werkbund*. Its work and output characterized the German adaptation of the English domestic style into mass production. The simple machine

Germany's AEG combine grew huge on the second industrial revolution: electricity. This AEG electric kettle was designed by Peter Behrens in 1908. C.R. Mackintosh, architect of the Glasgow tea rooms, 1898 (right), was the darling of the Vienna Secession.

aesthetic of its by-now standardized objects echoed the functional and constructional ideas of the British Arts and Crafts Movement. In 1914 the Werkbund had its first major exhibition, in which its ideals were expressed to the world, and in that year a debate between van de Velde and Muthesius about the importance of individualism or standardization highlighted the differences between the nineteenth and twentieth centuries.

## THE INFLUENCE OF C. R. MACKINTOSH

The other direction in which the English domestic revival had an effect was over the border in Scotland, where Charles Rennie Mackintosh, with his group of three co-workers, was aware of the English developments as propagated in the pages of the periodical *Studio*. Here again was an example of arts and crafts becoming proto-Modern in the use of materials, structural ideas and aesthetic concerns. Mackintosh stands on the sidelines of art nouveau with his use of rectilinear and occasional curvilinear forms in which decoration *is* structure, while maintaining its symbolic powers. His individual ideas about design, his modification of traditional Celtic motifs and his references to Scottish baronial architecture give Mackintosh a unique position in the development of modern architecture and design. The Glasgow School of Art, begun in 1897 and finished in 1909, makes use of the 'functional grid' system, while incorporating art nouveau details like the huge curved entrance and the metal window decorations which were there to help window cleaning. The building is an example of inner space dictating outward appearance (a characteristic of the later functionalist approach), the large studios lit up by the large windows which create the north-facing façade. The building is constructed on steel girders and cast-iron beams, with exterior walls made of local stone. Inside, the studios have removable wooden partitions, allowing an amount of flexibility and 'open-planning'. In spite of its obvious nineteenth-century affiliations, the building is an early example of twentieth-century thinking, in which function, structure and construction determine form. Mackintosh and his group exhibited in Vienna in 1900 and it was in Austria, not England, that the full effect of his work was felt.

## THE SECESSION

Like Germany, Austria invested its architecture and design with great significance. A breakaway group called the Secession included architects, designers and artists among its ranks. J. M. Olbrich built the Secession Building in 1898—a building which was both a defence and a prosecution of art nouveau with its decorated dome and severe façades. A use of the straight line characterized Austrian developments, and Otto Wagner's Majolika House and his Savings Bank

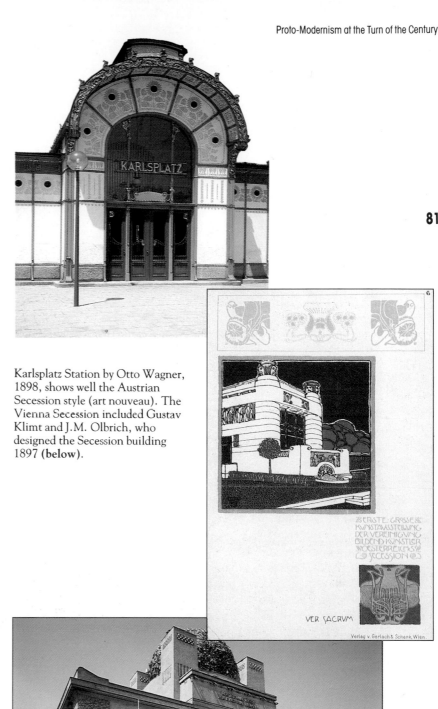

Karlsplatz Station by Otto Wagner, 1898, shows well the Austrian Secession style (art nouveau). The Vienna Secession included Gustav Klimt and J.M. Olbrich, who designed the Secession building 1897 **(below)**.

81

There is a sense of Dr Caligari's Cabinet about this Berlin cigar shop, designed by Henri Van de Velde in 1898. Note the stylized painted decoration representing cigar smoke.

combined art nouveau detail with engineering rationality and simplicity, rejecting the previous pervasive Austrian use of classical motifs. Wagner wrote his *Moderne Architektur* in 1895, in which he maintained that 'architecture should orientate itself to modern life' and that 'using new materials should lead to a new style more or less automatically'. This question of a new style which was simple and plain without unnecessary detail was discussed at length by Adolf Loos. His attitude embraced a total cultural approach to architecture and design, rather than treating them merely as a practical or functional justification of simple form. He wrote in his *Ornament and Crime*: 'Remember, the path of culture is the path away from ornamentation towards the elimination of ornament. The evolution of culture is synonymous with the separation of the ornamental from the functional. The Papuan covers everything within his reach with decoration, from his face and body down to his bow and rowing boat. But today tattooing is a sign of degeneration and is only used by criminals or degenerate aristocrats. And the cultured man finds, in contrast to the Papuan negro, that an untattooed face is more attractive than a tattooed one, even if the tattooing were the work of Michelangelo or Kolo Moser himself, and man in the nineteenth century wants to feel that not only his face, but also his suitcase, his dress, his household effects and his house are safe from the artistically trained latter-day Papuans. The Renaissance?

We have reached further. Our temples are no longer painted blue, red, green and white, like the Parthenon. No. we have learnt to discover the beauty of bare stone.'

## AMERICA AT THE TURN OF THE CENTURY

In America there was also a move towards a functional definition of architecture within the very different cultural context that existed there. In Chicago, the commercial centre of the Midwest, a fire in 1871 had wiped out many of the important buildings. Because of the price of the land and the commercial necessity of being in the centre of town, the 'skyscraper' emerged as an answer to this practical problem. The French architect Viollet-le-Duc had described such a building in the 1860s as 'a tall multi-storey building, supported by a steel frame and clad by non-structured brick masonry or glass walls'. The use of the steel frame enabled these buildings to employ large areas of glass in place of structural walls and aided the development of a new architectural aesthetic which emphasized the skeletal frame.

Louis Sullivan developed these ideas in Chicago at the turn of the century, evolving his organic thesis that 'form follows function', in which he showed how form grew out of internal necessity, as in a flower. His buildings followed a functional code which put services in the basement and the attic, used the ground floor as a commercial outlet onto the street and the rest of the floors as office space. The external appearance followed the logic of the plan, incorporating floral decoration on ground floor level and an arched top to the 'classical columns' between the rows of windows.

Frank Lloyd Wright, the other important American architect from this period, applauded these buildings and the machine aesthetic and predicted the mood of Marinetti and Le Corbusier in his statement that: 'The tall modern office building is the machine pure and simple . . . the engine, the motor and the battleship [are] the works of art of the century.'

Wright's own work, however, was at this time mainly in the field of domestic architecture. He worked on houses for private clients in which he developed his ideas about spatial continuity in the planning of a house, an open internal structure which dictated the form of the exterior, and, above all, the harmony of the built structure with its environment. Although his concerns were predominantly functional, he had a firm belief in the symbolic nature of the house, retaining the pitched, overhanging roof as a means of expressing the role of 'shelter', and employing a central hearth in his houses, again emphasizing their psychological protective function. Emphasis on horizontality showed the houses' connection with the earth, and the careful use of surroundings showed the relationship between man and his environment. These theories, developed at the turn of the century, were to be extremely influential on European and American Modernism in later years. Other

Department store, Chicago 1904, by Louis Sullivan. It has a steel structure and white terracotta surface. Sullivan and Adler's 1894 Chicago Stock Exchange **(left)** shows a geometric art nouveau. The oak chair (1904) is by Frank Lloyd Wright, a protégé of Sullivan.

countries contributed to the architecture of the early machine age, especially France with its use of reinforced concrete and its plans for a new industrial city. By about 1910 all the strands of modern architectural theory were firmly established in an international arena, just as the last flower of art nouveau was fading. The theory is predominantly an architectural one because of the stress upon technique, materials and form. The minimalist formal ideas, with their emphasis on the absence of decoration and ornament, were ultimately less important than the roles of construction and structure which derived from the ideal of machine production. The exigencies of industry were demanding simplicity to keep the cost of mass production low and to permit standardization, and the democratic emphasis necessitated a classless, simple design which was available to all.

Engineering principles had superseded those of the artist; logic and rationality ruled over imagination, and economic necessity precluded artistic fancy. The absence of an 'artistic' model was soon to be filled, though, by a return to inspiration from the visual arts once they had also evolved their own reductive 'machine aesthetic', that of analytical

Oak Park House, Illinois (above), and Kauffman department store, Chicago (below): Wright's imagery was rooted in natural forms and consequently his simple work was never barn-door plain.

cubism and its offshoots. By about 1912, the twentieth-century architectural theory was complete with a ready-made style to accompany it, a total new architectural language. Everything that came after this early formulation of the modern aesthetic, up to the Second World War, depended on it and was merely an extension of its laws. In the words of architectural historian Reyner Banham, speaking in 1960: 'The cultural revolution that took place around 1912 has been superseded, but it has not been reversed.'

By 1914 many of the idealistic theories of architects and designers had become much more directly aligned with modern practice and with the requirements of contemporary life. The ideas owed much to their nineteenth-century precursors—to the proto-functionalist ideas of Pugin, Morris and others—but they were born in a very different world and were to have more far-reaching effects. The backcloth for design change was by now an international one, but it was still dominated and manipulated by architects, whose ideas about the mass environment were highly influential across a wide spectrum of objects.

TORTURING WOMEN IN PRISON

VOTE AGAINST THE GOVERNMENT

THIS IS "THE HOUSE" THAT MAN BUILT.

AND this is the policeman all tattered and torn

Who wished women voters had never been born,
Who nevertheless
Tho it caused him distress
Ran them all in,
In spite of their dress:
The poor Suffragette
Who wanted to get
Into THE HOUSE
that man built.

**FEMALE SUBJUGATION**
Middle class women
were expected to keep house like the one here,
Manchester, 1900. Brave women, beginning the
twentieth-century fight for rights, were horribly
treated. Patterns of urban life changed as cities
grew. Stations like Waterloo enabled London to
grow south of the Thames. Office work became
the chief occupation of the lower middle class but
until the First World War it was mainly men's
work.

# PART TWO

**1915**

**1939**

Periods are not homogeneous in their styles: nations differ, classes differ, tastes differ. If we were to say these three pictures express the dilettante, the utopian and the ideologically hidebound, which label would we assign to which work?

In the years between the two world wars, all the factors we have come to associate with 'modern life' became a reality for the majority of people in the western world. At the same time modern design began to make a significant impact. Industrialization and urbanization—by now mature forces—brought into being a new life-style, characterized by the continued presence of 'masses' of people and by huge increases in consumption. In turn, this raised the standards of living and the material expectations of large sectors of the population.

The period was also characterized by an acceleration in the pace at which events influenced people's lives, and by the participation of the majority of the population in wage-earning employment outside the home. Later on, however, it became a time of plenty for some and of scarcity for others. The effects of the economic depression of the late 1920s and 1930s were widespread, causing considerable hardship at the lower end of the social spectrum in the US and a number of European countries.

The notion of the avant-garde took on a special meaning in this period and was a force to be reckoned with in the years immediately following the First World War. Experiments in Holland, Russia, France and Germany—followed later by others in Sweden and Italy—developed into a fully-fledged progressive modern architecture and design movement, influencing many of the efforts to revitalize the environment and to move away from nineteenth-century historicism and eclecticism. The Modern Movement was closely linked to the progress of mechanization, standardization and mass production—or rather to the *idea* of these new concepts—proclaiming the birth of a new design which would transform the physical appearance of the modern world and the life-styles of its inhabitants. It accepted, again as an abstract concept only, the idea of the new, mass society, and claimed to be the first design movement to embrace essentially democractic principles. Yet it failed to understand the basic laws of a capitalist economy, which required not universal but expendable objects, not absolute but temporary solutions. The gap between avant-garde ideals and the socio-economic reality of the new inter-war world was enormous. With the exception of the short-lived situation following the Bolshevik uprising in Russia in the years after 1917, the Modern experiment in design in its early, most radical phase failed as the Utopian society it envisaged, and upon which it ultimately depended, did not emerge.

The years after the First World War saw sudden and far-reaching change. In the area of manufacturing, for instance, the pre-war forays into mass production by the American automobile and domestic appliance industries became fully-fledged realities after 1918. The 1920s saw huge increases in production, followed, inevitably, by an expansion of consumption; it looked, for a while, as if the dreams of men like Henry Ford had been realized. What he, and a few others, had not fully understood, however, were the expectations of more affluent consumers, who now demanded more variety in the products they bought. Ford was soon forced to revise his famous ideas about the nature of standardization. The missing element in many discussions about design in the years leading up to the Wall Street Crash of 1929 was the consumer. It was not until the following decade that the industrial designer emerged, on American soil, to focus on his needs—both aesthetic and symbolic. Politically, the years after 1918 were highly volatile, as the revolutions in Russia, Germany and Austria clearly demonstrated. In the following two decades the major nation-states sought ways of stabilizing themselves internally and in the field of international relations. The economic depression of the '30s aggravated the uncertainties of the period causing a number of countries to opt for totalitarian leaderships. The relationship of these regimes with design will be discussed in the first chapter of this section, as will the implications of the hardening distinction between totalitarian and democratic regimes.

Many of the themes which become prominent in the years between the two world wars both influenced and were influenced by design developments. The expansion of retailing, the decline in the number of servants, the developing role of the housewife and hence the growth of a range of labour-saving domestic appliances presented new challenges to the new generation of industrial designers. So too did the emergence of new materials such as rayon, aluminium and plastics, and the growing trend for the designer to work as an adjunct to mass-production industry.

This section will examine a number of these themes, showing how they related to the context which created and sustained them. Chapters 4 and 5 will concentrate on the influence of social and political changes on design; and Chapters 6 and 7 will examine the theoretical background to the Modern Movement in architecture and design, and contrasting its avant-garde and popular manifestations.

# CHAPTER FOUR

# POLITICS SOCIETY & DESIGN

> " IN THE NEW ORDER OF SOCIETY IN WHICH WORK WILL CEASE TO BE SLAVERY, IN WHICH THERE WILL NO LONGER BE SMALL GROUPS PRODUCING LUXURIES FOR A RESTRICTED STRATUM OF SOCIETY, BUT WHERE WORK IS BEING DONE BY EVERYONE FOR EVERYONE, IN SUCH A SOCIETY WORK IS GIVEN FREE SCOPE AND EVERYTHING WHICH IS PRODUCED IS ART "
>
> *EL LIZZITZKY, QUOTED IN C. GRAY, THE GREAT EXPERIMENT: RUSSIAN ART 1863-1922 (1982)*

The relationship between political events and design change took on a new intensity in the years immediately following the First World War. Prior to then, design had been seen as an important element within international relations and the fight for hegemony, and a number of individuals—among them William Morris and Walter Crane—had considered it an essential element of the Socialist revolution. It had not yet had to prove its potential within a situation of political change. With the Russian Revolution of 1917, design was given an opportunity to demonstrate its work as a political tool and to show that it was imbued with the power to transform society and to realize the aims of Socialism in a tangible form.

At the turn of the century, modern design had been part of a crusade in a number of countries for economic nationalism. The drive towards nationalism in fact lay behind the growing international rivalry in all sorts of areas in the years up to 1914—ultimately, indeed, it was one of the factors which led two world wars. Through a 'national style', newly unified countries such as Germany and Italy sought to establish a special identity on the world market and thereby to achieve a powerful position within it. Others such as the US and Great Britain claimed their positions through their respective commitments to advanced technology and to tradition, but, generally speaking, the aesthetic of the product assumed an increasingly important role. The world exhibitions in the second half of the nineteenth and the early years of the twentieth century provided shop windows where countries could view the material achievements of competing nation-states. The main message to be promoted abroad was that of technological and cultural progress. A high design profile indicated that a nation was in control of its means of production and able to present itself with an assured image on the world market. The Paris exhibition of 1867, the Vienna exhibition of 1873 and Philadelphia's 'Centennial Exhibition' of 1876 all provided opportunities for this kind of national self-promotion. Even Japan, the first of the Asian countries to

industrialize, was keen to advertise its progress at these venues. Alternatively the harnessing of national traditions could indicate the extent to which a country was in touch with its own past, and the decorative arts of Britain, Sweden and Japan, among others, showed many signs of this more conservative approach to design. The US and Germany were much more committed to a futuristic, machine-inspired aesthetic, and took every opportunity to express this to the rest of the world.

With the advent of the First World War, technology and production were, inevitably, focused on the war effort and its material and technical needs. Many developments in the application of electricity and experiments in new materials resulted from the war, and the expanded production of the post-war years owed much to initiatives taken under war conditions.

Much avant-garde art, architecture and design in the post-war years owed its emergence to a particular political context. The Russian movement grew out of the actuality of the Bolshevik Revolution, and the *De Stijl* Movement in Holland was a direct result of that country's neutrality during the First World War.

In Russia after 1917 peasants and workers were exhorted to terrify the bourgeoisie (left), but before the First World War Russia had seemed more likely to develop into a bourgeois capitalist society, sustained, as in Germany, by market-led industry. Peter Behrens designed these electric fans for AEG in 1908.

## PEOPLE AT WAR

The First World War destroyed old Europe, quickened the graphic arts of the propagandist and increased the sum total of industrial knowledge. Under the necessity of war, chemicals, machine tools, auto engines and metallurgy all underwent rapid development. Women did men's work, but only while it was convenient to the British government. After the war, the gender demarcations in factory work returned.

# Avant-garde design in Russia

Before the war, the Italian futurist movement had anticipated the possibility of design's intervention in everyday life through its absorption and depiction of the qualities of mechanization and speed. As Banham has explained in his book *Theory and Design in the First Machine Age*: 'Apart from the introduction of gas-lighting, the appearance of the streets of most capital cities hardly altered between 1800 and 1880, after which the increasing use of buses and trains, and their subsequent mechanization began to alter the urban pattern more rapidly.'

This new, exciting environment inspired the futurist painters, poets and architects—among them Marinetti, Balla, Carrà and Sant'Elia—to produce works which both reflected and celebrated their world. It was the 'new spirit' that they exalted and which led them, as a group, into the politics of Fascism, which depended upon an emotional involvement with modern life and the new, mass environment. As Benedetto Croce

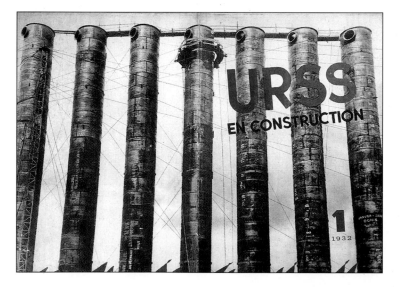

Years after this Russian poster was produced in 1932, Nikita Kruschev, visiting America, thought the New Jersey industrial landscape beautiful: generations of Communist leaders were in thrall to smoke stacks.

explained in 1924: 'The ideological origins of Fascism can be found in futurism, in the determination to go down into the streets, to impose their own opinions, to stop the mouths of those who disagree, not to fear riots or fights, in its eagerness to break with all traditions....'

The mood behind the work of the Russian constructivists in the years after 1917 depended upon a similar emotional commitment to modern life. Their work was clearly 'futurist' in inspiration, exalting the forces of mechanization and speed, but their political circumstances and their ends were very different. They sought to provide a new aesthetic and life-style for post-Revolutionary Russia, to reinforce the principles of the Socialist revolution which depended upon groups of people acting together, and upon the necessity for radical change rather than gentle evolution.

In 1913 a group of Russian painters who called themselves the Rayonists had proclaimed, in true futurist spirit, that: 'The genius of the day is: trousers, jackets, shoes, tramways, buses, aeroplanes, railways, magnificent ships—what an enchantment, what a great epoch unrivalled in world history.'

After the Revolution it was to the design of many of these products that some Russian designers turned, determined not simply to be inspired by them but to create them. After 1917, the movement called 'constructivism' developed as a means of bridging the gap between objects, buildings and culture, and of defining the 'artist' in terms of his relationship with the industrialized world.

The Russian artists, among them the painter Kasimir Malevich and the sculptor Vladimir Tatlin, set out with the specific intention of changing society rather than merely depicting its new character. This was a development of their pre-war avant-garde activities, and Tatlin explained that: 'What happened from the social aspect in 1917 was realized in our work as pictorial artists in 1914, when materials, volume and construction were accepted as our foundation.'

For Tatlin the materials from which his constructions were made and their intended use were paramount, and in his corner-sculptures of around 1913 he had already begun to formulate the necessity for a direct relationship between the artist and the age in which he lives by using metal. Equally, in his abstract 'non-objective' paintings of the years before 1917, Malevich saw his own work as 'anticipating the revolution in economic and political life of 1917'.

After the Revolution both these artists turned to the design of practical artefacts, from clothing to buildings, although they differed in

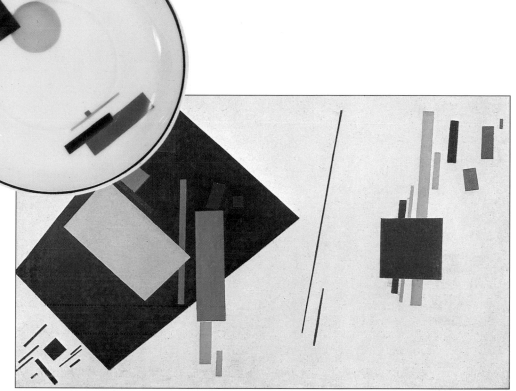

PROPOSAL FOR A MONUMENT TO THE THIRD INTERNATIONAL
by Tatlin (Front View)

Stalin loathed modern art and design even though its protagonists called them Revolutionary. Tatlin's tower **(far left)**, Malevich's painting **(above)**, Suetin's ceramics, and Popova's textiles **(left)** were among the flowers crushed by the dictator.

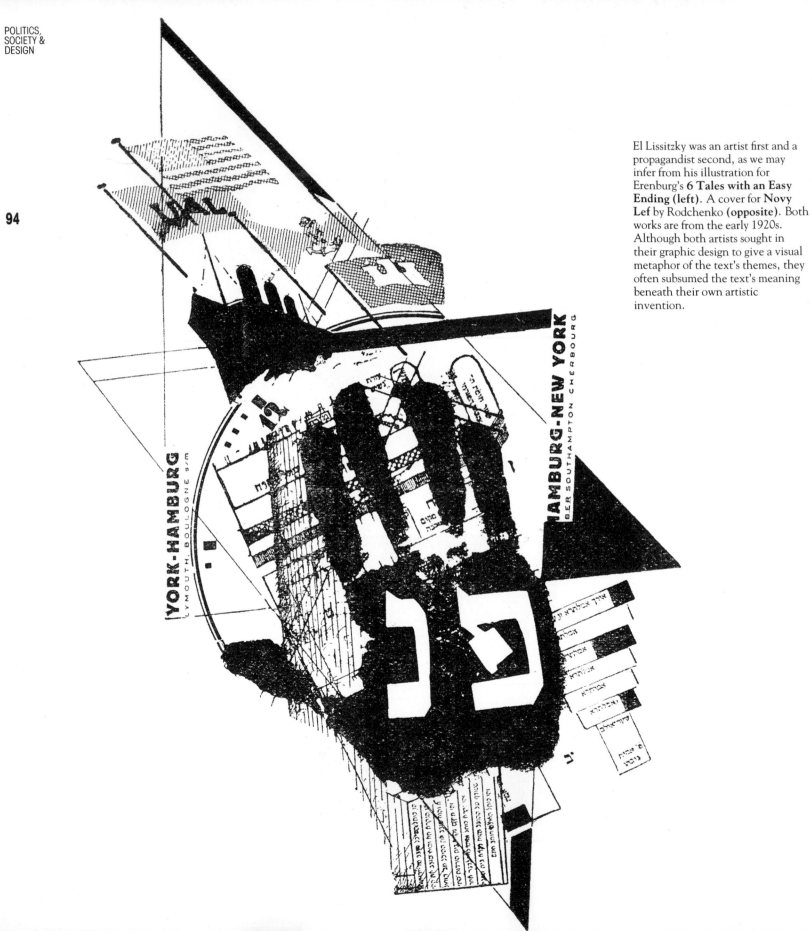

El Lissitzky was an artist first and a propagandist second, as we may infer from his illustration for Erenburg's **6 Tales with an Easy Ending (left)**. A cover for **Novy Lef** by Rodchenko **(opposite)**. Both works are from the early 1920s. Although both artists sought in their graphic design to give a visual metaphor of the text's themes, they often subsumed the text's meaning beneath their own artistic invention.

their theoretical positions. While Malevich saw this activity as essentially one of 'applying art' in the tea-sets and theatre scenery he worked on, Tatlin became more closely involved with the idea of engineering and the importance of 'function'. He wrote that he saw an 'opportunity emerging of uniting purely artistic forms with utilitarian intentions' and, in the designs for his *Monument to the Third International* and for his workers' clothing, concerned himself with these aims. Tatlin's ideas inspired other artists and designers working in the post-Revolutionary period—among them Rodchenko and El Lissitzky whose graphic 'constructions' from those years were primarily designed to serve the needs of the Revolution.

It was in providing the props for the Revolution that the Russian designers came into their own: they created the agitation posters, decorated the streets for the May Day parade, designed boiler suits for workers, as well as factories for them to work in and communal housing complexes for them to live in. In these last projects they were able to unite theory and practice by making communal living possible, and they used the language of Modernism to express the ideology they were embracing. One of the Vesnin brothers described a 'constructivist' building in the following terms, showing the importance of its context and function. 'The building is characteristic of an age that thrusts after glass, iron and concrete. All the accessories that a metropolitan street imposes on a building—illustrations, publicity, clock, loudspeaker, even the lifts inside—are all drawn into the design as equally important parts and brought into unity. This is the aesthetic of constructivism.'

The constructivists' ultimate ambition was for the proletariat to create its own houses and objects of everyday life, and for the artists and designers to hand over those responsibilities. Their role was essentially that of a catalyst.

The poster provided the most appropriate combination of utilitarian function and expressive power—and it was in this field that El Lissitzky flourished. Trained as an architect, he went on to produce posters, book jackets and letterheads and to champion what came to be called the 'new typography', a particularly expressive version of the international modern idiom. He expressed the aims of his colleagues when he wrote, in the 1920s: 'In the new order of society in which work will cease to be slavery, in which there will no longer be small groups producing luxuries for a restricted stratum of society, but where work is being done by everyone for everyone, in such a society work is given free scope and everything which is produced is art.

'Thus the conception of art as something with its own separate existence is abolished.'

In his continued commitment to the concept of 'art', El Lissitzky shared some of Malevich's idealism, unlike Rodchenko and Tatlin, for whom technique and function were the ultimate goals.

For just over a decade, until Socialist realism was promoted by Stalin

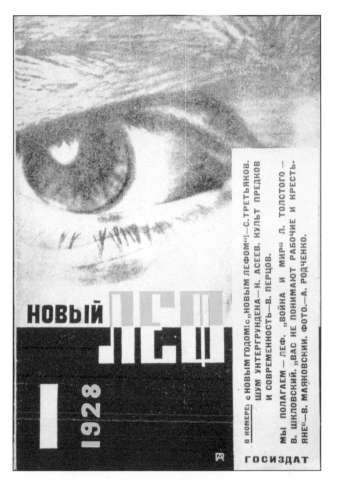

in 1932, the Revolutionary Russian designers had an opportunity to turn their ideals into tangible forms, and to bring both the aesthetic and the ideology of Modernism into line with political reality—however naive their understanding of that political reality may have been. It was a unique set of circumstances as, generally speaking, Modernism remained at odds with the ideology (of capitalist mass production and consumption) which created it.

### REVOLUTION
The inspired graphics romanticize a revolutionary programme that had no mass support, but it had Rodchenko's designs – a Civil War poster **(above)**, and a Bolshevik postcard 'Long Live the Revolution' **(left)** were appropriately aggressive.

# De Stijl

The other major experiment in avant-garde design took place in Holland in the years after 1917. Dutch neutrality during the 1914-18 war had given a number of Dutch avant-garde artists, designers and architects the time and the incentive to evolve a new theory of form whose essence was idealistic, philosophical and very far removed from the basic necessities of everyday life. The objects they developed were more concerned with the articulation of space and volume than with practicalities, but, in ideological terms, they reflected a commitment to a uniform, undifferentiated, non-hierarchical society which denied class distinction and artistic élitism.

The *De Stijl* movement was essentially Utopian in nature and while it influenced the design of a number of shops, buildings and interiors commissioned by enlightened clients and became the philosophical and aesthetic basis of international Modernism in the 1920s, it failed to penetrate the mass-produced environment in a significant manner.

*De Stijl* differed from futurism in its commitment to order and objectivity. Banham writes that: 'They had crossed the watershed that divides the pre-war futurist attitude to machinery as the agent of private, romantic, anti-classical order, from the post-war machine aesthetic that saw machinery as the agent of collective discipline and an order that drew nearer and nearer to the canons of classical aesthetics.'

An altogether cooler approach to technology therefore characterizes the *De Stijl* aesthetic which claimed the mass-produced artefact as its

MAANDBLAD GEWIJD AAN
DE MODERNE BEELDENDE
VAKKEN EN KULTUUR
RED. THEO VAN DOESBURG.

*De Stijl* was not just an elaborate theory of metaphysics but a club, a meeting point, a movement.

starting point. In a discussion of the objects which inspired his work, the *De Stijl* architect J.J.P. Oud, for instance, asserted that it was 'automobiles, steamers, yachts, men's wear, sports clothes, electrical equipment, table-ware, and so forth' which he saw as the point of departure for a new aesthetic. Like all their international avant-garde counterparts, the *De Stijl* artists and designers, including Mondrian, Theo van Doesburg and Gerrit Rietveld, were concerned with the idea rather than the actuality of mass production. As a result they developed a highly abstract picture of its implications for design. Theirs was basically an emotional commitment to the new world. Van Doesburg (see p.00) was adamant, however, that the movement had a practical base and wrote in 1922 that: 'It is not the result of some humanitarian, idealistic or political sentiment, but of that amoral and elementary principle in which science and technology are based.' But his words remained, on the whole, unconvincing. The group took on the name *De Stijl* ('The Style'), the title of a publication which first appeared in 1917 and which served as a platform for the articulation of their ideals, and a shop window for their paintings, sculpture, architecture and furniture. The *De Stijl* aesthetic was based on a neo-Platonic belief in such abstract concepts as the 'reality behind appearances', 'unity in plurality' and 'individuality in universality', from which its protagonists developed a strict language of pure form. Rietveld's

famous red-blue chair of 1919 epitomized the 'elementarist' aesthetic they all aspired towards. It was an abstract exercise in the formal problems of chair design and construction, showing not how it is used, but the means of its manufacture. It is a kind of meta-chair, functioning as a comment rather than as an object to sit on. The historian Peter Collins has said of this problematic chair: 'Where *De Stijl* was original as regards furniture design, was in creating the first chair deliberately designed not for comfort, not for dignity, not for elegance, not for rational assembly according to commonly accepted principles of woodwork, but simply "designed".'

While the chair was not, at least at the time, mass produced, it incorporated a statement about mass production and was conceived within the context of mass production.

Such rarefied ideals lay behind all the *De Stijl* experiments in the years 1917 to 1928, including Rietveld's Schroeder House and van Doesburg and Oud's architectural projects. The movement stands, perhaps, as a bid for collectivism in a world of advanced capitalism—a bid too Utopian to succeed in the complex mass environment without substantial political underpinning. Nevertheless, the style played an important role within international avant-garde design in these years.

Utility was not the soul of the Modern Movement. Men like Theo van Doesburg had loftier, metaphysical ambitions. Gerrit Rietveld, the carpenter turned designer and architect, designed this house in Utrecht **(below)** in 1924.

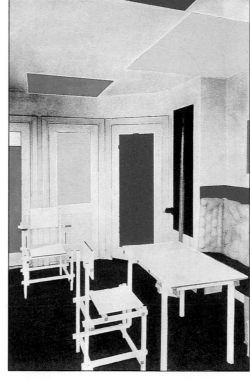

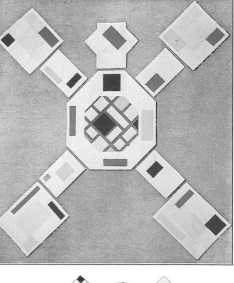

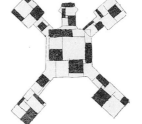

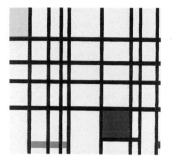

The painting **Red, Yellow and Blue** by Piet Mondrian encapsulated the aesthetic that others, such as J.P. Oud, wanted to build.

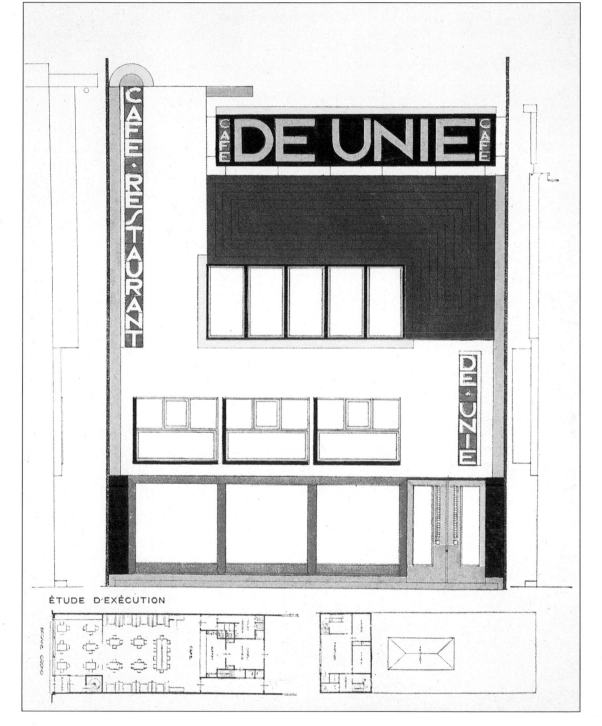

# Politics and design in the 1930s

**W**hile the political aftermath of the First World War encouraged the emergence of a highly theoretical avant-garde movement in art, architecture and design, the relationship between politics and design changed later in the inter-war period.

In Russia, Stalin outlawed avant-garde experimentation; and the emergence of Fascism in Germany brought to an end the expansive and radical projects of the earlier Weimar period. Hitler closed the Bauhaus (see p.00) in Dessau, the home of German experimental design, in 1933. The intervention of the state in avant-garde design became a characteristic of the early 1930s in those countries whose economic insecurity had aided the rise of totalitarian regimes.

In Italy, the country with the oldest Fascist government (Mussolini came to power in 1922), the relationship between modern design and the state was highly complex. Unlike Hitler, Mussolini had a certain amount of interest in modern architecture and was not averse to its manifestations. A number of Italian rationalist architects, among them Giuseppe Terragni and Giuseppe Pagano, continued to work through the 1930s— Terragni even designed the Fascist Party's headquarters. On the whole though, the official architecture and design of Italy in the 1930s became that of the 'novecento' style, a fusion of rationalism and neo-Classicism.

In Germany Hitler supported the rationalization of industry in the 1930s, particularly where arms production was concerned and he sponsored the development of modern road systems. Where national style was concerned, however, Hitler favoured neo-Classical for his official buildings, and a revival of the German craft aesthetic also took place in this period.

The countries with a democratic system in the 1930s operated a much more open-ended design programme and within the capitalist economies, design continued to be largely controlled by such forces as competition in the market place and mass consumption. At one end of the spectrum, in the US, design was sponsored purely by manufacturing industry and ignored by the state. In Sweden the Social Democratic government sponsored many of the community-oriented architectural projects of the decade. In Britain there was a certain amount of state patronage through bodies like the Council for Art and Industry, set up to help promote design as part of the export drive, but with few significant results.

The influence of party politics, whether directly through wars and

### DICTATORIAL KITSCH

Nazism, like Fascism, was a nightmare and, like many dictatorships, chronically prone to kitsch – possibly the result of having instantly to generate recognizable symbolism to impress the party's presence on the public's mind. So many twentieth-century despots have been inimical to good architecture, but some good product design emerged: the Volkswagen (**above**); the Fiat 508 (**right**) – cars for the people.

revolutions, or through decisions about neutrality, or state intervention in matters concerning design, was a major component in the push towards or pull away from Modernism in different countries in the inter-war years.

In the inter-war years, a few designers allied political with design radicalism, but this was a relatively rare phenomenon. As a politically subversive tool, design has not had the strongest of voices in this century.

Political art: a sycophantic socialist realist painting by K. Aksenov celebrates Lenin's return to Russia; John Heartfield developed the subversive art of radical discontinuity – the photomontage – while Nazi propagandists played Pied Piper to German youth.

# Society and design

The changing shape and nature of the market were among the strongest influences upon design in the inter-war years. In the number of people purchasing new products for the first time, the US clearly led the way. Urbanization took a leap forward there in the 1920s, and was accompanied by a huge consumer boom, unequalled until the 1950s. The main causes were high wages and employment, caused by the expansion in manufacturing and the tendency towards smaller families. Additional factors were the increased status symbolism attached to the ownership of consumer objects such as vacuum cleaners, electric refrigerators and automobiles, and the expansion of department stores and other retail outlets.

Changed consumption patterns in the US put pressure on manufacturers to meet the market's growing needs. Whereas in pre-war years the average American family had been content to run a model T Ford and manage with the minimum of household appliances, by the 1920s it was prepared to pay a little more for those products that had 'consumer' appeal. By the middle of the decade, General Motors, which had pioneered the annual model change, was selling more cars than Ford, whose principle of standardization was rapidly becoming outmoded.

The influence of the market on mass-manufactured goods was crucial in defining the appearance of new products and the way the manufacturer sold them. Advertising expanded in response to the need for a 'hard sell', and producers became increasingly aware of the 'image' of their products.

These forces were felt most strongly in the products of the new industries, as the traditional industries—ceramics, glass, textiles and furniture—had long ago established their markets and their 'identities'. Cars, and other new products had, up to now, sold on the basis of their technological novelty and utilitarian qualities, combined, in many cases, with a traditional image. With increased consumption this had to change, and the car, for instance, became not just a useful tool but a sleek projectile symbolizing the new values of speed and optimism.

Where kitchen appliances were concerned, a rather more complex social situation existed, influencing the way that manufacturers marketed their goods. Appliances manufactured in the first decade of the century had been sold primarily on the basis of their cost-cutting and labour-saving qualities. This was related to the so-called 'servant problem' and the attempts being made to systematize housework along the lines of the 'scientific management' newly introduced in factories.

By the 1920s the problem of finding good servants had become very

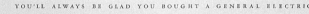

While the old world was menaced by social engineers like Stalin and Hitler, the Americans got on with designing the new world good life. General Electric, 1939.

**DEPRESSION**
Steinbeck's novel *The Grapes of Wrath* captured the pain of the near starving American itinerants in the Depression. Other Americans were more fortunate – summer meant, not ailing crops, but new fashions.

severe in the US. Labour-saving goods had previously been seen as an incentive for servants to remain in service, rather than taking up alternative employment in a factory, office or shop. As the housewife took over the sole responsibility for household work in the 1920s and '30s, however, appliances were marketed not just as servant substitutes but as desirable status objects in themselves. They were aimed directly at the housewife, and it was claimed they would improve the quality of life in all sorts of magic ways.

An interesting example is the way that the refrigerator was designed and marketed. Prior to 1914, before it was perfected technologically, the gas or electric refrigerator had not really superseded the ice-box. After the war rapid advances were made and by 1930 large companies like General Electric, Westinghouse and Kelvinator all had an electric refrigerator on the market. Whereas the refrigerator of the early '20s had been a large wooden cabinet, looking more like a piece of furniture than an item of kitchen equipment, with the use of sheet steel, it gradually took on the familiar metal box shape. The little 'cabriole' legs were retained, and there was a problem in integrating all the parts of the machine into a single box. General Electric's refrigerator, for instance, had a 'bee-hive' compression unit perched on top of it right up until the mid-1930s, and it was not until the industrial designer Henry Dreyfuss was brought in that an integrated white metal box was finally achieved. In the mid-1930s Raymond Loewy created his famous 'Coldspot' refrigerator for Sears Roebuck, introducing elements from automobile styling into his design. The modern image he provided for the refrigerator lasted well into the 1950s.

The pressure to provide a modern visual identity for such products derived from the market need for object symbolism, which was due, in turn, to the general increase in affluence and consumer power. It brought the application of 'fashion' concepts to otherwise utilitarian products, which meant that designers became as important in this area as they had been in the creation of women's clothing, for example. The idea of the annual model change, which originated in the automobile industry, was quickly applied to many other products, and became the norm for mass production in this century. This tendency was fundamentally opposed to the ideal of universality and objectivity that the Modernists were proposing. It meant, instead, a much more relativist attitude towards the design of everyday goods. It was during the inter-war years that these two approaches to modern design, the idealistic and the pragmatic, began to manifest themselves, but they did not clash openly until after the Second World War. While idealism underpinned the major design movements throughout the century, pragmatism became the manufacturing and practical design norm, operating within the laws of mass production and consumption. These laws decree that, in order to keep the wheels of the economic capitalist system turning, consumption has to be continuous and on an ever-increasing scale. Object obsolescence becomes a *sine qua non*, and one of design's primary roles, therefore, is to produce continuous object innovation. Consumers may then be sold goods on their visual novelty, social cachet and so on, rather than for any obvious functional benefit, and the designer injects 'added value' into products. The concept of 'conspicuous consumption' derives from this law of economics; design is one of the major means whereby consumption is, in fact, made conspicuous.

The role of women as the major consumers of goods aimed at the domestic context was also important in the relationship between society and design during the inter-war years. Women's position in society had changed dramatically since the middle of the nineteenth century. They had taken on an important role in the household and, increasingly, in paid employment as well.

In the US the number of working women expanded enormously in the inter-war years. In Britain and Europe, in spite of the advances made during the First World War, many women then went back into the home, and only came out of it again after the Second World War. Yet in general women had more money to spend on the household than ever before in these years and, knowing this, advertisers pushed many goods in their direction. The flood of goods aimed at the home environment brought with it auxiliary products such as soap powder for washing machines, all of which were bought avidly by the housewife. While there is no doubt that many back-breaking tasks were either eliminated or speeded up, at the same time standards of cleanliness and hygiene were raised. White was adopted as a symbol of hygiene and the colour for the new 'labour-saving' kitchen appliances, but it showed up dirt more easily. So time spent in housework was not necessarily reduced, and in fact in many cases it actually increased.

The twentieth-century 'industrial revolution' in the home parallels the one that took place in the male-dominated factory in the previous century and had as important an influence upon the progress of modern design.

The idea of hygiene was a dominant social theme in this period, central to the housewife's concerns. It became increasingly important in discussions about design. As Adrian Forty has pointed out in *Objects of Desire*: 'From about 1920, the design of a very disparate range of articles and complete environments began to embody ideas of cleanliness, while the advertisements for the same products warned of the consequences of neglecting health and cleanliness, which ranged from emotional rejection by loved ones to social ostracism, illness, death and national downfall.'

This stemmed from the 'germ theory of disease' which had had a strong hold in the 1890s and which provided a rationale for keeping the household spotlessly clean and for washing clothes very frequently. By

the 1920s it had become a prerequisite for all appliance advertising, particularly for products such as vacuum cleaners.

By the 1930s these ideas were reinforced by other popular themes such as 'speed', which symbolized modern life and an optimistic approach towards the future in the same way as it had for the futurists twenty years earlier. This provided a means of escapism, just like the products of Hollywood.

**107**

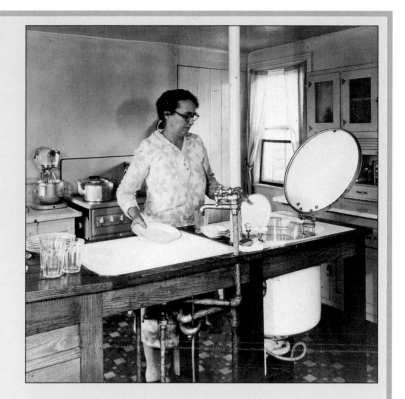

**WOMEN'S ROLES**
Brand naming became recognized as a formidable marketing tool and Coca Cola led the way, linking itself with healthy happiness and light sex. Women were recognized as new consumers and manufacturers devised new products for women, like the dishwasher **(above)**. In the Second World War it again suited the British Government to put women in 'men's' jobs.

Between the wars working women were more numerous in America than in Britain, and firms like Hoover took advantage of their spending power.

# CHAPTER FIVE

# INDUSTRY TECHNOLOGY & DESIGN

> **" A GREAT EPOCH HAS BEGUN. THERE EXISTS A NEW SPIRIT "**
>
> *LE CORBUSIER, TOWARDS A NEW ARCHITECTURE (1923)*

The relationship between industry and design in the inter-war years hinged most significantly on intensified mass production and mechanization in some quarters, and on the retention of craft techniques in others. Automobiles, domestic appliances and other products of the new industries, dependent upon a high level of scientific research and technological innovation, were manufactured in ever greater quantities with an increased use of machinery within 'rationalized' factories. The production of more traditional goods such as furniture, ceramics, glass and textiles was mechanized to only a limited extent and generally relied on existing technology. Inevitably the balance between mechanization in these two kinds of industry varied in different countries according to the scale of production and the nature of the different markets involved.

It takes time for a new technology to obtain its own design imagery; radios were once encased in wooden boxes but Wells Coates' round, plastic Ekco wireless, 1934 **(left)**, radiated modernity. Some years earlier, Ford, facing competition like the Cadillac from General Motors, learned that new styling was a commercial necessity.

CADILLAC · LA SALLE

# American industry and design

Noted for the relative homogeneity of its market from the mid-nineteenth century onwards, the US was at the forefront in developing mass production in this period. The nineteenth century initiatives in the introduction of specialized machine tools and highly organized division of labour systems, combined with the tradition of high capital investment in manufacturing industry, meant that the US was ready to supply the new, affluent market with all its needs. The principle of manufacturing goods in quantity, rather than supplying goods to fulfil needs on an individual basis, meant that a sophisticated system of marketing had developed to ensure that all the products would be bought and the company would not be left with surplus stock on its hands. High investment, quantity production and mass marketing combined to create a special formula which became the norm for many American companies concerned with consumer goods in the early years of the twentieth century.

Even Henry Ford, who claimed to supply the 'ultimate automobile', indulged in subtle model changes to meet the ever more sophisticated needs of his fashion-conscious market, although his advertising gave no suggestion of this in the years up until 1926. In his book *From the American System to Mass Production*, David Hounshell has argued that these model changes did occur but were only slight. By the late 1920s, however, when Ford realized that he had to introduce a completely new model to compete with the stylish products of the General Motors Company, he had to shut his River Rouge plant completely in order to retool for the model A.

The Ford experience taught that a commitment to single-purpose tooling and a highly mechanized and centralized production system did not allow for the flexibility needed to supply a market demanding not simply utility but aesthetic novelty as well. The introduction of design into production required a revised formula which combined quantity production with flexibility—a *sine qua non* for model variation.

General Motors succeeded in staying abreast of the increasingly fickle American market of the 1920s by keeping its lines—Cadillac, Buick, Pontiac, Chevrolet and others—quite distinct from each other, thereby offering choice of styles. In reality, of course, the basic frames of several models were shared, and only superficial details such as the trim distinguished one model from another. The Modernist principle of 'unity in diversity' was replaced by its reverse—'diversity in unity' in this marketing-led approach to design.

Between the wars American industry pioneered consumer-orientated industrial design – good examples of which were GM's Pontiacs and GEC refrigerators.

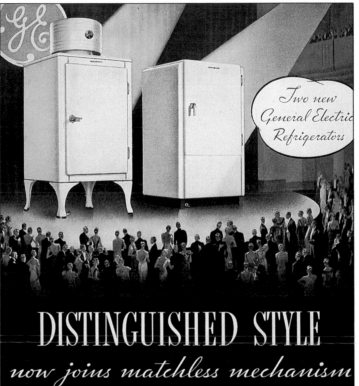

General Motors' strategy was adopted by nearly all the other American manufacturers of technological consumer goods through the 1930s. The pattern of a few, very large companies taking over from a much greater number of smaller, craft-based ones was repeated in other areas as well. While Ford, General Motors and Chrysler led the way in the field of automobile production, the giant firms of General Electric and Westinghouse dominated that of electrical appliances. Many methods of production, especially that of steel stamping, were also transferred from automobile to appliance production, and as a result the same companies often produced both kinds of goods. Frigidaire, for instance, was a section of General Motors, and Kelvinator belonged to the American Motor Company. With improved methods of steel pressing, the 'white' goods or kitchen appliances they produced changed from having an iron frame to being made entirely without joints.

# European industry and design

The American mass-manufacturing model provided an ideal which other countries sought to emulate, although they did not often succeed, as they were too reticent in embarking on marketing programmes. In Britain in the 1930s, for example, Morris Motors Ltd borrowed much from American methods, while others retained the older, small-scale coach-building approach. The Fiat factory in Italy also developed along American lines, as did a few European manufacturing firms such as the Italian Olivetti typewriter company and the German electrical companies, Siemens and AEG.

In general, the European craft-based industries were little changed in these years. Mechanization and electrification were introduced, but few factories undertook the full-scale reorganization that would have been needed to operate along Fordist lines. In Britain, for example, the furniture industry remained fairly conservative, both in its production methods and in the furniture it offered its customers. Based in High Wycombe, where it had developed in the last years of the nineteenth century, it continued to operate from modestly sized units in which hand-work, particularly where finishing was concerned, was still common. Gradually, however, as the market expanded through the inter-war years, new materials such as laminated wood and veneers were introduced to replace carving and hand-work. These innovations served not only to speed up and increase the scale of production, they also encouraged the emergence of simpler, more 'modern' furniture. Coupled with the changing market which, increasingly, sought modern-looking furniture for its new semi-detached homes, these technological changes were an important factor in moving Britain a small distance from its exclusive commitment to traditional furniture.

Compared with the Americans and Germans, the English, although dabbling in modern design and industry, preferred their Modernism to have a craft look. They preferred wood to metal, and a hand-finished joint to a machined weld. This sitting room was designed by Gordon Russell, 1930.

The Fiat Balilla 1933 **(above)** demonstrates the Italian flair for styling that, 30 years later, gave an edge to Italy's post-war manufacturing boom. In England new industry chose the affluent South East. This Hoover factory, 1932, is in west London. Today the factory is closed, but the building is still used.

# Craft and design in Scandinavia

The countries that were most successful in imparting a modern aesthetic to their traditional craft industries were the Scandinavian ones, especially Sweden, Denmark and Finland. They were countries with small, fairly homogeneous populations and few natural resources which had developed strong craft traditions in producing decorative domestic items. With the breakdown of the craft guild system in the mid-nineteenth century, they established a number of institutions to protect them from an influx of inferior, foreign mass-produced goods. In Sweden the Svenska Sjlödforeningen, established in 1845, served to maintain high standards in Swedish craft production. The turn of the century saw changes in the Swedish ceramics and glass industries with artists being brought in to redesign their otherwise essentially conservative output. The Gustavsberg ceramics factory, for instance, hired the painter Gunnar Wennerberg. He introduced a series of pieces which owed much to the international fashion for art nouveau but which had, at the same time, a specifically Swedish feel to them.

This move into modern forms had no effect upon the manufacturing processes at Gustavsberg, which remained and still remain essentially craft-based. The introduction of the artist Wilhelm Kåge into the company in 1917 reinforced the Swedish design philosophy of 'more beautiful everyday things' but, once again, had more effect on the aesthetic and social front than on the technological one. The Swedish decorative arts managed, even with their craft base, to fulfil a democratic ideal by supplying simple, modern ware for a substantial market.

While this model remained common across the spectrum of decorative art production, from ceramics to glass to textiles, another part of the Swedish manufacturing leant more heavily upon the American mass-production model, if not on quite the same scale. The Swedish car manufacturers Volvo and Saab, and the electrical appliance company, Electrolux, took their manufacturing principles from the US, and became strong companies with an international market. While the

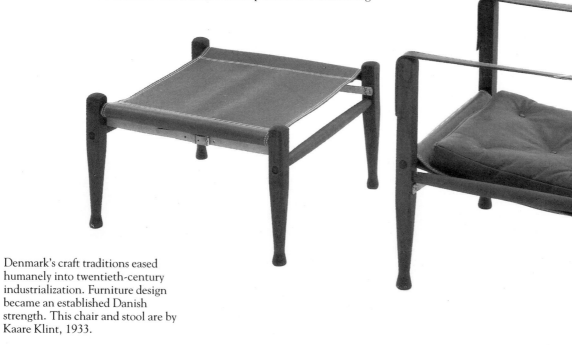

Denmark's craft traditions eased humanely into twentieth-century industrialization. Furniture design became an established Danish strength. This chair and stool are by Kaare Klint, 1933.

**SCANDINAVIAN SENSIBILITIES**
The Swedish decorative arts managed to fulfil a democratic ideal by supplying modern wares to a substantial market. The scenes here are from Gustavsberg in 1890.

products of the craft industries were directed primarily at the Swedish home market, Electrolux quickly saw the need to go in search of foreign markets, and by the 1920s divisions of the company had been established in both the US and England.

### THE DANISH FURNITURE INDUSTRY

Perhaps the most consistently and determinedly craft-based Scandinavian industry was Danish furniture-making. The pioneering work of men such as Kaare Klint, Borge Mogensen and Hans Wegner, working as, or with, individual craftsmen, established a tradition of high-quality, hand-made furniture which was greatly respected internationally in the post-war years. Like Sweden, Denmark had not experienced the violent changes that industrialization had brought about in Great Britain, and the craft tradition continued unbroken into the twentieth century. The presence of a relatively small, fairly affluent market put no immediate pressures upon this situation, although by the 1920s a small number of mass-manufacturing companies such as Fritz Hansen began to emerge, using new materials such as plywood.

The Danish craft furniture tradition remained strong, however, through the inter-war years. It looked to a modern aesthetic, rather than simply reviving traditional items. Klint's Safari Chair and Deck Chair, dating from this period, referred to conventional furniture types but reworked them in such a way as to create strikingly modern forms. In a similar way, Mogensen and Wegner leaned heavily upon such vernacular chair types as the Windsor and ladder-back chairs, but reinterpreted them as modern Danish pieces. While Wegner worked with a small craft-based manufacturing company, Johannes Hansen, Mogensen's designs were produced on a slightly larger scale by the Danish Cooperative Society. Along with furniture, Danish ceramics, glass and silver depended upon the concepts of the designer-craftsman as the initiator of new forms, and goods were manufactured on a modest scale. Mechanization in these industries was limited and, where it was used, was restricted to machines which had been installed at the end of the nineteenth century.

The Scandinavian design movement of the inter-war years did not, therefore, unreservedly espouse the high-technology mass-production ethic that American manufacturers were so proud of, but exploited instead the link between traditional production methods, aesthetic innovation and wealthy markets in its decorative arts.

**117**

Sweden developed socially useful but sensitive design: designers there did not impose aesthetic ideologies on people. Wilhelm Kåge's crockery **(above)** is modern and traditional. The consumers' continuing pleasure in the decorative was not ignored; as witnessed by Josef Frank's **Anakreon** textile design, 1938 **(far left)** and the pots, 1897, by Gunnar Wennerberg. New industry was also successful. The innovative Electrolux Co. **(left)** competed with Hoover.

# New materials and modern design

**118**

While mechanization and volume production were the main preoccupations of mass-manufacturing industry in the inter-war years, the question of new materials also played an important role.

The main innovations occurred in the US, and a number of the larger companies invested vast sums of money in researching the potential of new materials. The Toledo Scale Company, for example, set up a research post in a university in the late 1920s to look into the development of a plastic scale body.

The earliest changes occurred in metal production. Pressed steel gradually replaced iron and other forms of steel manufacture, while lighter metals such as aluminium and magnesium became increasingly popular. The Ford Motor Company, for instance, made its own steel and pioneered advances in pressing the material. This method led to the body-shell concept, which became a characteristic of many technological consumer goods, from automobiles to irons, in the 1920s and '30s.

The addition of a chromed surface to steel in small consumer goods also became a feature of the 1930s. It served as a means of preventing steel from rusting and as a means of turning mass-produced goods into decorative items. The development in steel which had one of the most dramatic impacts upon furniture design, however, was that of seamless tubular steel. This technique was developed by an inventor called Mannesman, and it provided a new material with the combined advantages of being light, strong and, above all, modern. The appropriation of tubular steel by German and Dutch furniture designers associated with the Bauhaus, and the designs of Mart Stam, Marcel Breuer and Mies van der Rohe in this material have repeatedly been chronicled. The designs have become icons of modern design, symbolizing the use of a new material to create a new, light furniture aesthetic which made a clean break with the conventions of furniture design which went before.

The main problem with tubular steel furniture was its lack of consumer appeal, except to a very exclusive, sophisticated market which understood and sympathized with the aims of the Modern Movement. Tubular steel was produced in large quantities by the Pel Company in Britain and the Chicago and Grand Rapids Companies in the US, but it never succeeded in becoming fully integrated into the domestic interior, except perhaps as part of a kitchen dining set. For the most part, the tubular steel chair became an institutional item, associated with church halls, hospitals and the lobbies of the more modern hotels. France and

### INVENTION AND PACKAGING

Modern design involved more than styling as this elegantly utilitarian operating theatre in England, 1952, demonstrated. Raymond Loewy's famous design for the Gestetner duplicator was skilful repackaging. Indeed, product designers frequently leave the mechanical guts of a model unchanged through successive restylings. Loewy led the art of creating appropriate – hence saleable – 'looks' for modern environments like Frank Lloyd Wright's design for the Johnson Wax Co. Buildings, 1936-49 **(below)**.

New materials and new techniques
broadened the vocabulary of the
designer: a dining suite by Marcel
Breuer in bent plywood, 1936
**(right)**; the sumptuousness of –
bakelite **(below)**.

Modern furniture design became relatively popular in Britain through a handful of companies such as Practical Equipment Ltd. A tub seat and bed, 1932-6 **(below)** and goods from the Bandalasta catalogue, 1927-32 **(right)**. Early plastic goods were not cheap but chic.

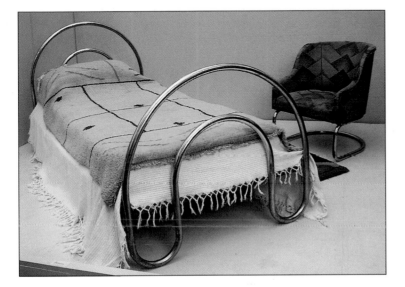

Italy produced their own highly expressive versions of tubular steel furniture, but these remained, for the most part, avant-garde experiments, failing to deter the majority of the population from continuing to buy traditional and reproduction furniture.

## DESIGN AND NEW MATERIALS

Metal was not the only material to encourage the emergence of a modern furniture aesthetic. New forms of machine-processed wood, such as bent and sheet plywood and laminated wood, also encouraged designers to experiment with new forms. The Scandinavian designers Alvar Aalto and Bruno Mathsson provided some of the most striking experiments in this area, and Marcel Breuer, working for the British company Isokon, also produced some memorable items. By the end of the 1930s new materials had had a considerable influence upon the appearance of much of the furniture available on the mass market.

Without doubt, however, the materials which did most to make products available to a wider audience were plastics. Plastics had developed in the nineteenth century as a substitute for more expensive materials like horn, ivory and jet. Celluloid, the earliest form of plastic,

was first adopted commercially in the US where it was used for billiard balls in the 1860s. In the 1890s Parkesine was introduced in Germany for insulating telegraph wires, and in 1909 Leo Baekeland, the American chemist and inventor, developed bakelite, initially for electrical fittings. While metal had developed as a replacement for wood in the move towards large-scale production, plastics were developed as an even cheaper alternative. As such, they gradually replaced metal, particularly as the material for the body-shells of technological products. As early as 1929 Raymond Loewy had used bakelite as the material for his restyled Gestetner duplicating machine, and quite quickly pressed metal was replaced by this new material, which was cheaper and easier to manufacture in bulk.

It was in the first thirty years of this century that huge advances in plastics research were made in the US largely as a result of the Du Pont chemical company taking celluloid on board in 1915 and ploughing funding into its development. In the 1920s plastic became an increasingly widespread material in the US, used in small objects such as powder boxes, manicure sets, ear trumpets and fountain pens. With the discovery of cellulose acetate, which replaced the highly flammable celluloid,

122

plastic could be made in a variety of bright colours, and its aesthetic potential became more apparent.

The application of plastics to industrial design occurred in the 1930s and, in addition to Loewy's Gestetner, Walter Dorwin Teague used it for the case of his new camera design for Eastman Kodak. Radio cabinets soon became an obvious medium for plastics, both because they were an easy shape to get out of a mould and because they were new products without an established visual identity. Pioneering work was undertaken on both sides of the Atlantic in developing them. In Great Britain, the designs of Serge Chermayeff, Wells Coates and Misha Black for Ekco stand out as landmarks in this field, demonstrating how plastics could escape from their role as substitute materials. Plastics became ubiquitous in many countries in the 1930s, moving into the areas of tableware, cheap jewellery, houseware and domestic appliances, when they were used for features such as control knobs and door handles.

Chairs such as this by Marcel Breuer, 1936, give the lie to the received opinion that modern design lacked expressiveness: this agitated work is also a technical *tour de force*.

# Technology and design

**W**hile a wide range of industrial and technological advances had a direct influence upon manufacturing and design in the inter-war years, others had indirect influences. The invention and domestic application of electricity, for example, gave rise to all the home appliances which depended upon that power source. Developed initially to provide a use for the electricity supply during the day when lighting was not in use and promoted as such by the electricity supply industry, electrical appliances quickly became important items in the home. By the inter-war period, they were competing for attention with furniture and the traditional decorative arts as items inviting 'consumer desire'. Domestic electrification in the US and Britain expanded steadily through the 1920s and 1930s, in the urban areas at least. By the end of that period, most urban homes contained a number of electrical items.

Technological and design developments also went hand in hand in the development of the products themselves. The futurists had seen cars, ships and aeroplanes as the most potent symbols of modern life, but the new electrical appliances for the home came to be equally evocative of the modern world. While their invention took place a generation or two earlier, it was in the inter-war years that typewriters, cameras, cookers, vacuum cleaners and countless other newly invented products took on identities other than those of technical, utility items. With the help of designers their social meanings were made explicit and their function became as much a symbolic as a practical one. Design gave technology a visual form, helping to create the modern life-style and providing a set of symbols which expressed the very meaning of modernity.

**MACHINE METAPHORS**
This AEG hairdryer, 1927, shouts its belief in the superiority of machine manufacture. Peter Behrens was a master of machine metaphors. This Bauhaus design, 1924 (**right**), was not mass manufactured until the late 1970s, in Britain.

On this page we see an interior, 1924, and a poster selling the art nouveau style in electrical fittings. Ten years later **(facing page)**, we see the sharp radicalism of the new, clean graphics and the Wells Coates radio. Thus, in a decade, designers went from ornament to reductivism. Now both styles provoke nostalgia, and both will be recycled in the future. Popular taste, of course, does not always follow the ebb and flow of designer interests.

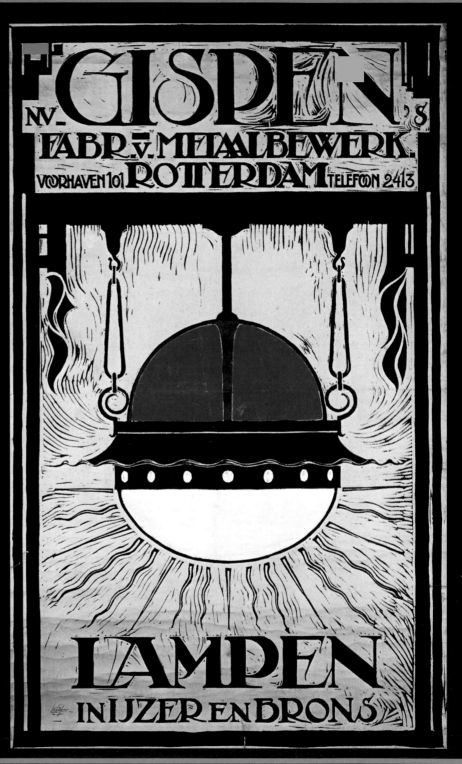

# CHAPTER SIX

# THEORY
# & DESIGN

> **"THE DANGER WE RUN IN A MACHINE AGE IS THAT WE SACRIFICE ONE SET OF VALUES AND CONFINE ART TO AN INTELLECTUAL PREOCCUPATION WITH 'FORM AND FUNCTION'."**
> *H. READ, ART AND INDUSTRY (1936)*

Most accounts of design in the early twentieth century stress the idea of the 'machine aesthetic' without placing it in its socio-economic and technological framework. They emphasize the abstract philosophical statements of the modern protagonists, failing to set these alongside the objects that were produced. In recognizing the limitations of this perspective and the need for a wider context, it remains important to take account of the relationship between design and high culture (in particular fine art and architecture) in this period. This relationship influenced many designs, in an avant-garde and later a mass-environment context.

The aesthetic roots of modern design lie in the artistic revolution that took place in the first decade of this century, a revolution that Banham has described as 'a wave of self-examination unparalleled in the history of art'. The new approach had its intellectual and emotional basis in the inward-looking, psychoanalytical theories of Sigmund Freud, in the death of religion as signalled by Karl Marx and in the inexorable scientific logic of Charles Darwin's evolutionary theories. While there are multiple dangers in embracing the *Zeitgeist* concept uncritically, there can be little doubt that the 'self-examination' that Banham has described grew out of a broad cultural climate and found its outlet in literature, music, fine art, architecture and design around the turn of the century.

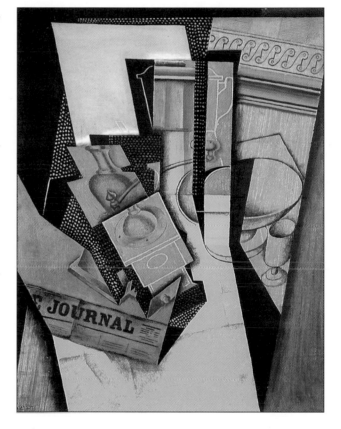

Cubist painting, such as that by Juan Gris **(above)**, was later exploited as a decorative art and soon found its way into printed fabrics.

The Bauhaus **(left)**, Europe's most famous school of design, established its reputation with its 1923 exhibition in Weimar. The catalogue cover is by Joost Schmidt.

# The influence of cubism

**128**

Where painting and sculpture were concerned, the examination involved looking further into the world of 'reality' as presented through the post-Renaissance artistic conventions of representation, perspectival space and pictorial content. 'Behind' that world was one which was thought to consist of essential geometric units. The neo-Platonism that underpinned the work of Cézanne and the cubists was fundamental to modern design. The new questioning mood coincided in society with the loss of belief in a unified, God-centred world which had previously held men together, creating an a priori purpose for all cultural activity. Modern society was further atomized by the new emphasis upon the production system instead of traditional allegiances. Following on from the discoveries of the French impressionists, the cubists revolutionized accepted notions of pictorial space, composition, perception and form. The painting process became 'interiorized' in the works of men such as Georges Braque, Pablo Picasso and Juan Gris. This kind of abstraction was highly influential upon modern architecture and design, and its major protagonists, Walter Gropius, Mies van der Rohe and Le Corbusier, all stressed the close relationship between architecture, design and the fine arts. Each of them discussed eloquently the concept of abstract form pioneered by the cubists and in many ways their work represented a three-dimensional extension in real space of the two-dimensional pictorial aesthetic that the cubists developed.

Modernist architects and designers were in thrall to fine art's avant garde: the apparently analytical approach of painters such as Cézanne in work like **The Bathers (right)** and Picasso in his work **A Bottle of Pernod (far right)** excited designers because it provided new recipes for handling form. Intellectuals were not afraid to embrace 'ugliness'. The vase **(top)** was made by Theodor Bogler and decorated by Gerhard Marcks.

# Modernism: ideology and style

The key features of modern design were commitment to the notion of functionalism—the idea, derived from modern architecture, that inner structure dictates outer form; to rationalism; scientific objectivity; a moral and aesthetic abhorrence of decoration; and a belief in the concepts of universality and standardization, or the theory of type-form. While the cubists, and even more so the futurists, based their new vision upon a commitment to mechanization, the modern architects and designers based their theories upon the rational system implied by mechanized mass production. Le Corbusier's phrase that a house is 'a machine for living in' has been frequently misinterpreted. It has been taken to mean that he envisaged a highly mechanistic environment. What he really meant was that a house should be conceived and designed in the same spirit of rationalism as underpin-ned mechanized mass production. The machine, both for the artists and the Modernists, was a useful metaphor which served to align painting, architecture and design with the essence of twentieth-century life. That metaphor was, however, often taken as fact, and Modernist theory translated directly into 'style', resulting in an over-simplification of the intentions of the Modernists. A weakness of much of the Modernist theoretical writings from the 1920s was that they ignored the possibility of this distortion. They were also more concerned with the metaphor of production than with the concept of consumption—a limitation which many of Modernism's critics have subsequently noted.

What Banham has called the 'uniform of Modernism' grew inevitably out of the abstract theories articulated in the first three decades of this century. In an attempt to penetrate beyond the superficiality of style, several Modernists aligned themselves with engineering which, they believed, valued mathematical and functional exactitude, rather than aestheticism. While they saw this as a means of associating themselves with modern technology, they were in fact, as Reyner Banham has pointed out, relating to the only branch of technology that was not at all new, but which derived from the world of Greek Classicism.

The Modernists' understanding of mass-production technology was at times idiosyncratic. In his book *Towards a New Architecture*, for instance, Le Corbusier uses the car as the characteristic symbol of a mass society, but failed to point out that the model he illustrated in his text was a very expensive, hand-made automobile.

Modernism turned, almost inevitably, into a style as much as an idea, and as such failed to convince its public of the full significance of its theoretical understanding. As Banham has written: 'In Europe, the architect-philosophers had their own strong artistic image of a suitable machine-style and used functionalism to justify it morally.'

This 1930 Modernist interior was heavily influenced by the Bauhaus, *De Stijl,* and the example of Le Corbusier. However, even Modernism could be too extreme. With the hindsight of 50 years, this interior is a caricature of Modern Movement puritanism and lacks humanity – a complaint that the petitioners of post-Modernism always press against the Bauhaus.

**THE WHITE GODS**
Le Corbusier on the left with
Walter Gropius. In **From Bauhaus to Our House**,
journalist Tom Wolfe, scourge of modern architecture,
called Gropius 'White God No 1' and wrote of Le
Corbusier: 'He was Aquinas, the Jesuits, Doctor Subtilis
and the Scholastics, Marx, Hegel, Engels, and Prince
Kropotkin all rolled into one.' The Fagus factory, 1911-14
**(below)** by Gropius and Adolf Meyer.

# Elementarism and constructivism

It has already been seen how special social and political circumstances enabled the Russian constructivists and the Dutch *De Stijl* artists and designers to bring their ideas to fruition in the years immediately following the First World War. Yet their aesthetic theories grew out of Modernism as a whole.

The experiments that went on in Holland and Russia from 1917 onwards were the direct descendants of cubism, although several stages nearer to total abstraction. They side-stepped the commitment to easel painting as their emphasis was placed firmly upon the role of utility objects, from clothes to furniture to architecture—upon production rather than aestheticism.

## DE STIJL

*De Stijl* was not a closely-knit group, but linked only through associations with van Doesburg and the magazine. The art magazine played an increasing role at this time in disseminating avant-garde ideas internationally. Most of what we know about *De Stijl* stems either from the magazine or from statements made by van Doesburg. The first *De Stijl* manifesto appeared in the magazine in November 1918, and was signed by van Doesburg (painter), Robert Van't Hoff (architect), Vilmos Huszar (painter), Antony Kok (poet), Piet Mondrian (painter), George Vantongerloo (sculptor) and Jan Wils (architect).

There was a definite sense of a collaborative artistic effort. The tone of van Doesburg's writing was strongly dogmatic (however much he claimed to be against dogma), and it remained so for his entire career. The degree of inflexibility and dogmatism contained in the group was demonstrated by the breakdown in communication between Mondrian and van Doesburg when, in the early '20s, van Doesburg included diagonal lines in his compositions. The enumeration of a list of artistic requirements in the manifesto resulted in a creed which had to be followed to the letter.

The tone of the manifesto was also reminiscent of futurism. Van Doesburg called vaguely for the idea of 'consciousness of the age', meaning an age in which technology and social events had produced a new environment which should in turn produce its own new aesthetic.

Collectivism, order and classicism were seen as synonymous, as necessary conditions of a post-war democratic society, and these in turn were seen to determine a new aesthetic, Banham's *Machine Aesthetic*. There was a quasi-philosophical element in van Doesburg's writing also

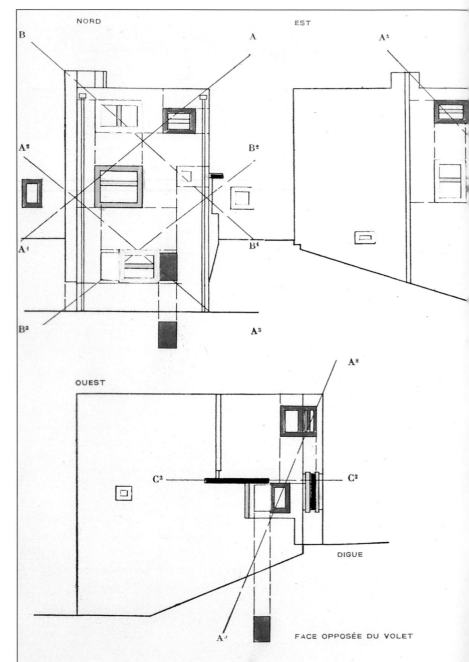

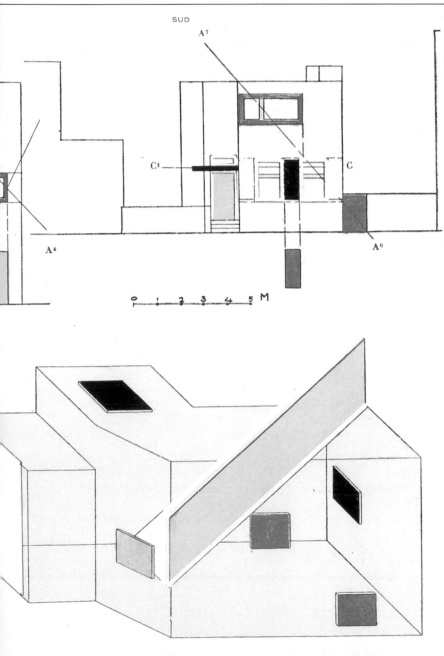

SUD

A⁷

C¹      C

A⁴      A⁶

0 1 2 3 4 5 M

VESTIBULE D'ENTRÉE ET HALL

which revealed the abstract, idealistic and in some cases, spiritual aspect of the movement. Mondrian's theosophical leanings drew ideas from the mystic M.H.J. Schoenmaekers about the spiritual implications of the horizontal and the vertical. Theory was seen to be an essential addition to artistic activity in the particular cultural situation in which they found themselves.

The search for a new aesthetic in the new age of rationality and collectivity was, however, the underlying concern of the group. Their name, 'The Style', gives an idea of the nature of the aesthetic, as do the words repeated in van Doesburg's text, such as 'pure', 'logical', 'rejection of the natural' and 'universal'. The post-cubist aesthetic they developed was epitomized by the works of Mondrian, who moved further and further away from naturalism in the years up to and after 1917. In the early '20s he

Gerrit Rietveld's 1918 chair joined Mondrian's painting with Frank Lloyd Wright's structures, and in one image broke with the decorative orders of the past. An architectural drawing **(left)** by Theo van Doesburg, co-founder with Mondrian of **De Stijl** magazine.

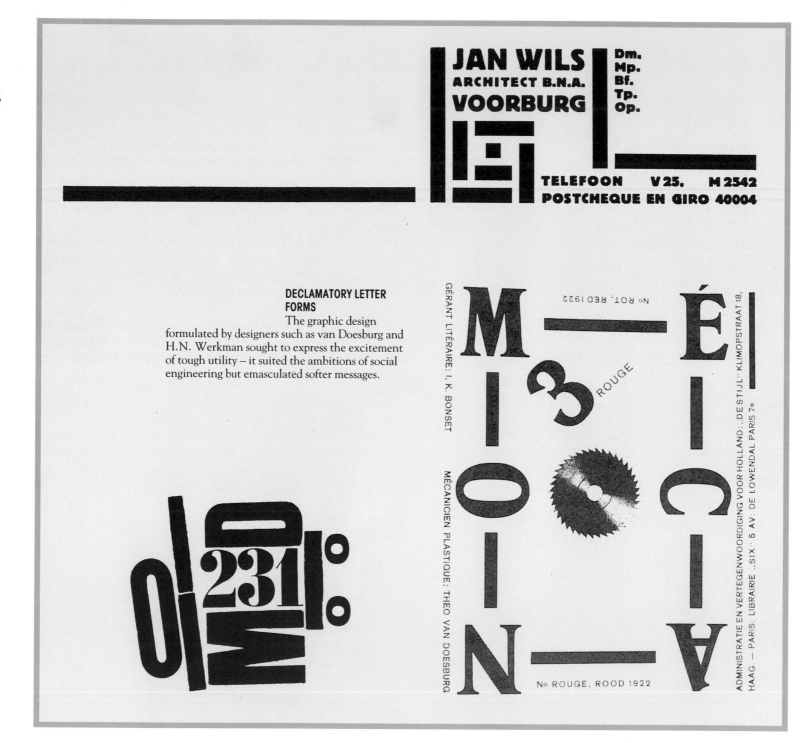

**DECLAMATORY LETTER FORMS**
   The graphic design formulated by designers such as van Doesburg and H.N. Werkman sought to express the excitement of tough utility – it suited the ambitions of social engineering but emasculated softer messages.

Housing, 1922, by J.J.P. Oud. In retrospect we can see in the radicalism of the ascetic regularity a continuation of traditional Dutch housing.

American architect Frank Lloyd Wright, who was concerned with the aesthetic relationship between horizontal and vertical lines, with the juxtaposition of volume and line, and with the use of space as a constructive tool. This became the essential formula for all *De Stijl* three-dimensional objects. Added to these concerns was an interest on the part of the architects with technical innovations—new materials and standardization—resulting from prefabrication.

## OBJECTIVISM IN RUSSIA

In Russia, a clear division can be made between those artists who believed in art as an abstract ideal which could, and should, be applied to three-dimensional objects, and those who thought that art had become redundant and that objects had their own functional and constructional requirements which were sufficient for a theory of design.

As in Holland, the pervasive idea was the development of an 'objective' machine aesthetic, and cubism again provided the formal inspiration. Malevich had visited Paris and developed his 'suprematist' painting as an abstracted extension of both cubism and futurism. Malevich pursued reductionism to its logical conclusion with his *White on White* series. Tatlin began his corner relief sculptures in the same period, making 'object' sculptures from raw materials which determined their own form through construction. Tatlin's approach focused attention upon the essential qualities of materials and construction, and once the Bolshevik Revolution had put a specific ideology in the hands of the artists, this was added to the all-important notion of function.

Post-Revolutionary Russia gave great scope to the artist willing to portray Socialist ideals and incorporate them in his own working theory. There was official encouragement for artists through the formation of *Khukemas* (art schools). In a state of relative freedom from restrictions—at first anyway—artists set about designing anything and everything that would further the ideals of the Revolution.

The division between suprematism and constructivism continued and hardened. Malevich turned to the design of functional objects and built some models of architectural structures, but maintained to the end that 'art' was an abstract ideal which could be put into a functional object but without which the object could not exist. In 1927 he wrote in *Suprematist Architecture*: 'The architect looks with regret upon the unavoidable necessity of fulfilling a purpose, and ardently seeks to combine within himself the engineer and the artist, in order to unite in every task "the attractive" with "the useful". This fusion becomes his primary task. Yes, he is even convinced that architecture free of purpose does not exist. Looking back at history, however, he would realize that his art lives on as a mark of beauty and that it is pure form. From this, I draw the conclusion that architecture is basically a pure art form and that God's

reduced his forms to horizontals and verticals and his palette to the three colours—black, white and grey. He provided the two-dimensional prototype for an aesthetic which by its simplicity emphasized the 'objectness' of the work itself, its tensions and contrasts, and which lifted the spectator to a world of real, pure forms.

In 1918 van Doesburg stated the concern of a work of art: 'Pure thought, in which no image based on phenomena is involved, but where numbers, measurement, relations and abstract line have occupied its place, manifests itself by way of the idea.'

The move from two dimensions to three in *De Stijl* suggested the importance of real objects for the movement. Chairs could more easily stand for themselves alone and be 'objective', than paintings, which tended to be seen as two-dimensional representations of the real world, however 'abstracted' they were. The idea of collectivism also encouraged these artists to concern themselves with 'useful' objects. In the end, however, the aesthetic code of *De Stijl* prevented them, in most cases, from creating anything more than 'symbolic' objects.

Many of the architectural schemes remained in the planning stage, as no more than Utopias. Oud, Van't Hoff and Jan Wils were among the first *De Stijl* architects. They based their aesthetic strongly on the work of the

Constructivism, *De Stijl* and Suprematism gave typography an illusion of three dimensions: it made the printed page architectural and, through the Stravinsky-like symphonies of diagonal and vertical lines, created a sensation of energy. Sometimes a gentler note was struck, as in this collage by Granovsky, 1923.

Kingdom on Earth resides in this pure form, which we can only observe, but cannot "use" for any purposes because that which serves a function cannot have originated in God's Kingdom on Earth or in Heaven.'

This ultimately spiritual view of form, which Malevich shared with Mondrian, contrasted with the more materialistic view of Tatlin, which was nearer to Marxist ideology in its emphasis upon the material and the role of production. Tatlin was in fact the only one of these artists who entered a factory at any time.

Malevich's views were shared by the brothers Naum Gabo and Antoine Pevsner in the *Realistic Manifesto* of 1920, in total opposition to those expressed in the *Programme of the Productivist Group* written by Rodchenko and Stepanova in the same year. They wrote that: 'The task of the constructivist group is the communistic expression of materialistic constructive work. It tackles the solution of this problem on the basis of

scientific hypotheses. It emphasizes the necessity of synthesizing the ideological and formal part, so as to direct the laboratory work on to the tracks of practical activity.'

They went on to list the components of the group's programme, which combined the *De Stijl* aesthetic code based on 'light, plane, space, colour and volume' with political activism.

Theoretically speaking, they shared many ideas with both *De Stijl* and the suprematists but took a more extreme position politically. In practice their emphasis was more upon creating objects of utility—clothes, houses and other practical accompaniments for the 'workers'.

The Russian painter and designer El Lissitzky provided a link between his country and Holland, as he met van Doesburg and contributed to *De Stijl*. It was in the early '20s that Dutch elementarism moved into its international phase, having absorbed many of the intellectual and artistic ideas deriving from Russia, but lacking the political fervour of its counterpart in that country.

**137**

(**Left**) A double page spread by El Lissitzky, 1922, and a poster advertising books by Alexander Rodchenko (**right**), 1921.

# Le Corbusier and the purist aesthetic

The architect-designer who had the most to say about the modern aesthetic was Le Corbusier. His variations on the cube as a basic living unit, in which the properties of space, light and volume played such important parts, were combined with a manipulation of new materials—particularly, at first, concrete—and a commitment to the idea of producing standard 'types'.

The metaphor of the machine was the central stimulus to the entire Le Corbusier oeuvre. At the beginning of *Towards a New Architecture* he wrote: 'A great epoch has begun. There exists a new spirit. There exists a mass of work conceived in the new spirit: it is to be met with particularly in industrial production. Architecture is styled by custom. The architecture styles are a lie. Style is a unity of principle animating all the work of an epoch, the result of a state of mind which has its own special character. Our own epoch is determining, day by day, its own style.'

The Utopian, poetic tone of this piece typified all Le Corbusier's writings, which were prolific and which accompanied all his architectural projects. The emphasis was upon finding an architectural language which would express the Utopia he envisaged—a Utopia which could be described in terms of 'the good life'. For Le Corbusier, this meant sunshine, relaxation, order, harmony and being in tune with one's time, while at the same time achieving timelessness and stability. He sought a language of form which would contain and express all these qualities.

Le Corbusier was born Charles-Edouard Jeanneret in 1887 in Chaux de Fonds, a Swiss watch-making town, and attended a local art school to learn the skills of engraving. He was self-taught as an architect, deriving his ideas from the many different countries he visited during his well-travelled youth. The inspiration from these places provided the vocabulary of the architectural language which he developed throughout his long career. One of the greatest stimuli of his early years was the Parthenon, exemplifying the universal order achieved by the Greek architects. He wrote of his discovery: 'It is a question of pure invention, so personal that it may be called that of one man. Phidias made the Parthenon...There has been nothing like it anywhere or at any period...The mouldings of the Parthenon are infallible and implacable...we are riveted by our senses; we are ravished in our mind; we touch the axis of harmony. No question of religious dogma enters in; no symbolical description; no naturalistic representation; there is nothing but pure forms in precise relationships.'

If we were to substitute Corbusier's name for that of Phidias in this description we would be near an understanding of what his work was all about—the key words were 'pure' and 'harmony'. Corbusier's aesthetic approach to form resembled the classical aesthetic in its use of simple geometry and universality. Phidias, however, was not acquainted with the aeroplane, the car and the ocean liner, but took natural forms and their proportions as his starting point, while Le Corbusier relied on the mechanized 'type' objects about him as a means of expressing the age he lived in.

The early architectural experiments of Le Corbusier were attempts to resolve the problem of minimum dwelling. In 1914 he developed the idea of his Domino (Domus and Domino) System, which was based on the idea of a single cubic load-bearing frame with a wall surrounding it. This basic unit, which was to be made in reinforced concrete and built from standard, repeated elements, was to provide a prototype for all Le Corbusier's work up to the late 1920s. It was used singly in his schemes for workers' housing or artists' studios, and in combinations in his urban plans, his projects for blocks of living units, or in the more sophisticated villas built for individual clients.

The emphasis on a free interior which could be divided up by partitions emphasized the contribution that Le Corbusier felt the inhabitant should make to his dwelling-place. The empty, functional shells he provided allowed for flexibility, modification and humanization. Le Corbusier's fundamentally extra-functional intentions were evident in his reaction to the austerity of German rational architecture of the same period. He condemned their absence of aesthetic joy and wrote of the essential difference between building and architecture: 'The purpose of construction is to make things hold together: of architecture *to move us*. Architectural emotion exists when the work rings within us in tune with a universe whose laws we obey, recognize and respect.'

Function, felt Le Corbusier, must be surpassed by an emotional relationship with a building. Le Corbusier saw this emotion as a product of simplicity, order and pure forms.

The emphasis upon 'purity' was extended when Le Corbusier finally

Le Corbusier's purist imagery was severe but not punitive. The hole for a tree in his 1925 prefabricated **New Spirit Pavilion** is a graceful gesture, anticipating the freer sculptural inclinations of his later work.

settled in Paris in 1917 and, with the painter Amédée Ozenfant, started a movement which they called 'purism'. It was based on a post-cubist approach to form and developed a particular approach towards the 'type-objects' of mechanical production—bottles and so on. The work emphasized the pure form of such products and played with the formal/spatial relationships between a number of such objects in search of a harmony. The response by the senses to such abstracted forms was described by Le Corbusier and Ozenfant as existing on two different levels, the intuitive and the learned.

For Le Corbusier the architect, both levels were equally important. His abstract works could communicate on an immediate level and on a more sophisticated level at the same time, both to the general public and to the person proficient in the language of architecture.

It was during these early years in Paris that Jeanneret changed his name to Le Corbusier: 'Le' to give an objective effect and 'Corbusier' from the French *corbeau*—crow—because of his profile. He was an intro-

In the 1920s Le Corbusier's buildings evinced a mechanical form and rejected adornment – the apotheosis of this formal aesthetic canon being the Villa Savoye at Poissy, 1931 **(opposite, top and bottom)**. His 1931 Salvation Army building **(above and top)** is not quite as he designed it, for it was refurbished after the war by his former partner, Pierre Jeanneret.

verted, often isolated man, with a reputation for distancing himself from other people, a hard taskmaster and uncompromising in everything that he did.

In his architecture of the 1920s Le Corbusier began to put many of his ideas into action—ideas which were expressed in the periodical *L'esprit nouveau*. The Maison Citrohan was a development of his single cube idea—the name acknowledged his debt to the motor car—and his early villas consolidated his commitment to the flat roof (by now embellished with roof gardens as a means of replacing nature); and to the pilotis—supports which took the living area away from the flow of traffic and the bustle of the streets. His structure paid tribute to the traditional ideal of living on the ground surrounded by a garden.

In 1922 Le Corbusier developed his ideas for a *Ville Contemporaine* (contemporary town) which was based on a central axis with tower blocks arranged back form the road and set on pilotis. Le Corbusier's ideas for collective or commercial living were based on the concept of linked single modules which afforded privacy, and central service areas, shops and so on which provided focal areas. His Weissenhof Building of 1927 and his Unité d'Habitation at Marseilles (1946-52) took his idea through to a logical conclusion.

The pavilion Le Corbusier exhibited at the big International Exhibition of Decorative Arts which took place in Paris in 1925 was a single cell of a much larger block, and showed many of his ideas about open interior space. Le Corbusier's reverence for nature and the site caused him to make a hole for a tree, and he showed the importance of

Le Corbusier's work at Chandigarh is a composition in both abstract and symbolic form. His intention in designing this General Assembly Building (1953-61) was to create a monument that could be read from many miles away.

outside access and of the penetration of light into all his buildings by the presence of the patio. No areas were enclosed in a Le Corbusier structure without the possibility of the access of light. In this pavilion he played with the flexibility of the interior, using a balcony to split the different levels. In 1925 Le Corbusier also made clear his views on furnishing his cells, writing: 'Demand bare walls in your bedroom, your living room and your dining room. Built-in furniture takes the place of much of the furniture which is expensive to buy . . . Demand concealed or diffused lighting. Demand a vacuum cleaner. Buy only practical furniture and never buy "decorative" pieces. If you want to see bad taste, go into the houses of the rich. Put only a few pictures on your walls and none but good ones.'

This ascetic approach towards the interior demonstrated Le Corbusier's commitment to 'good taste' and economy. He used cheap, mass-produced furniture, particularly the bent-wood chairs made by the firm of Thonet, and provided built-in fitments wherever possible.

By the mid-1920s Le Corbusier had perfected his 'purist' aesthetic and developed a set of five points for such an architecture. They were:
1) Pilotis
2) Roof garden
3) Free plan
4) Ribbon windows (to allow maximum even light)
5) Free façade
He used these as a foundation from which to move on and express the

true meaning of architecture, which was, for him, contained in the human response to form manipulated in a sculptural way. Among the villas he built for private clients in the late 1920s was one at Garches for the Stein family, and one for Madame Savoie which was built at Poissy just outside Paris.

The site for the latter villa was a bare expanse of field with a small rise in the centre. Le Corbusier saw this as a perfect setting and built what has often been described as his most perfect structure. The approach by car took one into the area between the pilotis which was for car-parking and provided the servants' quarters. The structure of the villa was that of a cube on stilts, but a cube whose interior space had been cut away in such a way as to provide an open structure with use made of light, glass and a sun terrace to emphasize its open quality. The cube itself was a mammoth piece of white concrete sculpture in which every angle was thought out, leading the inhabitant from place to place within the static cube. The basic horizontals and verticals were transversed by the diagonal of the ramp, which led right through the house from the ground floor to the roof garden.

The villa at Poissy marked the high point of Le Corbusier's involvement with the Purist aesthetic, and demonstrated how it was founded on an abstract conception of form which could simply be copied or reproduced in an *ad hoc* manner. Le Corbusier's biggest problem were his imitators who took his formula rather than the spirit informing it as their model.

# The Bauhaus

Some of the most sophisticated theories of modern design were developed and expounded by individuals associated with the Bauhaus—a German design school which was set up in Weimar in 1919 and which moved to Dessau in 1925.

When Walter Gropius opened the school he wrote a manifesto which expressed the following conviction: 'the complete building is the ultimate aim of its visual arts,' thereby bestowing upon architecture the role of the leading art. Ironically, no architectural teaching took place at the Bauhaus under Gropius' reign, whereas the fine arts played a very significant role in the early years. An integration of fine art and design occurred at the Bauhaus primarily because many of the teachers that Gropius employed were practising fine artists. Paul Klee, Wassily Kandinsky, Lyonel Feininger, Johannes Itten and Gerhard Marcks were all there in the early period, and succeeded in creating a role for their own fine-art approaches within the school curriculum. They shared a commitment to post-cubist abstraction in one form or another.

The particular branch of post-cubist fine art that fed into the early theories of form at the Bauhaus derived from the movement called German expressionism which had flourished in the years after the First World War, spurred on by the revolution in Germany in 1918. It was an essentially dynamic movement, which combined post-cubist abstraction with a strongly emotive element that had particular socio-cultural implications. It stood in direct opposition to the highly rationalist strain of thought emerging from Holland, which was also to feed into the Bauhaus through van Doesburg's presence in Weimar in the early 1920s.

One aspect of expressionism was an architectural movement which, although it produced more drawings and visionary projects than built forms, was still significant in the progression of modern architecture and design. It tended until recently to be ignored, as it did not fit into the neat pattern of reductionism described by most historians of the Modern Movement, but in terms of its impact on the early Bauhaus it deserved attention. Erich Mendelsohn, one of the leading expressionist architects, described the movement's preoccupation when he wrote that: 'Certainly the primary element in architecture is function, but function without sensual contributions remains mere construction.'

The tenets of Modern architecture, as defined by the theory of functionalism and by such well known slogans as 'truth to construction' and 'truth to materials', were cast aside by the expressionists and replaced by a deliberate differentiation between inside and outside; an interest in

The Bauhaus, Dessau, 1925, designed by Gropius who, when he emigrated to America, assisted in the transformation of the 'factory' style into the International Style. Most people never accepted its severity.

144

### THE IRRESISTIBLE EGO

Before the Modern Movement hardened into the uniformity of Internationalism, there was eccentricity. A sense of the decorative kept seeping in, as seen in the Einstein Tower, Potsdam, 1921, by Erich Mendelssohn **(above right)** and in the ceramic benches by Antonio Gaudi, Barcelona **(right).** German art was not clamorous in its rationality like Dutch *De Stijl.* Lyonel Feininger **(below right)** drifted from analytic cubism to expressionism. Johannes Itten, until 1923 a mystically inclined guru of the Bauhaus, completed the painting **(below)** in 1917.

creating an expressive rather than a neutral space; a reliance on traditional materials rather than new, machine-age ones, and on the concepts of individualism and craft rather than standardization and mass production. Many of these ideas harked back to aspects of art nouveau architecture in which function and expression had been fused.

The main preoccupation of the German expressionist architects was a political one, the creation of an environment for the new communal society. As Dennis Sharp had explained: 'There was a desire to build great public buildings which would sum up the new Socialist age.'

The buildings for which the architects Bruno Taut and Hans Poelzig were responsible, for example, for the Werkbund glass pavilion of 1914 and the theatre in Berlin, were intended to dazzle their audience. As Poelzig wrote: 'It is better to do violence to the purpose and create a true work of art than to let purpose, ie cold reason, get the better of you.'

Their sharp, architectured details contrasted with the softer, organic forms created by Erich Mendelsohn and best expressed in his Einstein Tower in Potsdam.

Strong expressionist elements were present in the early days of the Weimar Bauhaus. Gropius himself had been a member of the 'Working Council for Arts'—the architectural section of which was headed by Taut—and some of his architectural creations, especially his Total Theatre of 1927, reinforced his interest in the expressive role of architecture. His claim, in the manifesto he wrote, that the Bauhaus would 'find forms to symbolize the world' also had an expressionist ring to it.

The artists at the Bauhaus formulated specific approaches towards the creation of abstract form, and applied them in the way they taught the students on the foundation course. They developed a system which was based upon the study of pictorial elements. Klee was concerned with the way pictures were constructed, with the relationship between points, lines and plane. Through experimentation, the students learnt how an objective analysis of a two-dimensional construction could be made, and how the same concepts could be applied to three dimensions as well.

Kandinsky placed a strong emphasis upon colour analysis and encouraged a full examination of the spectrum. His philosophy of form differed from Klee's inasmuch as he saw physical form as a reflection of a spiritual reality which both preceded and determined it. Klee's approach was very much more empirical, concerned with the physical construction of form.

Spirituality was, however, of vital importance in the early Bauhaus years. Gropius had introduced it by referring back to the spiritual unity of the medieval world: he saw the possibility of reviving such a unity by closing the gap between art and craft. He associated the spiritual with the aesthetic in statements such as this: 'The aesthetic satisfaction of the human soul is just as important as the material. Both find their counterpart in that unity which is life itself.'

In the early years of the Bauhaus, it was individuals—Feininger, Marcks, Itten, Oskar Schlemmer, Klee and the rest—who *were* the school. The subjects taught were dictated by their skills and interests, and it was a combination of the spiritual aspect of the teaching and the necessary individualism of the artists that caused the first of many internal disturbances in the Bauhaus.

## FROM EXPRESSIONISM TO RATIONALISM

An incident occurred which centred around Johannes Itten, who taught the preliminary course. Everybody was obliged to attend his course for six months and follow a non-academic training of 'learning by doing', an educational method which lays stress upon the experience of the individual. The students undertook a detailed study of nature and use of materials, composition studies and analyses of old masters.

Although the emphasis was upon 'analysis' and relearning—the Bauhaus method—the tendency was to stress the individual, spiritual experience, and not the construction. Itten, who had trained with a mystic, followed through this stress upon mystical, intuitive experience by introducing special breathing exercises, diets and dress for his followers.

Gropius saw this as a move away from collective work and a dispute arose between the two men which went to the heart of the philosophy upon which the Bauhaus was founded—the problem of individuals or teams. Gropius decided that Itten had gone too far and asked him to leave in 1923.

In the same year the Bauhaus was asked to present an exhibition and Gropius delivered his lecture, 'Art and Technology: A New Unity', thereby hoping to redress the balance and undo the harm that had been done. The very delicate line between art as individual expression and design as a socialized art integrated into the production system had been clearly shown.

The school attracted leading men from all over Europe. Van Doesburg, the spokesman of the *De Stijl* movement, came to Weimar but was too purist in his attitudes to be integrated into the Bauhaus. El Lissitzky visited and he and Laszlo Moholy-Nagy, who took over the preliminary course with Josef Albers after the departure of Itten, introduced the Russian constructivist element which led after 1924 to an increasing emphasis on the objective analysis of form and colour. Ironically, this was also the year in which outside disapproval led to the closure of the school in Weimar. The State authorities were antagonistic towards teachings which suggested affiliations with left-wing politics. The German Socialist Revolution of 1918 had been put down, but the

fear of Socialism remained.

Gropius wanted to adapt design to the economic and social requirements of his day, while at the same time changing the contemporary materialistic attitude to a humanistic one. The Bauhaus' move to Dessau coincided with its move towards an art and design synthesis as students like Marcel Albers, Breuer and others, who had been trained in the principles of both art and craft, took over the workshops. This meant that the syllabus could now be workshop and production based, and therefore more objective. In reality, not very much was produced and it seems that more debate than work took place. Some links with industry were forged, but at this stage it was only wallpaper that was put into mass production—

Among architects, Marcel Breuer's **Wassily** chair became a Modern Movement archetype – architecture writ small. Designed for Wassily Kandinsky's house in 1925.

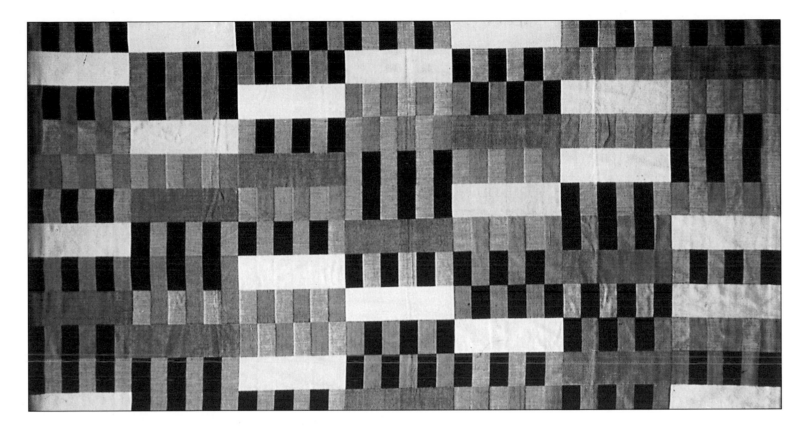

a relatively simple product in technological terms. Although Gropius saw the division of labour which resulted from the Industrial Revolution as the determining factor in design, there was little involvement in team production at the Bauhaus. Only a few artists and craftsmen worked together, such as Otto Lindig and Gerhard Marcks, who collaborated in the pottery department.

Gropius realized in theory how important the organization of the production system was to modern design. Art had become isolated and separated from society by adopting an 'art for arts' sake' attitude, and he set out to find a way of reuniting art with production. He wrote: 'I tried to put the emphasis of my work on integration and co-ordination. . . .'

Because modern art was using objective information for its material, Gropius saw the possibility of allying it with rational mass production. The designer had first to be a craftsman, who in turn had first to be an artist—this was his way of bringing art into production. He used the expression 'simplicity in multiplicity' which meant one essence behind everything that was standardized in mass production.

Gropius considered that every designer had to be efficient in a craft in order to understand every stage of the mass-production process. For him,

Design historians believe that formal 'industrial' Bauhaus design such as Anni Albers' textile hanging **(above)** and the lamp by Christian Dell has given the Bauhaus a misleading posthumous reputation for single mindedness, whereas in its heyday it was faddish, experimental and fissile.

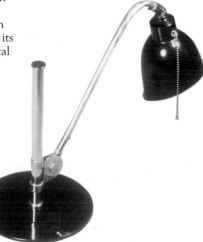

148

Ludwig Mies van der Rohe's Barcelona chairs, shown first in 1929 in the German Pavilion at the World Exposition, Barcelona. The chairs, which were then hand crafted, remain a high quality status symbol gracing the foyers of business corporations to this day.

the machine was just another tool. The crafts covered in the Bauhaus workshops were carpentry, stained glass, pottery, metal, weaving, stage design, wall painting and typography.

From 1923 onwards, when a more rational approach was introduced, the emphasis was less and less on individuals and more on the materials. Yet, in spite of Gropius' belief that the designer should be familiar with all the stages of the production process in order to conceive a unified product, he was unable to accept the individual designer's anonymity with ease.

Hannes Meyer, who took over the directorship of the Bauhaus in 1928, encouraged a more systematic approach towards design, and emphasized the role of engineering and technology in general. Few designs were produced during this period. Standardization became more and more the byword of the whole institution, and stress was laid increasingly on process rather than product.

The design theory contributed by the Bauhaus spanned a scale from, at one end, the aesthetic symbolism of the new age through geometric form to the 'styleless' functionalism of Hannes Meyer. It was the breadth of this programme and the apparent contradictions within it that created

problems for the subsequent generation.

In 1954, Mies van der Rohe, the final director in the Berlin period, wrote, 'the Bauhaus was not an institution with a clear program—it was an idea', and Hans Hess reiterated in 1970 that 'what made the Bauhaus was not so much its achievement, but its spirit'.

Whatever the fallacies of the emergence of 'styleless universal, functional form', following the dictates of technology and economics of production, in the words of Hess again, 'if they were not the right answers, at least they were the right questions'.

By attempting to ask questions about the implications of technology and to come to terms with problems like standardization, the Bauhaus, while still retaining the humanism of the craft ethic and aesthetic, confronted a real twentieth-century problem.

# The international style

While Bauhaus-inspired ideas about form and the shaping of consumer goods for the mass market did not find their way into the public arena until the years after the Second World War, the architectural Modern Movement became a fully-fledged reality in the 1930s. This was primarily a result of its transference to American soil with the closure of the Bauhaus by the Nazis in 1933 and the emigration of leading architectural figures across the Atlantic. It was in the US that the idea of the 'international style' first crystallized and was seen at an exhibition of the same name held in New York in 1932.

The Museum of Modern Art had been established in 1929 and in 1931 the director, Alfred Barr, asked H.R. Hitchcock and Philip Johnson who were both active promoters of the international style, if they would organize an exhibition of international architecture. This was the Museum's first venture outside painting and it took upon itself an extremely ambitious task—representing the contemporary architecture of fifteen countries. The fundamental promise of the project was that: 'Today a single new style has come into existence. In the last decade it has produced sufficient monuments of distinction to display its validity and its vitality. It may fairly be compared in significance with the styles of the past. In the handling of the problems of design it is more akin to the Classical. In the pre-eminence given to the handling of function, it is distinguished from both.'

The exhibition expounded this central thesis dogmatically. In many ways this tendency was responsible for the limited way in which the Modern Movement was handed down to succeeding generations. The exhibition resembled an exercise in American imperialism. Its organizers took every opportunity to stress the dependence of the Europeans upon the Americans Frank Lloyd Wright, and before him, Henry Richardson and Louis Sullivan. Without them, they claimed, the new style could never have been formulated. Hitchock and Johnson wrote: 'But it was in America that the promise of a new style appeared first, and, up to the war, advanced most rapidly. Richardson in the '70s and '80s often went as far as did the next generation on the Continent in simplification of design and in direct expression of structure.'

Furthermore they said, 'Wagner, Behrens and Perret lightened the solid massiveness of traditional architecture; Wright dynamited it,' implying strongly that the American impulse was the most radical and highly influential.

Many innovations were American in origin but just as much American architecture of the first decades of this century was revivalist in tendency and lacked the 'new spirit' almost totally. The 1893 World's Columbian Exposition in Chicago had brought the Classical Revival into predominance and, in the words of Alfred Barr, 'neatly styled the thread from Richardson, to Sullivan, to Frank Lloyd Wright'. Up to the '20s, American designs continued to be largely imitations of Renaissance, Roman or Gothic architecture. The Americans themselves were convinced that they led the world in architecture because, firstly, they felt that they imitated European styles more tastefully than the Europeans, and secondly, they led the field in technical proficiency.

In 1922 the American architectural profession received a jolt with the Chicago Tribune Tower Competition. All the American submissions were in revivalist style, and all the European ones, according to the judges, 'genuinely modern'. The Americans Raymond Hood and J.M. Howells were given first prize for their Gothic design, and the Finn, Eliel Saarinen, came second with a design which was an eclectic compromise but which derived in principle from Sullivan. The competition shook the confidence of American architects in the sufficiency of historical styles for modern purposes. Ever hopeful that America would take the lead with her skyscrapers, however, H.R. Hitchcock wrote in his book *Modern Architecture* of 1929: 'The skyscraper awaits the first American New Pioneer who will be able to take the engineering as a basis and create directly from it a form of architecture.'

Hitchcock pointed out that American buildings like grain elevators were modern in style and had inspired European architects, but that they could not be included in the international style category as 'the only spirit that informs them is economic'. American architecture received another blow in 1925, when the Exposition of Decorative Arts in Paris contained no American work at all. It was explained that America had no designs which were sufficiently modern. The American interior designer, Paul Frankl, retorted indignantly that they had their skyscrapers which, if they could be shipped over, would put all European work to shame.

Yet there is no doubt that the American styles would have looked dated against the work of Hoffmann, Le Corbusier and Melnikov displayed at the 1925 exhibition. In fact, America drew yet another surface style from the exhibition—this time the 'moderne'—and combined it with other decorative motifs, such as those found in Aztec temples. As Barr wrote: 'The Modernistic style has become merely another way of decorating surface.' And Hitchcock reiterated: 'The

The Gothic-topped Tribune Tower, Chicago, 1925 was designed by John Mead Howells and Raymond Hood. European Modernists eventually weaned American architects off the past, but America retained a taste for symbolic form, for example, 1950s car design.

zig-zag has become as tiring as the sensuous curve.'

With very few exceptions, American architects were unable to grasp the new European spirit of modern architecture. The International Style Exhibition of 1932 was strongly dogmatic in its assumptions because of the message it had to put across to its own architects and public. As Barr wrote: 'The present exhibition is an assertion that the confusion of the past forty years, or rather of the past century, may shortly come to an end... A number of progressive architects have converged to form a genuinely new style which is rapidly spreading throughout the world. Both in appearance and structure this style is peculiar to the twentieth century, and is as fundamentally original as the Greek, Byzantine or Gothic.'

Many historical and cultural assumptions were made by the exhibition. It assumed the presence of a *Zeitgeist*, a spirit of the age, which inspired all who were open to it and which determined the independent style of the age. It assumed that convergence was a natural direction, and that there was an ultimate style to be found, one which all architects would eventually stumble upon if they searched long enough. It assumed that an avant-garde led the way, showing the path to the unenlightened, and these premises were based upon a belief in the path of history progressing logically towards a single goal.

The final and largest assumption made by the exhibition's organizers was the presence and importance of style, or the formal properties of architecture, as a meaningful way of analysing it and placing it in history. They developed a strong architectural formalism, stressing at every point the 'aesthetic' qualities of the buildings they discussed and neglecting the social and psychological properties clearly intended in many of the structures. They also took a somewhat patronizing and élitist position on the relationship of this new architecture with the public. Barr wrote: 'The lack of ornament is one of the most difficult elements of the style for the layman to accept... The modern public must adjust itself to what seems new and strange.' Avant-gardism was seen to be a necessary condition, and the struggle one of keeping up with the New Pioneers at all costs, if America was to enter the international arena.

In his historical account of the growth of the international style, Hitchcock differentiated between two stages. He saw the first taking place up to 1914, a 'New Tradition' in which individuals—including

Berlage in Holland, van de Velde and Behrens in Germany, Perret in France and Saarinen in Finland—took over from the historicism of the nineteenth century and cleared the path for future innovation.

The second stage was that of the 'New Pioneers', who appeared simultaneously in France, Germany and Holland around 1922.

In his account of the Modern Movement, Hitchcock dismissed art nouveau and expressionism and concentrated only on those phenomena which pointed directly towards the international style.

The leading architects of the day were categorized thus: Le Corbusier—the greatest theorist; Gropius—the most sociologically minded; Mies van der Rohe—the most luxurious and elegant; Oud—the architect with the greatest discipline. Apart from these individual qualities, the exhibition and those who wrote about it chose to emphasize the common characteristics of the architects. Their discussions were thematic and general. Significant factors were considered to be the influence of engineering, and of abstract painting after 1910; the possibilities of the machine as an art tool, and the role of international reviews such as *De Stijl* and *L'Esprit Nouveau*.

## THE RULES OF THE INTERNATIONAL STYLE

The aesthetic of the international style was said by Hitchcock and Johnson to combine the following four qualities:

1. An emphasis on volume, not mass. 'The effect of mass, of static solidity, hitherto the prime quality of architecture, has all but disappeared; in its place there is an effect of volume, or more accurately, of plane surfaces bounding a volume. The prime architectural symbol is no longer the dense brick but the open box. Indeed, the great majority of buildings are in reality, as well as in effect, mere planes surrounding a

There is a strong echo of the Hollywood film set in both these two buildings by Frank Lloyd Wright: Hollyhock House, 1920 (**above**) and Imperial Hotel lounge, Tokyo (**right**).

A housing development in
Stuttgart, 1927, by Mies van der
Rohe. Seen from the air, it has the
order of an abstract sculpture.

Finesse of line, reflected even in the arm chairs in Mies van der Rohe's Tugendhat House, Brno, Czechoslovakia, 1930.

volume—volume is felt as immaterial, and weightless, a geometrically bounded space.'

2. Concern with surfacing materials. 'The ubiquitous stucco has the aesthetic advantage of forming a continuous even covering. But if the stucco is rough, the sharpness of the design, which facilitates apprehension of the building's volume, is blunted.'

3. Regularity. 'Good modern architecture expresses in its design this characteristic orderliness of structure and this similarity of parts by an aesthetic ordering which emphasizes the underlying regularity. Bad modern design contradicts this regularity. Regularity is, however, relative and not absolute in architecture.'

4. The avoidance of applied decoration. 'Absence of ornament serves as much as regular horizontality to differentiate superficially the current style from the styles of the past, and from the various manners of the last century and a half.'

Hitchcock and Johnson felt that applied decoration detracted from the decorative effect of the total construction, in terms of its composition and structure. Sculpture could be included in a building, but it ought not to be combined or merged with architecture itself.

These two writers were establishing an aesthetic rule-book for American architects so they could imitate the stylistic concerns of European architects. Little or no analysis was made of the intentions of the individual architects involved, and it was assumed that they are all aiming at a common aesthetic goal. Frequent references were made throughout the book to the inability of many American architects to follow the rules established by the European avant-garde.

One example of European architecture which served to support Hitchcock and Johnson's 'convergence' theory was the work shown at the Deutscher Werkbund's Weissenhof Siedlung, which was an exposition of twenty-two complete houses and apartment houses built by architects selected by Mies van der Rohe. The aesthetic idiom was clearly that of the internationalism in the late 1920s. The 'Siedlung' or town planning became a feature of the international style, in which the traditional notion of the home was replaced by new concepts in living.

A number of American architects were included in the 1932 exhibition and were described in detail in the catalogue and the book which accompanied the exhibition. Among them were three immigrants of Austrian origin—Richard Neutra, Richard Schindler and Frederick Kiesler—who clearly stood in the European tradition. The Americans included Raymond Hood, the skyscraper architect, George Howe and William Lescaze, and the young Buckminster Fuller. The intention was to push these architects into the international arena, and to show that America was in no way behind the Europeans.

In fact an even stronger assertion was made—that America might take over the lead. Hitchcock wrote: 'Besides France, Holland and Germany, it is already America which appears to have the greatest significance for the development of a new architecture. There, very possibly, in the future it will take the most individual and characteristic form.'

In many ways the concept of the international style was an American invention—an attempt to keep up with Europe at least stylistically, if not philosophically. Its chroniclers propounded many fallacies which were harmful to architectural history and theory, but it cannot be denied that they were perceptive and alert in spotlighting the 1920s so soon after the decade had finished. They stood at an interesting historical crossroads, before the spread of Fascism changed the course of history in the 1930s. Hitchcock himself wrote: 'By the early '30s the stream was certainly beginning to widen and meander again.' Whatever the shortcomings of the international style in its over-emphasis upon form and the spirit of the age, the exhibition and books served to pinpoint, in the words of Hitchcock, 'an account by young and enthusiastic contemporaries of the new architecture of the '20s at the moment when it reached its peak of achievement at the opening of the next decade'.

# POPULAR STYLE IN THE 1930s

The high-minded theorists of modern design worked from an idealized notion of machine production, and from the theory of fine art, which they applied directly to architecture. The idea of craft was also central to their discussions, providing the 'moral' base for a theory of 'good making'.

Where the production of actual goods for the mass of the population in the inter-war years was concerned, these theories had little relevance. They were soon associated exclusively with the strange, white, flat-topped buildings that suddenly appeared on the scene and with the rather unwelcoming tubular steel chairs which became standard in certain austere, institutional settings. The majority of people made do with reproduction items in their homes or, if they decided to buy 'modern', with one of the more popular 'modernistic' styles which had, by the 1930s, penetrated the mass market.

The first modern style to make a significant impact, both in the US and in Europe, was art deco, which had its origins in the French decorative arts of the 1920s.

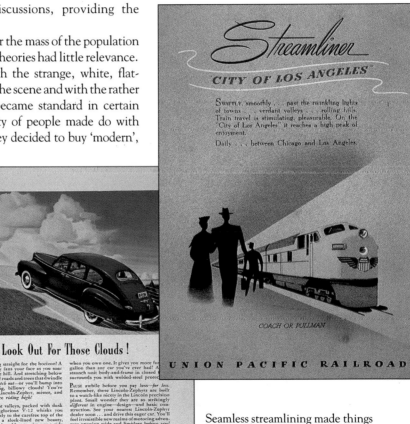

Seamless streamlining made things both modern and mysterious: it proved a commercially successful fantasy (even though its scientific benefits were marginal). Meanwhile, decoration such as that seen at the Park Lane Hotel, London **(left)**, mixed modernity with the reassuring gravitas of useless ornament. People liked it.

# The Decorative Arts in France in the 1920s

While Art Deco became the hallmark of the popular environment by the early 1930s, its origins were much more exclusive. In France, the concept of style had traditionally been associated with craftsmanship and individualism. In the 1920s, these factors were to reassert themselves and form the basis of the style which we now refer to as art deco.

The roots of art deco lie in art nouveau, which was brought to the notice of the general public at the Paris Exhibition of 1900. Art nouveau's public appeal resulted in a commercialization which eventually brought about its demise, and designers then looked around for a new style which had not been so exploited and which took into account French styles from the late eighteenth century without falling into the trap of historicism. It was thought that art nouveau had gone too far in its rejection of the past, and that what was needed was a synthesis, combining the best of the old and the best of the new.

In 1901 the Société des Artistes-Décorateurs was founded, consolidating an attitude which linked art, and not the machine, with design. Designers like Maurice Dufrêne and Paul Follot moved away from art nouveau, adopting a simpler approach towards the 'decorative arts', and emphasizing the unity of the interior, from furniture and wallpaper to decorative items. It was during these early years that the *ensemblier* (interior decorator) emerged as a dominant figure in the world of the French decorative arts. Firms like the partnership of the architect Louis Süe and the painter André Mare grew up, bringing different specialists together to provide complete interior decoration. Because of the luxury nature of their goods, these firms worked only for the wealthy. Paris in the 'Gay Twenties' was still the home of an affluent, upper-middle-class sector of French society, who patronized the decorating firms and enabled them to work in exotic styles and with sumptuous materials. The furniture designer Emile-Jacques Ruhlmann wrote: 'We must make *de luxe* furniture. I know that it is regrettably contrary to those generous beliefs for which I respect my colleagues. It would be preferable to educate the masses, but it is necessary to proceed otherwise. We are forced to work for the rich because the rich never imitate the middle-classes. In all periods craftsmen have followed the leaders whose work is addressed to the rich. And the rich, without grudging it, are prodigal with the money—and time—necessary for the solution of problems. It is the élite which launches fashion and determines its direction. Let us produce, therefore, for them.'

The general tendency to look back to the past for inspiration was altered around 1910 by a new influence upon the development of style. An exhibition of decorative arts in Paris showed the advances that had taken place in Vienna and the debt owed to Mackintosh by the school of rectilinear art nouveau.

The French couturier Paul Poiret was one of the earliest to put these ideas into practice. He saw how important it was to link the decorative arts and find a new style, and he opened a school, named after his daughter Martine in 1911. The following year he founded his 'Atelier Martine', selling fabrics, curtains, wallpapers, rugs, embroideries and decorated porcelain, pottery and glass, screens and panels. Poiret was directly influenced by art from Germany and Vienna, and wrote: 'In 1910 I visited exhibitions of decorative arts in Berlin and Vienna, and became acquainted with the artists leading the trends, such as Hoffmann, the creator and director of the Vienna Workshops, Karl Witzmann, Mulhesurs, Bruno Paul and Klimt... I spent whole days visiting modern interiors constructed and furnished with a wealth of new ideas which we had never seen at home. I dreamed of revolutionizing interior design... I even went to Brussels specially to see the Palais Stoclet.'

Poiret went on to develop his own style of interior decoration, which was luxurious and expressed the twin ideals of this period, comfort and elegance.

The bright colours imported by the Ballets Russes, who first danced in Paris in 1909, had an influence upon the mature decorative styles of the 1920s. The aesthetic discoveries of cubism were also incorporated as decorative motifs in many fabrics in the post-war years. René Gimpel (quoted in Battersby's *The Decorative Twenties*), described the particular way in which the French decorative artists interpreted cubism. 'Cubism is a decorative art, though the cubists didn't suspect this at the outset... Once cubism passes from a canvas to textiles, paper or bindings, everyone understands it; women gladly wear dresses with cubist designs but are loath to have a cubist picture in their home.'

After the First World War these tendencies were consolidated and the decorative arts took an even stronger hold in France. In 1919 Ruhlmann opened a business for his furniture; René Joubert founded the Decoration Intérieure Moderne, and Dufrêne opened a shop called 'La Maîtrise' within the Galeries Lafayette; while in 1923 Follot became the head of 'Pomone' at Bon Marché. The exhibition of French colonial art which took place in 1922 inspired much of the primitivism evident in the decorative arts afterwards.

**HIGH DESIGN**
Jacques Ruhlmann's pavilion at the 1925 Paris exhibition of decorative arts. **(Right)** Erté in fancy dress in Monte Carlo and a drawing by George Barbier of the dancer Nijinsky in Scheherazade.

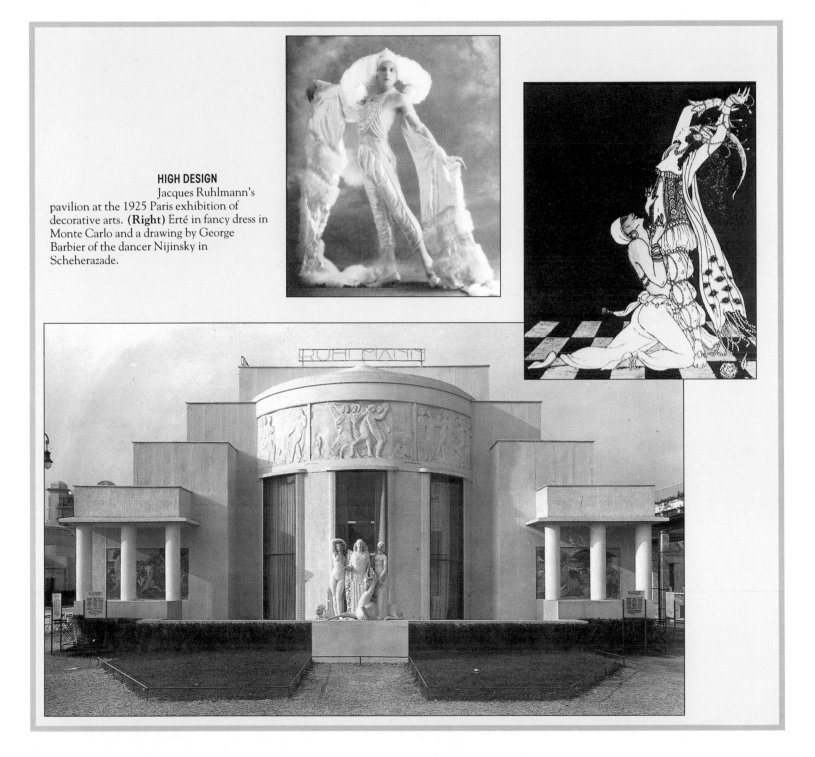

**158**

As early as 1910, the Société des Artistes-Décorateurs had suggested holding an exhibition to restore the place of France as the leader of the decorative arts. Italy had asserted her influence through the 1902 exhibition in Turin, and then Germany had taken over the lead with the Werkbund exhibition of 1914. France had apparently fallen behind and desperately wanted to change this situation. An exhibition was first suggested for 1915, then successively for 1916, 1922, 1924 and 1925, when it finally took place in Paris. As early as 1911 its aims had been set out clearly by the Société: 'By the collaboration of the artist, the manufacturer and the craftsman, to reunite all the decorative arts in an International Exhibition—these include architecture, woodwork, sculpture, metalwork, ceramics, glassware, fabric etc—whether they are objects of utility or simply decoration, in all their functions, whether the exterior or interior decoration of public or private buildings. This exhibition must be exclusively of modern art. No reproduction or stylistic pastiches will be admitted.'

Paul Follot (much in demand in the 1920s) produced work for wealthy Parisians – a clientele that not only demanded fine workmanship but insisted on it being highly visible. This carved chair, 1913, is in sycamore.

## THE 1925 INTERNATIONAL EXHIBITION

The International Exhibition of Modern Decorative and Industrial Arts of 1925 was a gigantic affair which took place down both sides of the River Seine, with the Alexander III Bridge used to connect the two parts. The bridge was covered with shops selling decorative items—one of the most interesting being the shop selling the 'simultaneous fashion' of the artist/designer Sonia Delaunay.

The gates which surrounded the exhibition area typified the spirit of the whole enterprise, the main purpose of which was to consolidate national prestige. Huge, unadorned classical columns, topped by sculptures by Emile Bourdelle, Aristide Maillol and others, formed monumental entrances. All the architecture on show was solid and monolithic, and attention to exterior details provided the decorative aspect. Each pavilion had a garden around it with fountains fed from the river, and sculpture was used as a landscape feature throughout. The grandiose style used traditional motifs in an entirely new way to provide a 'contemporary' aesthetic. It was an inclusive aesthetic, exploiting all the decorative styles at its disposal but somehow still managing to achieve a unity.

The pavilions were temporary structures made of plaster on wooden frames. The great majority were French, emphasizing their superiority in every field, but there were also contributions from Holland, Russia, Britain, Austria and some Oriental countries. The most notable absentees were Germany and the US—the former for obvious political reasons and the latter because America felt that it had nothing to contribute at that time.

The strongest element in the 1925 Exhibition was the work of the French *ensembliers*—decorators and craftsmen—among them the furniture designers Rhulmann, Dufrêne, Dunand and Legrain; the glassworkers Lalique and Marinot, and the metalworkers Puiforcat and Edgar Brandt.

Four of the French pavilions were presented by the studios of the big department stores: Primavera for Au Printemps, Pomone for Bon Marché, La Maîtrise for Galeries Lafayette, and Studium for the Louvre. They showed the work of the *artistes-décorateurs* who provided complete interiors for their rich clients, at its best. Waring & Gillow in England

159

Royal Doulton saltglaze ware, 1920-35, **(top left)** fed a middle-class demand for a return of the 'craft' element in design. A Lalique table lamp from the early 1920s **(left)**.

Pierrot and Pierrette by Demetre Chiparus, 1925. Made in ivory and bronze on a marble and mosaic base, the literalness of the modelling is rooted in photographic 'realism'.

**A SOFTER MODERNISM?**
In spite of the continued
rigour or puritanism of Marcel Breuer – a dining
room, 1927 **(below)** – the stylists of the modern
domestic landscape were obliged (and most were
willing) to build in obvious comfort. **Man's Den**
by Joseph Urban, 1929 **(far left)**, furniture by
Eileen Gray, 1925-30 **(left)**.

were soon to follow the French example, employing Paul Follot and Serge Chermayeff to design for them.

But it was two other French pavilions that dominated the exhibition. *Le Pavillon d'un Ambassadeur*, presented by the French Ministry of Fine Arts, consisted of twenty-five rooms containing textiles by Dufy, metalwork by Brandt, watercolours by Marie Laurencin and work from other top designers, decorators and artists. *Le Pavillon d'un Collectionneur* was a copy of a building that the architect Pierre Patout had built for Ruhlmann, and it held the best of the latter's luxury furniture.

The rich, luxurious style of these pavilions epitomized the contemporary French attitude towards decoration. As Battersby has written: 'Plain surfaces were embossed in a variety of textures, coloured or dusted with gold and silver powder.' Swags of flowers, flowing drapes and spiral shapes lying between the stylized roses of Mackintosh and 1920s champagne bubbles filled the interiors. Their lushness came to symbolize the extravagance of the French 'new rich'.

Some French pavilions were given over to manufacturing firms, for Sèvres ceramics, for example, and to the different regions of France, which played their part in the extravaganza.

A second French strain at the exhibition contrasted with these highly decorated pavilions. It owed more to modernism and the architecture of reinforced concrete, which had evolved an accompanying simple white style. Robert Mallet-Stevens' cubist trees and his Pavilion of Tourism employed this simple, undecorated aesthetic, whilst Le Corbusier's *Pavillon de l'Esprit Nouveau* juxtaposed the lightness of modern architecture against the heaviness of the decorative style—or *Moderne*.

Melnikov's Russian pavilion provided another dramatic contrast to the French decoration, epitomizing as it did the constructivist approach to architecture.

## FROM MODERN TO *MODERNE*

An interest in modern architecture and design was developing at this time in France, and by 1925 traditional wooden furniture was giving way to designs in metal. Designers like Eileen Gray crossed the barrier between the relative élitism of a medium like lacquer work, fashionable as this was amongst the wealthy in 1925, and machine-style tubular steel furniture. The advances that were taking place in Holland and Germany in metal furniture filtered through to France offering stylistic alternatives which were integrated into the ranges available on the market. The experiments of Le Corbusier and Charlotte Perriand in tubular steel furniture found a place in the French middle-class home.

After the 1925 Exhibition commissions came from offices, banks, bars and so on, and the decorative styles were immediately absorbed into a commercial context. As new materials such as plastics developed, they

162

replaced the more expensive ones and mass production gradually took over from hand-making. Modern and *Moderne* came to coexist as stylistic alternatives—ironically, the former becoming more élitist than the latter. As Banham explains: 'The clientele of modern architecture was composed of artists, their patrons and dealers, and a few casual visitors to the architectural section of the Salon d'Automme.' *Moderne*, however, developed into a definitely popular idiom. By the late '20s and '30s, the stylistic hotchpotch that Bevis Hillier describes in his book *Art Deco* had come into existence. In its more popular incarnation, he writes: 'It was an assertively modern style, developing in the 1920s and reaching a high point in the '30s. It drew inspiration from various sources including the more austere side of art nouveau, cubism and Russian ballet, American Indian art and the Bauhaus, it was a classical style in that, like neo-Classicism, but unlike rococo or art nouveau, it ran to geometry rather than asymmetry, and to the rectilinear rather than the linear, it responded to the demands of the machine and of new materials such as plastics, ferro-concrete and glass, and its ulitmate aim was to end the old conflict between art and industry, the old snobbish distinction between artist and artisan, partly by making artists adept at crafts but still more by adapting designs to the requirements of mass production.'

In England, motifs such as greyhounds, pyramid-stepped forms and sun-rays appeared as decoration putting the stamp of modernity upon the new factories, commercial buildings, cinemas, owner-occupied houses and ocean liners.

In America, Hollywood picked up what it called 'jazz-moderne' and developed it into a style associated with glamour, luxury and extravagance providing escapism in a period of economic depression. This zig-zag style, as it was called, characterized many architectural and mass-produced artefacts in the early 1930s, from the Chrysler building to cigarette boxes.

The market showed a ready acceptance of a style which symbolized modernity. Mass production and the utilization of new materials brought it within everyone's reach, and *Moderne* motifs proliferated throughout the '30s.

The agitated zig-zags of the Chrysler building, 1928-30, are by William van Allen – the spire **(left)** and elevator doors **(top)**. The noisy design caused critical uproar.

The foyer of the Daily Express Building, c.1933. Such film-fantasy imagery for a newspaper seems like irony today, but its vocabulary expressed the popular idea of what luxury should look like.

# Streamform

**A**ny discussion about popular rather than exclusive style hinges on the question of commercializing products, and the psychological links between objects and consumers. The early Modern Movement protagonists turned their backs on the market-led consumerism of industrial capitalism in order to emphasize the democratic ideals of mass production and the utility value of products. By the 1930s, however, Modernism had lost its critical base and become just another style available on the market. (Supporters of post-Modernism later criticized Modernism for its neglect of the essential symbolic relationship between product and consumer, seeing that gap as the reason for its demise.)

The design style which arose out of the most commercialized framework of all was American streamlining. 'Streamform', as it came to be called, went furthest in providing a modern design idiom which undercut the high-minded assumptions of Modernism. Kathleen Plummer has written: 'The streamlined Moderne's sleek expression seems to have been developed as a conscious reaction to the jumpy zig-zag Moderne of the '20s.'

This describes the replacement of one style by another, but it does not provide a rationale for streamlining itself. While the dynamics of mass taste are not precisely fathomable except by the sociologist, who can place them within a socio-economic context, a brief investigation of the commercialization of design which took place in the US in the 1920s and '30s, and its cultural background is essential. Why should the American public have been so keen to embrace a style which put the emphasis firmly upon the future?

Generally speaking, the attraction of streamlining lay in its relevance to the economic depression. Like the products of Hollywood, its drama and excitement provided the necessary release for a public which was otherwise preoccupied by inflation and unemployment.

The emotive value of streamling outweighed its functional qualities. Unlike art deco, it did not originate in an exclusive decorative art movement, but rather in the various aerodynamic experiments undertaken in the years following the First World War. The designs for cars, boats and planes that Norman Bel Geddes envisaged were prime examples of the 'teardrop' aesthetic that had been pioneered in Germany. The ideas, modelled on the forms of aeroplane fuselages, were inspired by the way in which dolphins and porpoises moved through the water. Analogies were made (mistakenly, it later turned out) with movement

### A PATCHY DEPRESSION
The effects of the
Depression on western economies were so
cataclysmic that recovery took years, but the
Depression was patchy in its effects. It depended
where you stood when the roof fell in.

166

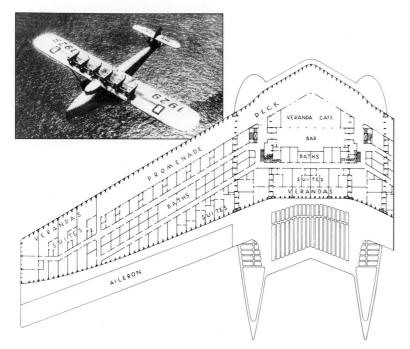

through air, and the round-nosed, tapered, rear-engined transport design emerged as the perfect foil to 'air resistance'. This style found its most evocative outlet in the railroad trains designed by Raymond Loewy for the Pennsylvania Railroad Company. They came complete with chrome trim and the 'speed' whiskers, taken straight out of comic books, which, by the mid-'30s, adorned the surface of nearly every streamlined object.

The rounded corners of trains and cars soon found their way into fridges and ovens, primarily because the same methods of steel stamping were used. Domestic objects came to suggest the same notions of speed and futurity as their outdoor counterparts. Eventually streamlining was applied to just about every metal or plastic object which was produced in the US in these years, from irons to staplers to radios. This style was closely associated with the industrial designers whose role it was to give goods 'consumer appeal'.

Contemporary commentators isolated streamlining's debt to modern art, showing that it had 'pedigree' roots as well as popular ones. The cubist painters and sculptors, from Cézanne to Picasso to Archipenko, were described as the fathers of streamform. More contemporary abstract painters such as Jean Hélion, and the 'art' photographers of the period such as Margaret Bourke-White were also cited. However distant these sources, they had in common an interest in the aesthetic of machine production and a commitment to abstract forms. In many ways, streamlining had more to do with futurism and expressionism than with cubism, as it was an expressive aesthetic, utilizing abstraction to emotional and evocative ends.

The style roused the ire of those designers who sought ways of promoting a 'pure', 'morally intact' international style, which made no concessions to commercialism. In the years following the Second World War, it was often equated with vulgarity and bad taste by such high-minded would-be reformers.

Streamlining became monumental. Norman Bel Geddes conceived wonderful flying sculptures, cruise liners of the air **(above)**. Henry Dreyfuss designed the Hudson locomotive, 1941 **(left)**.

# The American industrial designer

The commercial framework of streamlining was determined by its creator, the industrial designer. In order to understand why streamlining was so dramatically opposed to Modernism it is necessary to examine the background to the industrial design profession itself which emerged in the US in the late 1920s, and which became the model for many international variants in the years following the Second World War.

The pioneer American industrial designers—Walter Dorwin Teague, Norman Bel Geddes, Raymond Loewy, Henry Dreyfuss, Donald Dohner, Lurelle Guild and others—emerged as practising designers around the time of the Wall Street Crash. They were engaged by mass-production industry to improve the sales appeal of their goods during the economic recession—Teague by Eastman Kodak, Loewy by Gestetner and Bel Geddes by the Toledo Scale Company.

They all had backgrounds in the visual arts but their earlier professional experience was commercial. While Teague had worked in New York as a freelance typographer and advertising illustrator since 1908, Raymond Loewy had been an illustrator for women's magazines. Donald Deskey, another of the pioneers, had been the art director of an advertising agency before turning to design. Bel Geddes and Henry

A Kodak Camera by W.D. Teague, 1936. Designers of cameras emphasized simplicity to encourage everyone to take snaps – the profits lay in film and processing. Art deco suite by Donald Deskey, Radio City Music Hall, 1930s **(left)**.

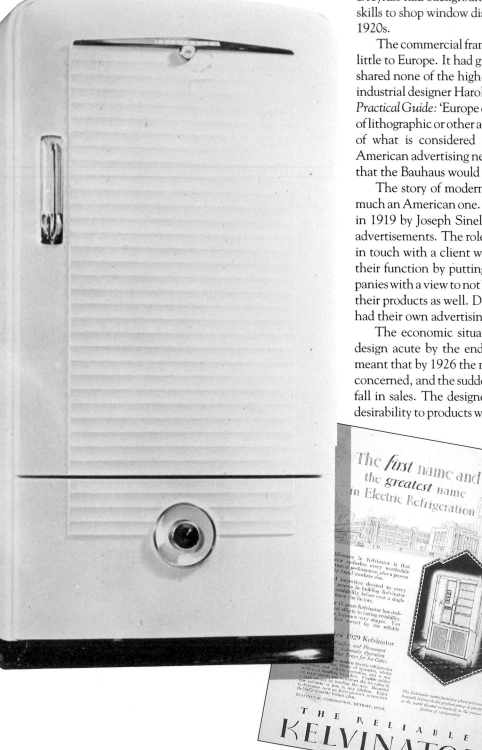

168

Dreyfuss had backgrounds in stage design but were quick to apply these skills to shop window display—a growing influence in New York in the 1920s.

The commercial framework that sustained these designers owed very little to Europe. It had grown out of American needs and expertise, and shared none of the high-minded ideals of the Modern Movement. The industrial designer Harold Van Doren, explained in *Industrial Design: A Practical Guide:* 'Europe exercises very little influence upon the character of lithographic or other advertising design in this country, largely because of what is considered to be the unsuitability of foreign designs to American advertising needs.' He reinforced this attitude when he wrote that the Bauhaus would find no place on American soil.

The story of modern advertising and marketing techniques is very much an American one. In fact, the term 'industrial design' was first used in 1919 by Joseph Sinel, referring to drawings of industrial objects for advertisements. The role of the advertising agency in putting a designer in touch with a client was crucial, and in the 1920s agencies extended their function by putting designers in touch with manufacturing companies with a view to not simply providing publicity material but restyling their products as well. Department stores and mail order catalogues also had their own advertising sections by this period.

The economic situation of American industry made the need for design acute by the end of the 1920s. The enormous post-war boom meant that by 1926 the market became glutted, where some goods were concerned, and the sudden recession, first felt in 1927, caused a dramatic fall in sales. The designer was brought in as the only means of adding desirability to products which had ceased to have any intrinsic consumer

Streamlining distanced the mind from the machine's mechanical guts and smoothed the path of the machine into the domestic kitchen.

appeal. The emphasis was upon technological goods—automobiles, domestic appliances and other small consumer machines—although even furniture and the decorative arts began to be influenced by the end of the 1930s. It was more difficult, however, to change the identity of an object such as a chair than a relatively new object like a fridge, which had not yet acquired a distinctive image. Streamlining affected those goods which the European Modern Movement had largely ignored, except as objects of inspiration. It provided new goods with an identity which they retained for a number of decades: it was not until the 1960s that the images created by the pioneer industrial designers finally faded from view.

The function of the industrial designer was very different from that of his counterpart in the studio of a decorative arts firm. Not only was he responsible for the design of the product in question, he also had to investigate the costs of any retooling required and undertake market research. As a result, projects were often very expensive and took a long time to complete. Teague, for instance, was retained by Eastman Kodak for a year before he came up with a proposal. The designers subcontracted much of the work to draughtsmen, engineers and model-makers, and gradually built up teams of people employed in their offices. On some

occasions the market research was fairly crude, but on others it was decided that a product should be presented as a range of alternatives, aimed at different sectors of the market. The international role of the industrial designer has been modelled closely on the work of the American pioneers ever since.

**169**

Advertisers gradually developed the advantage of linking glamour and perceived snobbery with industrial products: cars were among the first of the new century status symbols: a 1929 Oldsmobile Viking sedan **(left)**.

# The New York World's Fair

It was at New York's World Fair of 1939 that streamlining as a popular, modern design idiom came into its own, and with it the industrial designers. With the exception of the Chrysler 'Airflow'—the first commercially produced streamlined automobile—Chicago's Country of Progress exhibition of 1933 had owed more to French art deco and interior decoration than to indigenous American trends, but by 1939 they could not be ignored. The buildings and their contents, most of them designed by the 'big name' designers, all exhibited the well-known bulbous curves of streamlining and expressed a firm commitment to the future. It was a triumph of American commerce and industry and a celebration of the role of design, or more specifically streamlining, in communicating that ideology.

The main theme of the exhibition was 'Building the World of Tomorrow', and it attempted to answer the question where the products and processes of modern civilization were leading. The industrial designer, by now firmly established within the structure of American culture, was the obvious candidate to envisage this future world of high technology, and he replaced the architect in the construction of an exhibition area which covered over one thousand acres of waste land outside New York. Walter Dorwin Teague describes the appropriateness of using the industrial designer in this context. 'Because the industrial designers are supposed to understand public taste and be able to speak in a popular tongue as a profession and they are bound to disregard traditional forms and solutions and to think in terms of today and tomorrow, it was natural that the Board of Design should turn to them for the planning of the major exhibits in which the theme of the Fair is to be expressed.'

Teague was selected to represent industrial design on the Fair's planning committee and he was responsible for many of the constructions, including the Ford pavilion, and those for US Steel, Eastman Kodak and National Cash Registers. The style of the buildings was left open to the designers involved, and in most of the American pavilions a design vocabulary was achieved with the use of streamlining. This meant an emphasis on smooth, rounded surfaces, and a neo-futurist use of dramatic architectural punctuation. This was seen most clearly in the 3,700-foot Trylon and 200-foot Perisphere, two constructions which provided a focal point from which the 1400 exhibits radiated outwards.

A vivid use of colour was evident: each avenue out of the central point took on a darker hue the further away it got from the central white constructions.

Building **The World of Tomorrow** – New York World Fair, 1939. The shapes were percipient, although the technology to live in them – radar and nuclear reactors – had yet to be invented.

172

W.D. Teague's brilliantly simple
cash register became architecture at
the New York World Fair. Industrial
designers and architects were bride
and groom in the new age. The
reciprocity in their image-making
continues to this day.

The Sweden Square garden courtyard at the Swedish Pavilion, New York World Fair. After the war, Scandinavian style came to dominate American contemporary taste.

Henry Dreyfuss was responsible for the interior of the Perisphere which housed the City of Tomorrow, viewed from a revolving balcony dubbed 'The Magic Carpet'.

The American exhibits emphasized the role that transport and the new road and rail systems would play in the environment of the future. Raymond Loewy's 'Transportation of Tomorrow', which was exhibited in the Chrysler Motor Building, included a streamlined taxi, liner, car and trucks, as well as a rocketship which would travel between New York and London.

A model was set up to show the rocketship in action, and Teague described it: 'Accompanied by a brilliant flash of light, a muffled explosion, and ingenious effects which make it appear that the rocket vanishes in the skyline ceiling of the exhibit building.'

The industrial designer was undoubtedly the hero of the hour. As Teague explained: 'At the Fair the profession is coming into its own and emerging for the first time in its major, basic role, as the interpreter of industry to the public.'

Norman Bel Geddes showed the results of several years of his experiments in the General Motors Building at the Fair. His exhibit was called 'Highways and Horizons', and it envisaged a whole new network of motorways covering the US—an innovation that he claimed was necessary before transport could be developed.

The pioneer designers succeeded in capturing the popular American imagination through their involvement with the New York World's Fair. The purist international style was overturned by a neo-futurist interest in styling the World of Tomorrow—a world in which idealism, optimism and faith in technology ruled the day, and which was symbolized, in the words of Teague, by 'a dynamic architecture that shall be a true expression of our own materials and our own spirit'.

This dynamic concept of architecture and design was to become an internationally accepted style for many consumer goods in the years following the Second World War.

# Swedish modern

174

Among the foreign exhibits at the Fair to receive a lot of attention was an interior in the Swedish pavilion by the designer Josef Frank. Frank was Austrian by birth and had been closely involved with the architectural Modern Movement in that country, exhibiting at the Weissenhof Siedlung in 1927. In 1932 he moved to Sweden and settled there as a furniture and textile designer for the shop Svenskt Tenn. The 1939 World's Fair interior initiated the Swedish modern style but it was not until the decade after the Second World War that this style achieved maximum international popularity in the domestic living-area. Nonetheless, it had a great influence on the mass-produced furniture designed by men like Russel Wright and Gilbert Rhode in the US in the 1930s, and it established a furniture aesthetic which was embraced enthusiastically by the more fashion-conscious consumer. Swedish Modern never achieved the popularity of stream-form, but it became a widespread style, symbolizing ideas about human-ism, democracy, tradition and moderation. These qualities contrasted dramatically with those of streamlining, and provided a culture for the living-room which was quite different from that of the kitchen in the American home of the 1930s.

The term 'Swedish Modern', subtitled 'A Movement Towards Sanity in Design', was actually coined by a critic at the New York World's Fair of 1939 to describe Sweden's interior display. It became a general description for the furniture, ceramics, glass and textiles, which together constituted the Swedish interior style. It had already been seen at Chicago in 1933 and at the Paris exhibition of 1937, and its history went back to the early years of the century.

The term 'Swedish grace' had already been used to describe the products of the Swedish applied art industries in the 1920s. The artists Edward Hald, Simon Gate and Wilhelm Kåge had been put in touch with the glass company Iittala and the ceramics firm Gustavsberg by the Svenska Sjlödforeningen in 1915. Thanks to their work, a new, light, modern, decorative aesthetic had emerged in Swedish glass and ceramics which had no equivalent elsewhere. It was more humanistic than

Josef Frank left Austria to work in Sweden. At first his highly coloured textiles showed Bauhaus influence, but they became more popular in the 1940s when he introduced plants and figures into his designs.

A chair designed by Josef Frank in 1925 **(below)**. Alvar Aalto's design for Iittala Glass, Finland, 1930 **(above)**. The predominance of organic form made Scandinavian design the living-room's equivalent of kitchen streamlining.

176

Early 1940s student accommodation
at the Massachusetts Institute of
Technology, with furnishings by
Alvar Aalto.

German functionalist decorative arts, and lighter than the French and Viennese examples. In 1919 Gregor Paulsson, the director of the Swedish Design Council, had written a book, *More Beautiful Everyday Things*, in which he outlined the need for objects which were of aesthetic interest, as well as being widely available and non-élitist. This ambition underpinned all the experiments undertaken by the applied arts industries through the '20s and '30s. At the time of the Stockholm Exhibition in 1930, Swedish architects were briefly tempted to emulate the strict functionalism that they saw emerging in Germany, and the Swedish Social Democratic Government put many of their ideas into practice in communal projects. Yet the applied arts were only temporarily swayed by this move towards austerity, and by the early 1930s had reasserted their commitment to light, decorative forms with stylized natural imagery. A battle between the 'Funkis' and the 'Tradis' (the functionalists and the traditionalists) took place as a result of the Stockholm exhibition which had tended to favour the former, but it became quite clear by the mid-'30s that the Swedish commitment to the role of tradition in its decorative arts was undamaged.

In addition to the ceramics and glass produced primarily by Gustavsberg and Iittala in these years, a number of Swedish furniture and textile designers emerged who were to be highly influential in formulating the 'Swedish Modern' style. The textiles of Astrid Sampe for the shop Nordiska Kompaniet expressed the same humanistic ideals as her counterparts' ceramics and glass and, where furniture was concerned,

Bruno Mathsson, C. A. Berg, Carl Malmsten and Josef Frank showed that being 'modern' did not necessarily imply breaking absolutely with the past.

Frank, in particular, harked back to English eighteenth-century furniture in his search for a new idiom. He was vociferous in his condemnation of the German school, writing that: 'In beholding the currently fashionable functionalism, holding that form should be adapted to use, material and structural, the functional form has often been mistaken for the plainest geometrical one in the belief that it is closest to the most primitive.'

Frank went on to evolve a complete theory of interior decoration, which included the use of traditional materials—mahogany, brass, cane and upholstery—and which stressed the need to keep furniture up on legs, so as not to hide the structure of the room. It combined plain walls with patterned textiles,, and included personal mementoes and decorative objects wherever possible, as a means of humanizing the space. Frank stressed that furniture should be the servant rather than the master, and that design should not be linked with puritanical ideals. His interiors encouraged eclecticism and light decoration, and he relegated tubular steel furniture to the garden. His ideal interior, he wrote: 'Radiates repose, harmony and sophistication, and supplies the purist fragrance of the epoch called "Swedish Modern".'

In the 1930s, then, a number of popular styles co-existed on the international mass market, and manufacturers in many countries were quick to exploit their appeal, combing styles and infiltrating new elements into more traditional designs when the market was a cautious one, as in England.

By 1939 many people in the industrialized world had objects in their homes which expressed, in one way or another, the cult of modernity, and which showed consumers participating in contemporary fashion and taste. This phenomenon was to be cut short by the war, and it did not re-establish itself until a few years after hostilities had finally ceased.

Simon Gate's virtuoso but oddly lugubrious Orrefors glass vase **(above)**. Swedish 'Trivia-Brigg knock-down' furniture and 'Safari' chairs **(right)**. Between the world wars, Sweden pioneered the concept of socially useful egalitarian domestic design.

# PART THREE

# 1940
# 1985

T he question of international trade was one that preoccupied all the countries emerging from the Second World War. The first requirement was to turn their economies back to full production for peacetime needs, and this called for American financial aid. A loan scheme was initiated, and England, France, Italy and, a little later, Germany and Japan, were soon busy re-establishing their peacetime industrial manufacturing. The trade tariffs which had been imposed by the US before the war were gradually abolished and free international trading resumed. Recovery was slow at first, but it accelerated rapidly, initiating a period of unusually fast economic growth which, in North America, western Europe and Japan, was sustained for two decades.

The manufacture of goods played a major role in this economic rebirth. Between 1945 and 1958, for example, world manufacture increased by 60 per cent, while between 1958 and 1968 the figure rose to 100 per cent. These rises were paralleled by a growth in export figures, and by 1957 the world trade in manufactures exceeded primary produce for the first time ever. The reasons for this resurgence were complex. Social and economic factors played a part, but the strongest stimulus was the rapid development of technology. Many advances had been made during the Second World War, including developments in radar, aircraft production and the use of new materials such as plastics and light metals. Yet perhaps the most significant development of the late '40s was the transistor, which made possible the miniaturization of electronic equipment. This opened the way to computers which were to play a central role in the post-war period, both in the automation of production and in information retrieval. The role of technology in the post-war world, and its application to the space race and cybernetics research, to name but two areas, cannot be underestimated.

Manufacturing provided the industrial designer with his major challenge in these years. In several countries he provided the means by which goods were distinguished from their foreign competitors and made more desirable for the purchaser. The lesson taught by pre-war America that 'design sells' was digested and became a major strategy in the programmes of industrial reconstruction and international trading undertaken by many countries in the post-war period.

Countries such as Germany and Russia, where avant-garde design movements had been cut short by the totalitarian regimes of the 1930s, lost their predominance in the evolution of design. They were overtaken by the countries with a more liberal attitude towards the role of design in society, among them the United States, the Scandinavian countries and Great Britain. The wartime occupations of France and Holland laid the final nails in the coffins of their contributions to pre-war Modernism, so that all in all a total change of emphasis occurred in design after the war.

The war years themselves were characterized by a shortage of materials and manpower in the countries where design was an on-going concern, either as a craft tradition or as part of the industrial process. Immediately after the war, the rapid acceleration of industrial growth in many countries brought with it a new wave of design activity and ideas. This expansion can be viewed from a national perspective, with each country developing a theory of production and a language of form appropriate to the 'new face' it wanted to present to the world.

By the middle to late 1950s, alongside the national lines of development, an international design forum emerged, encouraged by the growth of multi-national corporations. Supported by a framework of conferences and publications, it introduced an 'international style' which shared many features with the architectural styles of the early part of the century. From this point onwards, design theory and practice were shaped by an international dialectic. A number of crises, followed by 'alternative' or 'post-Modern' philosophies and styles, characterized the late 1960s, helping to create the pluralistic situation which exists today.

Since the Second World War the West has run the gamut of excess, trendiness and seriousness in design: the Union Jack was frivolous in the 1960s **(top left)**; Arne Jacobsen's Swan Chair, 1957 **(left)**; and Herman Miller's revolutionary Action Office system, 1968. In 1959 pseudo-spaceship styling in American automobiles **(above)** peaked, together with American self-confidence. Both then declined.

# CHAPTER EIGHT

# RECONSTRUCTION & DESIGN

> **I SUBMIT THAT BETTER HOUSEHOLD EQUIPMENT AND BETTER MECHANICAL DEVICES ARE OF NO REAL VALUE UNLESS THEY ARE EASY FIRST ESSAYS IN THE FUNDAMENTAL REDESIGN OF OUR WORLD: HARBINGER OF A WHOLESALE REORGANIZATION OF OUR CHAOTIC SCIENCE**
>
> *W. D. TEAGUE, DESIGN THIS DAY (1940)*

Immediately after the Second World War, design was dominated by the need for realism and reconstruction. The Utopian visions of the 1920s and 1930s were no longer appropriate in a world which lacked the basic material accompaniments to living.

Two symbolic models of reconstruction presented themselves to manufacturers and to the design profession—one technological and the other artistic. In some countries industrial expansion was seen as a means of 'getting things back on their feet'. The US, Germany, Switzerland and Japan channelled their creative efforts into industrial production, evolving an industrial design style which emphasized mechanical efficiency, and devoting much of their attention to technological goods. In contrast, the Scandinavian countries, Great Britain and Italy envisaged their ideal future in terms of social equality with beauty being made available to all. They wanted to achieve an environment—symbolized by the domestic interior—which would reflect stability and individual fulfilment and with which the public could identify.

With the onward march of mass production, both paths led to a design formalism, whether based upon the classical German machine aesthetic or upon the romanticism of 'contemporary' Italian furniture. This formal emphasis reflected the new relationship between design and the public. The practical demands of post-war reconstruction had been replaced, by the 1950s, by stylistic demands, in which the power of consumer choice equalled that of its manipulators. The vacuum created by the absence of any extensive design theory such as had characterized the early part of the century was filled by this universal public awareness of design as more than a mere functional appendage to living.

This section describes the development of these tendencies in five of the countries that gave birth to them—Scandinavia, the US, Great Britain, Italy and Germany. It shows how many of the problematic features of design in the 1960s had their roots in this formative period of post-war design.

From 1945 until the late 1950s America led the world in manufacturing and design. Then Italy, by then industrialized for the first time, sprang its design culture on the West. Achille Castiglione, designer of the tractor seat, 1957 **(above)** is one of Italy's most inventive designers. Furniture designed by Americans Charles Eames and George Nelson, 1956 **(left)**, for the Herman Miller Company.

# Scandinavia and the craft ideal

In contrast with the products of the mechanized industries epitomized by Volvo and Saab, post-war Scandinavian design for home furnishings and fittings charted a traditional course. By 1940 an image of Scandinavian domestic design had been firmly established internationally. The Stockholm Exhibition of 1930 had contrasted the radical functionalism of Germany with the humanism of the Scandinavian craft traditions, and the New York World's Fair of 1939 had established 'Swedish Modern' as an international design concept.

In general terms, this image was recognizable by an emphasis on simple forms. This was the result of craft traditions, combined with the long-term poverty and shortage of materials in Scandinavia. The unpretentiousness also expressed the Scandinavians' humanistic approach towards the environment—the belief that man was at the centre of all things, and that it was he, not the machine, who determined the appearance of everyday objects. Faith in the importance of tradition as a foundation for innovation lay at the root of their attempt to fuse the work of the hand with that of the machine, old with new materials, and the twentieth century with the past. In an article in *Industrial Design* magazine, Jane McCullough described the essential qualities of these design principles as they were displayed in an exhibition which toured the United States from 1954 to 1957. 'Because they are in touch with a continuing craft tradition, Scandinavian designers have a sense of, and a respect for, the materials they work . . . this sympathy for materials, linked with what might be called a sense of justness in Scandinavian culture, has produced a remarkably high median of design.'

The democratic idealism which had remained a basic premise of Scandinavian design since the beginning of the century was manifested after the war in a determination to rebuild a democratic society with material equality for all. On the world market, this design fitted the general mood of regeneration and relief after the austerity of pre-war functionalism.

In Sweden, war conditions minimized the materials available but maximized the inventiveness of the new generation of artist-craftsmen who succeeded the pioneering architects. The restrictions encouraged the development of their 'aesthetics of economy' which had grown up in the pre-war period and continued to thrive after the war. Humanism, democracy and craft continued to inspire the designers after 1940, and in 1955 an exhibition was held in Hälsinborg specifically to reinforce this

This optimistic, life enhancing textile design was produced by Josef Frank in Sweden in 1944. Small wonder that European eyes looked to Sweden for design at the war's end.

Swedish design: a display cabinet by Josef Frank, Sweden, 1948, and tableware by Stig Lindberg, 1954 (above). Lightness and graceful good sense in design, together with an intact economy and manufacturing base, gave Sweden a head start in the post-war international market.

philosophy. A writer in *Form* magazine at the time reiterated the Swedish ideals of 1930 in his description of the aims of Hälsingborg '55: 'To renew what we believe in and work for today...beautiful and practical surroundings. The main idea was to put man in the centre before everything created by architecture and the utilities.'

Hälsinborg '55 was organized by the Swedish Council of Design, which was furthering the democratic idealism of Swedish design by pursuing anthropometric investigations into living spaces and making recommendations about furniture measurements from 1948 through the post-war period.

The exhibition at Hälsingborg showed its social awareness in sections entitled 'Living in Terraced Houses' and 'Living with Little'. There was a strong democratic and humanistic flavour in many of the stands which developed the general theme of 'Design for Living'. The exhibition was characterized by a light, open and ordered aesthetic, and it used aluminium architectural structures and display areas. It consolidated the traditional principles of Swedish design, bringing back into focus the twenty-five-year-old debate between the functionalist and the humanist approach to design, and demonstrating beyond all doubt the victory of the latter.

Bruno Mathsson, Carl Malmsten and Josef Frank were among the 'modern' Swedish designers who had helped to establish the philosophical foundations of the Scandinavian approach towards design in the 1930s. They continued to act as strong influences in the post-war era, and their attitudes towards 'furniture architecture' helped determine and preserve the light, humanistic atmosphere of the Swedish home, which

Swedish domestic ornament, like
this by Sven Palmqvist in 1952,
satisfied a demand for textile design
in a way that industrial designers
sometimes neglected.

provided an important psychological base for the family during the long,
cold winters.

Matthsson replaced solid wood with bent-wood-laminated veneers
and developed curved furniture shapes to fulfil his own idea that:
'Comfortable sitting is an art, it ought not to be. Instead, the making of
chairs has to be done with such an art that the sitting will not be any art.'
This philosophy of comfort influenced the selection of the material, and
flexible, natural materials such as woven strips of fabric and cane were
used by the younger furniture designers, among them Axel Larssen and
Carl-Axel Acking.

Austerity was avoided in the Swedish post-war interior by the use of
discreet abstract and floral patterns on most two-dimensional surfaces,
and by the inclusion of light, unobtrusive pieces of wooden furniture,
mostly in birch or elm. Glass and ceramic decorative objects also played
an important psychological part in the settings, blurring the distinctions
between art and craft. Tradition and innovation coexisted happily—a
Windsor chair frequently accompanying the 'contemporary' tapered-leg
furniture. The Swedish home, a microcosm of Swedish society, expressed
the country's design ideals, showing at the same time the importance of
designed objects and the environment in the country's cultural rebirth.

Sweden's greatest contribution to post-war design lay in glass and
ceramic production. This was the responsibility of a few companies
only—among them Gustavsberg, Rorstrand and Orrefors, all of which
employed artists. Stig Lindberg became the art director of Gustavsberg in
1949 and determined the appearance of their products until 1957,
hand-making prototypes for mass production. The barrier between
ceramics and sculpture was eliminated in the work of Lindberg, Karin
Björquist, Lisa Larsen and others, and the hand-made aesthetic was
evident in the use of texture and rough finishes.

The two principal glassworks, Orrefors and Kosta, pioneered the
policy of employing an artist to design for them. Sven Palmquist began his
work with the 'Kraka' and 'Ravenna' techniques in 1947—sophisticated
glass techniques which employed air bubbles and vivid colour. Describing
his own work for Orrefors, Nils Landberg wrote: 'I try to give the glass a
refined simplicity and I want to have it manufactured in the most natural
way, that is, to have it blown by skilled artisans . . . In this way the glass
gets its most natural and balanced shapes . . . Glass is very thin and to blow
it emphasizes the delicacy and elegance of this fascinating material.'

## DENMARK

Stemming from the same
nineteenth-century arts and crafts roots as Swedish design, pre-war
Danish design was characterized by a strong emphasis upon social realism
and scientific experimentation. This provided a twentieth-century
tradition upon which the post-war generation leant heavily.

One of the strongest support structures for Danish post-war design was
the establishment of a permanent exhibition in Copenhagen—*den
Permanente*. Originally the brainchild of the silversmith Kay Bojesen in
1931, this was re-established in 1945 after its eclipse during the war years
and the German occupation of Denmark.

Pre-war Danish design had reached high peaks in silverware,
ceramics, textiles and, to a lesser extent, glass. All were characterized by a
simple unpretentiousness which continued into the post-war years.
Bojesen's approach, demonstrated in his silverware, served as an
aesthetic model for many formal experiments undertaken by the post-war
generation of designers. The sculptor Henning Koppel, the architect Eric
Herlow and others worked with craftsmen creating the abstract sculptural
forms that typified the Danish style of the late 1940s. Danish ceramics had
been mainly the responsibility of firms like the Royal Copenhagen
Porcelain Company, and Bing and Grondahl. These firms continued
producing in the post-war period, developing the design of simple
stoneware items with the help of creative artists. They worked alongside
pottery workshops like Saxbo, whose earthenware and stoneware
reflected natural earth colours and the textures of indigenous craft
ceramics. In the late 1940s, a boom period for the Danish applied arts, an
expressive, sculptural interest in form developed in crafts, while a terser,

more functional aesthetic emerged in industrially manufactured objects.

The Danish design that had begun under the German occupation produced their greatest results in furniture. The experiments of Kaare Klint provided an early instance of anthropometric analysis, and Borge Mogenson also conducted a series of experiments for the Danish Cooperative Society, based on studies of English eighteenth-century and other traditional furniture. Using two experimental flats as a laboratory, Mogensen developed a set of light, simple furniture in birch and beech to meet the needs of the average Danish family. It was shown to the public in 1944.

This sense of social realism and experimental rigour ran parallel with an almost sculptural attitude towards form, concerned more with the symbolic than the practical interpretation of democratic ideals. Hans Wegner's famous 'chair' for Johannes Hansen was 'sculpture' rather than 'tool'. Poul Henningsen emphasized its expressive function: 'It fulfils its task in society with the modest consciousness expected of the good citizen.' Furniture was no longer merely the practical outcome of social awareness; it now expressed that awareness through its chosen aesthetic of simple elegance.

Scandinavian furniture was ostentatious in its space-saving, clean-living imagery. The emphasis on natural materials declares the commercially popular virtues of 'old-fashioned craftsmanship' but the modern technology producing it ensured quality at a reasonable price. The apartment was designed by Eva and Nils Koppel, the chairs by Kaare Klint.

Danish design: Poul Henningsen's lamp, 1957, functions well and was efficient to make. Similarly, Arne Jacobsen's 1952 chair has a simple, press-moulded, one-piece seat and back. The chair had excellent stacking ability.

in London in 1968, implying that this was a time for retrospection (the last British exhibition of Danish design had been held in 1948). The 1960s were characterized in Denmark by a move towards the more international rectilinear shape in stainless steel, glass and ceramic design. In the furniture trade, a number of avant-garde experiments were undertaken by new designers, many of whom worked for the firm of Fritz Hansen which celebrated its centenary in 1972. Among them were the architects Jorn Utzon, Verner Panton, Piet Hein and Paul Kjaerholm. Panton described his own work in 1969, showing the distance that new materials had encouraged them to move from conventional furniture forms. 'I try to forget existing examples even though they may be good, and concern myself above all with the material. The result then rarely had four legs, not because I do not wish to make a chair but because the processing of new materials like wire and polyester calls for new shapes.' Such radical attitudes towards furniture would not have been possible without the pioneering work of Wegner and Jühl. While the aesthetic of new materials took over from that of traditional ones, the overall emphasis was still upon sculptural elegance and quality.

## FINLAND

A completely different set of conditions prevailed in Finland. Geographical remoteness, political conservatism and the lack of a strong design tradition placed Finnish design in a context different from that of Sweden and Denmark. The Finnish industrial designer emerged comparatively late, growing into the 'superdesigner' of the 1950s who created an image of exotic exclusiveness and artistic individualism for post-war Finnish design.

Two parallel streams of design activity had emerged in Finland after the war. One stemmed from Arttu Brummer's emphasis on the artistic, visually expressive nature of hand-made objects; the other from Alvar Aalto's pre-war interest in the technological and constructional aspects of design, and their application to mass production.

The work of Finn Jühl, shown at the 1949 Cabinet-Makers' Guild Exhibition, was inspired by the tools and weapons of primitive tribes. Their formal simplicity provided a model of instinctive unity of form and function through the craftsman's hand. In the 1950s, industrially produced furniture by Arne Jacobsen, Poul Kjaerholm and others exploited new materials such as steel and plastic, moving beyond the formal wooden sculpture of the pioneers to the creation of symbolic forms where the material became a means to an end. Jacobsen's moulded chairs were expressions in abstract form, conveying physical and mental comfort through their ovoid, womb-like shapes.

Finn Jühl designed an exhibition for the Victoria & Albert Museum

There was a great demand for designed objects when these became almost unobtainable during the wartime period of drabness and general hardship. Several firms employed artists to develop their production. But it was not until 1951, with the Zurich exhibition and the Milan Triennale, that Finnish design finally moved into the international arena. Arabia and Iittala, manufacturers of ceramics and glassware respectively, provided financial backing for the Finnish contribution to the Milan exhibition. Tapio Wirkkala's artistic organization of the exhibits produced a stunning visual effect, which, however, provoked criticism of Finnish exclusiveness. The exhibition brought the Finns six prizes—a success which was repeated in 1954 and 1957. The use of exhibitions to propagate and promote national design was part of a deliberate policy of industrial expansion undertaken in Finland in the post-war period.

The daring technological and formal innovations of Finnish furniture first had an international impact at the Cologne Furniture Show of 1959. Alvar Aalto had founded Artek in 1935 as a shop window for his experiments in bent-wood technology alongside his textiles, glass and light fittings. His innovations in furniture included his 'Y' joint of the 1940s, which took bent-wood into the third dimension, combining the chair leg with the seat. Later on, the more complex 'X' joint resulted from his extensive experimentation. Aalto's furniture was light and unassuming, always harmonizing with its settings, which covered a large range of public and private areas, and conforming to the principles of mass

Poul Kjaerholm's chaise longue, 1965. Using steel rather than wood allowed Kjaerholm to pare this structure almost to nothing, letting the cane seating appear to float.

production by keeping its costs low. Artek expanded it concerns in the 1950s, sponsoring large exhibitions and employing young designers to extend Aalto's principles.

Another important Finnish furniture company, Asko, was founded on a more directly commercial footing, using mass production from the start. The emphasis in the 1950s and 1960s was on new materials, particularly plastics, and the aesthetic freedom permitted by these encouraged the Finnish love of sculpture and expressive form. This was demonstrated in the furniture designs of Ilmari Tapiovaara, who was art director of Asko from 1937 to 1940, and who acted for them as a consultant designer from 1940 onwards. Eero Aarnio's and Esko Pajamies' work for Asko introduced new chair types from moulded plastic, developing the theme of 'unfurniture' which Asko invented in the 1960s to describe its radical formal experiments.

Other notable areas of Finnish design in the post-war period were textiles, especially those of Dora Jung, and the silver and stainless steel work of Bertel Gardberg. Both fields demonstrated a characteristic simplicity, the roots of which were firmly entrenched in functionalism.

There were two distinct tendencies in Finnish design in this period: on the one hand, a desire for simple, mass-produced, anonymous items, and on the other, for highly individual artistic pieces. This second trend

Arabia, Finland's leading pottery factory, has always adapted its designs to the period. Around 1930 it opted for modern style. This collection is by Inkeri Leivo, 1965.

caused the very term 'design' to become problematic during the 1960s, as Richard Lindh realized in 1975: 'I think people are beginning to turn against the whole gibberish of Design, which has been made out to be something special.' The Scandinavian belief in the unity of art and society was one to which much Finnish design did not conform, and this initiated a debate about design as a reflection of individualism or a means of social equality. This subsequently became an important international issue.

# Styling and the US

The industrial designer was a figure of American origin, whose role developed during the expansion of the 1920s and who then 'styled' goods in the 1930s to increase profit margins during the economic depression. The position of this 'artistic' figure within the hierarchy of industry remained problematic throughout the post-war period. There were recurrent debates about the importance or otherwise of style and the rapidity of obsolescence in objects which were the products of an advanced capitalist economic system.

Before the Second World War, the new alliance between art and industry gave rise to a neo-futurist attitude towards the machine and, by extension, towards the objects of machine production. Idealized views of the newly electrified home with its accompanying gadgets, and of modern, speedy transport and the ensuring road and rail systems, resulted in a fresh, symbolic 'style for the age'. The pioneering industrial designer, Norman Bel Geddes, described the optimism of the era: 'In the midst of worldwide melancholy, owing to an economic depression, a new age dawned with invigorating conceptions and the horizons lifted.'

The evolution of a specifically American theory of industrial design in the post-war period depended upon these enthusiastic foundations and on a rejection of European Functionalism. In his *Industrial Design—A Practical Guide* of 1940, the designer Harold Van Doren remarked upon what he believed to be the irrelevance of European Modernism as brought to America by the design immigrants—among them Moholy Nagy, Gropius and Josef Albers. His dismissal of Europe signalled an intellectual break with the past and room for innovation in the 'new world'.

Van Doren and Walter Dorwin Teague, in his *Design This Day* of the same year, formulated a backbone of American design theory which provided a professional base and a theory of form for subsequent generations of designers. Paying verbal homage to many Modernist formal tenets such as 'simplicity' and 'honesty to materials', they went further than the Europeans in claiming that design, 'is one of the gears in a train that also includes management, sales promotion, advertising, engineering and research'. Both writers betrayed their fundamental commitment to style with descriptions of a refrigerator as a 'sleek, sanitary monolith', and a car as a 'sleek projectile'. They put forward an essentially anti-Modernist theory advocating the use of visually simple body shells to hide mechanical complexity. Van Doren rightly pointed out, for instance, the impossibility of finding an 'honest shape' for new mechanical products like the vacuum cleaner which had no one 'natural' form.

The point of divergence between the two theorists lay in the objects with which they felt industrial design should concern itself. While Van Doren felt strongly that cars were outside' the scope of the designer, Teague saw them as a central concern, alongside household equipment. Both shared the belief, however, that design should be less concerned with 'art' products, which Van Doren listed as 'ceramics, glassware, textiles, silver, jewellery, wallpaper and furniture'—all items which were dear to the hearts of the Scandinavian craftsmen.

The ideas of Teague, Van Doren and others gradually filtered through the mass-production system so that by the 1940s the flashy, swollen household gadget with 'bulbous corners' and accented chrome strips or plastic ridges was a familiar one. Designers deplored its excessive use, but justified it on practical and aesthetic grounds and were realistic enough to recognize its selling power. Edgar Kaufmann defined the word 'Borax',

America: even the toasters were styled up to look like automobiles. This one from Westinghouse, 1950, featured sophisticated timer and thermostat controls.

190

which came to describe this style, as 'a trade term for flashy, bulbous, modernistic design', and his defence of it as a 'popular' style was soon adopted as an argument for anti-élitist, mass design. The American designer transformed 'Form follows function' into 'Design follows sales' and 'Borax' became a descriptive term for any object which was styled in a non-purist manner and which exploited consumer appeal to increase sales.

The anti-Modernist aesthetic and the rapid obsolescence of objects which accompanied the increased affluence and consumption of the post-war population boom was nowhere more obvious than in American car design. The 1940's obsession with chrome and aggressive grilles was replaced, in the 1950s, by a taste for longer, jet-inspired, finned models, on which chrome served to highlight the formal features, symbolizing 'substance, speciousness and rich abandon'. General Motors' chief designer Harley Earl adopted an unequivocal attitude towards obsolescence: 'In 1934 the average car ownership span was five years, now it is two years. When it is one year, we will have a perfect score.'

The main characteristic of the American industrial designers was their commitment to 'total design'. As S. and M. Cheney described it in their book *Art & Industry*: 'Their work may and does range from a lipstick to a steamship, from a paper-clip to a locomotive, from an ash-tray to a model industrial community.' Most of the designers had established their consultancy services before the war and had assisted in the war effort, often working with the war authorities and defence organizations. Official recognition of their work was confirmed in 1944 by the foundation of the American Society of Industrial Designers, with Teague as the first President. Although he had first established his office in 1927, W.D. Teague continued to influence American industrial design up until his death in 1960. His commitment to the 'American dream'— 'Competition provides, in our opinion, maximum incentives to advancement and improvement'—encouraged him to work relentlessly throughout his life for American industry and governmental bodies. His designs covered a very wide spectrum of industrial and architectural possibilities, from the Polaroid camera in 1949 to the interior of the Boeing 707 in 1958.

### RAYMOND LOEWY

Raymond Loewy worked for a number of companies in the post-war years, including Frigidaire and Singer. His almost European sense of restraint was evident in his designs for the Studebaker Car Company from 1947 onwards. John Wheelock Freeman described the 1947 model: 'He reasserted the grille's function as an air intake rather than a cow catcher, and capitalized on large glass areas for both visibility and a feeling of lightness.' Loewy's theory of industrial design went beyond surface styling to a concern with the absolute

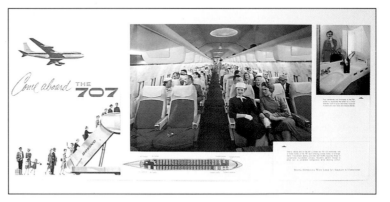

The inside of a long-haul civil aircraft is a uniquely modern space. W.D. Teague rose to the occasion with his 1957 interior design for the Boeing 707. Unlike cars such as Harley Earl's 1957 Chevvy **(top)**, there was no room for excess.

Sometimes a modern design intended as an up-market product (as were these plastic pedestal chairs by Eero Saarinen for Knoll International) caught the public's fancy. Saarinen's concept went from being *de rigueur* among the design conscious in the 1950s to being considered kitsch by the late 60s.

integration of the designer into the planning stage of industrial production. In 1967 his importance as a designer was recognized when NASA asked for his help on Skylab's habitability systems.

### HENRY DREYFUSS

After his work for the War Department, Henry Dreyfuss returned to his pre-war concerns with the design of consumer goods, capital goods and transportation. His work covered a wide spectrum of design possibilities, and his activity was unified through his fundamental belief in the anthropocentric base of design. He listed his criteria for good design as 'utility and safety, maintenance cost, sales appeal and appearance'. In his 1955 book *Designing for People*, Dreyfuss emphasized the importance of 'Joe and Josephine' at the centre of all design problems and research, stating that: 'What we are working on is going to be ridden in, sat upon, looked at, talked into, activated, operated, or in some way used by people, individually or *en masse.*'

### POST-WAR AMERICAN FURNITURE

The American furniture industry was relatively slow to gather momentum and develop independently of the new ideas about the design of consumer and mechanical goods. It was not until the 1940s that the Herman Miller Company employed George Nelson as a consultant designer; and Hans and Florence Knoll set up Knoll Associates. At the same time individual designers like Charles Eames and Eero Saarinen began to make an impact with their 'casual contemporary furniture'—a new style which owed much to the Scandinavians, Aalto and Mathsson, but which was also inspired by the work of contemporary artists and sculptors, particularly the surrealists.

Nelson's designs for the Herman Miller Company extended the feeling for simplicity of his predecessor there, Gilbert Rhode. Nelson's light wood, metal-framed pieces of furniture were in the direct line of descent from Scandinavian humanism, but they combined this with technological innovation which, Nelson maintained, was essential to 'real design', as opposed to mere styling.

It was Nelson who encouraged the Herman Miller Company to look at the work of Charles Eames. Trained as an architect, Eames developed a new chair through his use of moulded plywood bonded to rubber and metal, creating a chair which was elegantly light, functional, strong, and with the flexibility and comfort of heavier furniture. His earliest all-wood designs, prepared with Eero Saarinen for the 1940 Museum of Modern Art's Organic Furniture Exhibition, took two prizes and in 1946 he exhibited a new set of furniture with metal rod legs, which Herman Miller subsequently put into production. The combination of metal legs, or pedestals, with a moulded plywood frame provided the foundation of the Eames aesthetic, which juxtaposed new technology with humanism. For

SINGLE PEDESTAL FURNITURE DESIGNED BY EERO SAARINEN

the Museum's International Competition for Low-Cost Furniture in 1948 Eames designed a chair in stamped steel; while in 1949 he designed a house for himself from mass-produced materials, demonstrating his involvement with industrially produced design.

Variations on the moulded plastic frame with metal legs were produced in the late 1940s, and in the '50s overt comfort returned with the use of black padded leather seats and backs, which contrasted with their light aluminium base. Eames' 1956 lounge chair and ottoman, originally designed as a TV chair for Billy Wilder, included a traditional touch with its rosewood shells. The chair designs of the 1960s suggested at once a sense of simplicity and of controlled luxury, as Arthur Drexler explained in his description of a 1971 padded armchair. 'Sleek, polished, impeccably detailed, the moulded and padded shell of this chair suggests the world of aviation.'

Eames' grasp of the mood of the day led him to work with more than just furniture. He used juxtaposition as a communicative tool in films and multi-media productions as well. His contribution to American design was that of a unique mind confronting the technology of the day and proposing creative solutions which contained the essence of mid-twentieth-century western culture.

Knoll International served as a patron for many other furniture designers of the period. By the end of the 1940s Knoll had produced designs by Saarinen, the Swiss Hans Bellman, the Italian Albini, the Finn Tapiovaara and the American sculptors Bertoia and Noguchi. A Knoll design by Bob Knorr won the Museum of Modern Art's Competition for Low-cost Furniture. The sculptural tendency in 1950s furniture was described in an article by Nelson, which compared pieces of furniture to works by Lippold, Calder and Henry Moore. Saarinen produced a pedestal version of his 1946 womb chair in 1953, showing his fundamentally sculptural involvement with moulded plastic. Harry Bertoia was asked by Knoll to perform experiments with steel rod furniture, and in 1951 he created a chair which was a study in form and volume.

Design in post-war America derived, therefore, from both European and indigenous roots, but styling was more in evidence than European purism where the mass market was concerned. The affluence of the American market in the immediate post-war years made it the international centre of mass consumption and by the end of the 1950s obsolescence was widespread. Europe tended to recoil at first from the overt commercialism of the American model but, by the late 1950s, similar values had penetrated its mass markets as well.

**AMERICAN STYLES**
By the late 1940s
American interior design had established a style in which comfort and metaphors of sophistication were combined into cocktails – the combination above is of neo-neo-Classicism with a dash of art nouveau. But industrial design was dandy in the kitchen, and ascetic modernism was practical for gas stations. Fitness for purpose.

# Great Britain and the design establishment

By 1940 Great Britain had consolidated its own nineteenth-century Arts and Crafts tradition and assimilated a number of foreign influences, including Scandinavian humanism and American involvement with industry and technology. These cross-currents were clearly evident in the first years of the British Council of Industrial Design—a body which perpetuated the autocratic attitude of its nineteenth-century precursors towards 'good taste' and the public.

During the war many industries and industrial designers assisted the national struggle. The shortage of traditional materials meant experimentation with new ones, and the lack of wood for furniture led the Board of Trade to introduce standard furniture production through state control

Britain: utility fashions, designed by
Norman Hartnell, were launched in
June 1943.

of manufacture and supply. The 1942 committee's specifications for this furniture were vague; it was to be 'soundly made of the best possible material' and 'of pleasant design'. Gordon Russell was asked to head the committee, and his Arts and Crafts orientation undoubtedly determined the choice of the designs, which he described himself as 'simple and workmanlike'. These principles dominated the entire utility venture from 1942 to 1952. The Czech architect, Jacques Groag, and the textile designer, Enid Marx, were responsible for many of the designs which were all simple and functional. Ultimately the furniture came to symbolize austerity and drabness to the post-war public who were seeking gaiety and extravagance. As a writer in 1948 complained: 'Since the war, "Utility" has unfortunately become a synonym for something cheap and undesirable.'

Founded in 1942, the Design Research Unit—the first British design cooperative—was part of an attempt to keep up with the United States and its practice of professional teamwork. Herbert Read chaired a panel of architects, designers and engineers, and Milner Gray and Misha Black controlled the general practice of the unit, the aims of which were: 'To make available immediately a design service equipped to advise on all problems of design.' The unit undertook many architectural and design projects in the post-war period for both private and public concerns, and its effect upon British design was to encourage links with industry, the concept of 'total design', the subordination of the individual to the team, and the professionalism of the designer. In an attempt to bridge the gap between the Arts and Crafts tradition and the growing involvement of industry in contemporary society, the Council of Industrial Design was founded in 1944. Set up by the Board of Trade of the Coalition Government, it was to 'promote by all practicable means the improvement in the products of British industry'. Aware of American competition, the Council attempted to educate both industry and the public into an understanding of the difference between good and bad design by displays, publications, television broadcasts and so on. It was spurred on by the motto, 'Good design, Good business'. Democratic idealism was accompanied by a commitment to the notion of 'good taste' which derived essentially from Arts and Crafts principles and traditions.

### WOMEN'S WORK
The sexual equality promoted during the war was propagandist rather than real. Women at war could sew barrage balloons, drive vehicles, file papers and operate search lights but not anti-aircraft guns. Men did not let women do 'men's' work in the armed forces and expected women to look feminine.

196

Gordon Russell, the Council's second director, appointed in 1946, expressed his commitment to tradition in his book on furniture, *The Things We See*. He wrote: 'There is much in this to stimulate a sensitive designer, who will remember that there is no necessity to discard all old materials and methods. English oak remains a glorious material, if rightly used.' The contradiction between a theoretical commitment to industry and an emotional relationship with the hand-made object remained unresolved in the immediate post-war years.

The propagandist role of the Council was at its strongest in the decade following the war, and it used the exhibition as a publicity tool to spread the idea of reconstruction through design.

In 1946, with the backing of Sir Stafford Cripps, the director of the Board of Trade of the new Labour Government, the Council organized an exhibition entitled *Britain Can Make It*, in order to 'interest manufacturers in design, to interest the public in design, and to put Britain on the map'. The intention was to sell the idea of design, as well as designed objects, to the public and to the manufacturer, and the dominant theme, interpreted by the exhibition designer James Gardner, was exhibition design itself. Gardner's display techniques were described as 'a costly frame for a mediocre picture', although individual items like Ernest Race's aluminium-frame chair were highly praised.

Straightforward displays of consumer goods alternated with educational stands about the nature of industrial design and its role in society. Other exhibits encouraged audience participation, like the *Quiz Bank* at which visitors registered their design preferences. The general aesthetic evident in all the display techniques was that of pre-war surrealism, with much use made of lighting effects.

British design of the late 1940s was characterized by a humanism which implied the freedom of the individual through plastic expression. Many writings of the period stressed the psychological importance of pattern and colour. Noel Carrington wrote in 1947: 'I do not myself see why it should be considered necessary to eliminate ornament, nor do I consider it likely that either this generation or the next will easily consent to do without it.' Through the medium of its periodical, *Design*, which began in 1949, the Council of Industrial Design saw the possibility of a national boom in design, and encouraged the development of the 'contemporary' style.

Design in two dimensions succumbed most easily to the 'artistic' tendency, and artists such as Graham Sutherland and John Farleigh designed 'contemporary fabrics' which made use of curvy, organic surrealist forms. Poster design, illustration and advertising graphics also revealed surrealist tendencies. Glass and ceramics were frequently decorated, and furniture was dominated by the Scandinavian influence. Heals and Dunn's perpetuated their Arts and Crafts ideals, selling light wood items with the familiar tapered leg. A number of young designers

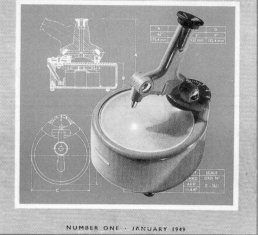

**Design** magazine began in 1949. Good domestic design of the post-war period was much concerned with fitting a lot of people into small rooms but the interior shots, although wall to wall with light furnishings, were strangely unpeopled.

developed light, flexible, multi-purpose designs made of new materials like plywood, steel and aluminium. Among them were Ernest Race, Ian Henderson, Austin and Ward, Goodden and R.D. Russell, Dennis Young, Dennis Lennon, Robin Day and Clive Latimer. The influence upon household equipment was American, but it was applied with restraint. As Jane Drew explained: 'Our poverty helped us to avoid many of the vulgarities of pre-war styling, such as bogus streamlining, though, alas, some of our refrigerators and washing machines still have them.'

## THE FESTIVAL OF BRITAIN

The idea of a festival to celebrate the centenary of the 1851 Great Exhibition was first mooted by the Royal Society of Arts in 1943. Conceived as a show of civilization and industry,

man's achievement.

It was as an experiment in town planning and landscaping that the exhibition was most successful. It developed what the *Architectural Review* dubbed, 'a picturesque landscape principle', which was unorthodox and informal, making use of contrast, variety of shape and scale, interrupted views and multi-levels. An emphasis upon the environment rather than individualized structures was achieved by concentrating on details like railings and street furniture. Jack Howe's litter bins and Race's 'Antelope' and 'Springbok' chairs were typical. A nautical theme dominated the Festival, with flagpoles, rigging, lookouts and other details completing the effect.

The Council of Industrial Design selected the objects for the *Homes and Garden* and *New Schools* sections. The accompanying design philosophy was once more formulated by Russell, who stated: 'A well-designed object should be pleasing to the eye, efficient in use and soundly made whether by hand or machine.' In contrast to the pre-war Modern Movement's abhorrence of decoration and the wartime drabness, the emphasis at the Festival was upon vibrant colour and strong surface pattern.

Inspiration derived from several sources among the fine arts. Abstract sculpture by Moore, Hepworth, Lyn Chadwick, Reg Butler and others was exhibited on the South Bank, as were the crystal structures developed by the Festival Pattern Group. This had been established in 1949 specifically to experiment with crystal structure diagrams, and its creations were chosen because they 'had the discipline of exact repetitive symmetry; they were above all very pretty and were full of rich variety, yet with a remarkable family likeness'.

The Festival stood as a symbol of public enthusiasm and pleasure at having been released from wartime restrictions. As a Labour-backed project, it was criticized by the Opposition as a waste of tax-payers' money, and it has been seen by some as a reason for the fall of the Labour government in that year. But it not only captured public feeling, it paved the way for the strong fantasy element which appeared in much British design in the decade which followed.

The problem of the public taking over the role of design arbiter from the establishment in a changing industrial and social context was one which concerned designers in the 1950s. The fact that 'the bonds of austerity had been loosened' led to a popular delight in pattern, colour and 'artistic' form. In interior decoration, different patterns and colours often coexisted in a single setting, while in furniture there was an imaginative use of 'jigsaw' shapes, 'knitting-needle' coat stands, plant holders and table legs. The Council stood out against this public enthusiasm and 'do it yourself' tendency, encouraging instead 'a decent well-bred elegance' which should, it claimed, provide a 'quiet background to living'. It also expressed criticisms of what it considered to be

it was planned in a spirit of campaigning reform, with the help of the Council of Industrial Design from 1947. A balance between education and celebration was sustained from the start. The travelling exhibitions, the display at the Science Museum and the architectural reconstruction project at Lansbury were educational, while Battersea Pleasure Gardens provided the fun.

The exhibition on the South Bank was the focal point of the Festival of Britain and provided a meeting place for the architectural and design establishments and the public. The architects and designers included Hugh Casson, Misha Black, James Gardner, James Holland and Ralph Tubbs, while the Council selected the objects to be shown. The South Bank 'story' was divided into three main sections, and the layout emphasized the narrative treatment of the topics showing the glory of

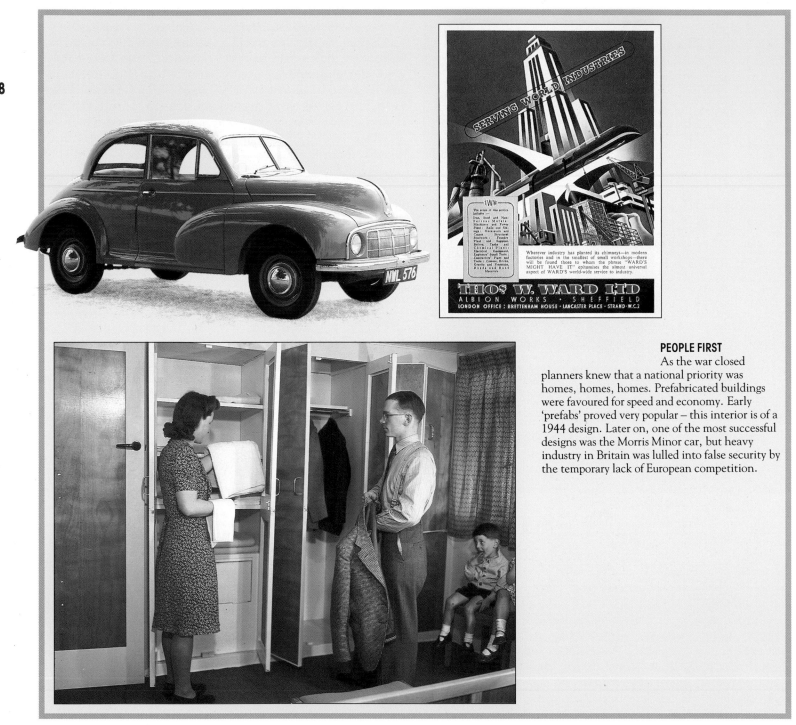

### PEOPLE FIRST

As the war closed planners knew that a national priority was homes, homes, homes. Prefabricated buildings were favoured for speed and economy. Early 'prefabs' proved very popular – this interior is of a 1944 design. Later on, one of the most successful designs was the Morris Minor car, but heavy industry in Britain was lulled into false security by the temporary lack of European competition.

the vulgar excesses of American streamlining.

A class-based dichotomy emerged in British design, in which the taste of the establishment clashed violently with that of the public. In 1953-4 the Design and Industries Association furnished two rooms at Charing Cross, one in the popular idiom and the other in the 'contemporary' style, in a last-ditch attempt to help the public see the light.

The 1950s also saw the growth of a new breed of 'realistic designers'—among them the furniture designers Ronald Carter and Robert Heritage, and the silver designers Robert Welch and David Mellor. All had been trained at the Royal College of Art which, since 1949, had been modifying its structure and curriculum to help educate designers for industry. These designers developed Scandinavian workshop-based principles, and the Council seized upon their work as exemplifying the 'decency and elegance' which was required of 'good design'.

In 1956 the Design Centre was opened in the Haymarket, consolidat-ing the Council's hold on design in Britain. The Centre's first Design Awards were presented in 1957. The conflicting influences of Scandinavia and the United States were still uppermost in the Council's projects in these years. Studies of the body derived from the early work of the Dane Kaare Klint, and the problems of design management were surveyed following research done in the United States. The Council's nineteenth-century philosophy underwent no radical change in the post-war period, however. The integration of the designer into industry was slow, and the problems of catering for popular taste in the changing mass were not tackled. When the crisis came in the following decade, it stemmed from a revolution in taste which sprang from the roots of British society.

**199**

The Royal Festival Hall was designed for the Festival of Britain, 1951. The site on the south bank of the Thames also featured a coloured canvas screen and the award-winning vertical Skylon, lit from the interior. The Festival expressed the post-war national mood of aspiration and self-confidence.

# Italy: style and individualism

The decade following the war was a formative one for Italian design. It emerged as a visible symbol of the affluence and material aspirations of the newly industrialized country, and it was characterized by daring experimentation and new design forms.

Writing in 1949 in *Design*, Leopold Schreiber exclaimed that 'the Italians have undoubtedly a genius for reconstruction'. The tremendous post-war Italian design effort took place on two fronts. On the one hand, design was seen as the tangible expression of democratic ideals, providing the foundations of a cultural renaissance in post-Fascist Italy; on the other, it became a receptacle for the various stylistic experiments which opposed the functionalist aesthetic. Both attitudes were evident in the pages of the architectural and design periodical, *Domus*. Ernesto N. Rogers, the editor from 1946 to 1948, a dominant voice in the cause of an anti-Fascist Italy, filled the journal with images of men constructing prefabricated, standardized units to replace the 'huge decay' of the immediate past. He believed that: 'It is a question of forming a taste, a technique, a morality, all terms of the same function. It is a question of building a society.' This social idealism was coupled with realism in the architectural sphere, where pre-war rationalism was still the prevailing code and where small living spaces and poverty were acknowledged as facts of everyday life. Realism dictated ideas about furniture and interior design too, and the pieces designed by Magistretti, Gardello, the Castiglioni brothers, Vigano and others at the 1946 RIMA exhibition of Popular Furnishings were simple and inexpensive, modelled on traditional types such as the deck chair and the safari chair. The programme of the eighth Triennale also took into account 'the social and economic climate created by the war'.

Rogers' idealism extended beyond the limits of materialism to include a general cultural dimension and a human perspective. His theme, 'The House of Man', combined the architectural with the human problem, and he wrote: 'We tried to insert the specific problems of architecture into the common framework of modern cultural problems.' Humanism in post-war Italian design took different forms—recognition of the importance of the family; juxtaposition of tradition (particularly that of the Italian baroque) with the avant-garde; and a strong emphasis upon the hand-made object.

In spite of Rogers' desire to mechanize the design industries, craft production was still the norm before 1950, particularly in the decorative arts. Ceramics, glass and enamelware were still made by the artisans who

## DESIGN CULTURE

Henry Moore went to Italy and won the sculpture prize at the 1948 Venice Biennale. Economist Kenneth Galbraith argues that Italian design flourished because of Italy's traditional rootedness in fine art, but too many architects with nothing to build but consumer goods and a burgeoning black economy also helped.

Gio Ponti's 1949 prototype design for a coffee machine resembles a Harley Earl car bumper. It was commercially manufactured by La Pavoni and became a feature of the espresso bars of the 1950s.

straddled the artist/craftsman barrier, in the Renaissance tradition. Furniture was either simple, out of practical necessity, or manifested a self-conscious formalism, which recalled traditional Italian styles. The works of the Turin architect-designers—Carlo Mollino, Romano and Rava among them—went beyond the controlled sculptural concerns of the Milan School. Mollino's fantastic 'streamlined surreal' forms, which suggested both Italian baroque and art nouveau, exploited exaggerated organic structures, recalling the twisted contortions of wood growing in its natural state.

The surrealist theme was common in this period, wherever form and decoration suppressed functional concerns and 'a need for fantasy' was felt. The fabric firm of Fede Cheti, for instance, which sponsored many new designs, produced advertisements in which the imagery recalled the ambiguous spatial effects of the Italian metaphysical painters of the early twentieth century. Theories of organic form, put forward by Max Bill, Brancusi, Henry Moore and others, provided a base for ideas about 'utility plus beauty', which became a familiar phrase for those who sought a new style.

202

Early industrial design in Italy succeeded in holding a middle position between these two extremes, and creating a recognizable family style which acknowledged both 'utility' and 'beauty'. In the industrial products of the late 1940s, new vision and formal innovation revolutionized the appearance and nature of many familiar objects. Innovations such as Gio Ponti's Pavoni coffee machine, and Piaggio's Vespa motor-scooter served to give Italy a new identity and confidence. As the British designer F.H.K. Henrion noticed on a trip there in 1949: 'A similarity of aesthetic values among different products—a similarity which might be called the style of the mid-twentieth century.'

In 1950 W.D. Teague wrote: 'This is the season of spring in contemporary Italian art, with all the freshness and vitality and experimentation of a great revival.' Magistretti, Zanuso, Ponti, Albini, the Castiglioni brothers, Nizzoli, Sottsass junior—the major names in Italian design—were established, and along with leading firms like Olivetti, Tecno, Artemide, Cassina and Azucena, they looked forward to a period of prestige and international renown.

Rogers' determination to create ' a new taste', which for him meant simple, humanized, democratic forms which were neither avant-garde nor élitist, developed, after Gio Ponti took over editorship of *Domus* in 1948, into an obsessive eclectic search for style.

In the early 1950s Ponti wrote: 'Our ideal of "the good life" and a level of taste and thought expressed by our homes and manner of living are all

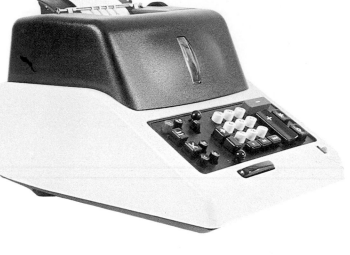

Marcello Nizzoli designed the Divisumma 24 calculator (above) for Olivetti in 1956. Nizzoli had studied ornament and figure drawing, as well as architecture. Olivetti employed artists and sculptors to aid its designs. Ettore Sottsass's secretary chair, 1969, proved so popular it is still manufactured today (right).

The Vespa motor scooter revolutionized Italian transport. The first version, designed in 1946, is of streamliner pedigree.

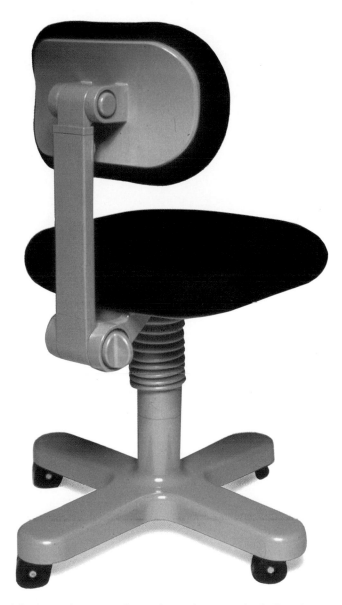

Italian design in the 1950s and early 1960s.

The theme of art allied to industry became a leitmotiv of the period. An exhibition at the Rinascente store in 1953 was entitled 'The Aesthetic of the Product', and the 1954 Triennale was devoted to the 'Production of Art'. The precedent frequently quoted was that of the artist of the Italian Renaissance, for whom painting, design and invention were synonymous acts. This link with tradition, coupled with rapid industrial organization and the challenge of new materials such as plastics and light metals, encouraged the Italians to leap into the field of industrial design. They brought to it their characteristic 'flair' for invention, their playful boldness and above all their commitment to the belief that novelty in design meant 'a bit for prosperity and for life itself', in the famous words of Ernesto Rogers, writing in *Domus* in 1946.

### THE MILAN TRIENNALES

The first Milan Triennale, an Italian world fair concentrating specifically upon design, had taken place in the purpose-built Palazzo dell'Arte in 1923. The Ninth Triennale of 1951 was the second post-war exhibition to demonstrate Italy's recovery and growth in the field of industrial design to the rest of the world. It unified in a single environment the disparate themes that had emerged since the war, among them the emphasis upon the cultural meaning of design, the link between 'beauty' and 'utility', the importance of tradition, and a strong emphasis upon fantastic form. One section was entitled 'The Decorative and Industrial Arts'. The former included some highly ornate pieces reminiscent of Miro sculpture, with decoration by the surrealist Lenor Fini among others, together with some Arp-like pieces of glass. The industrial section, 'The Form of the Useful', was arranged by Max Huber inside a lattice-work of string with ball shapes threaded onto it. A cross-section of products displayed the new, moulded aesthetic: digital clocks by Ritz Italora, lights by the Castiglioni brothers, typewriters by Nizzoli for Olivetti and car designs by Pinin Farina. All these items were set individually within a complex, enveloping space created by the intersecting strings. Lighting design provided a dual opportunity for expression in the exaggerated praying-mantis forms of the lights themselves, and in their use for creating shadows and environmental effects.

### THE DESIGNERS

Most of the designers who worked for the newly formed industries came from the architectural profession, and saw the design of mass-produced objects as an extension of their control of the environment. They were not limited to specific objects but undertook a large range, from interior design to engineering projects. Their notion of design as sculptural form meant that the nature of the object was, as a rule, regarded as secondary to its plastic possibilities.

part of the same thing—and one also with our method of production.' This clearly put forward a different conception of culture from that of Rogers. For Ponti, culture was synonymous with the desires and aspirations of the Italian *nouveau-riche*, a class created by the rapid industrialization of the late 1940s and early 1950s. Its values were more individualistic than collective; more concerned with formal innovation than with function and practical necessity. This attitude was to determine the predominantly 'artistic' relationship with creativity and form, and the preoccupation with the isolated object, which characterized

**204**

Gio Ponti began his work as an architect and industrial designer in 1923, when he first joined the firm Richard-Ginori. In the post-war years he was largely responsible for the combination of traditional and avant-garde tendencies in Italian design, conducting a campaign to bring artists, craftsmen, architects, industrial manufacturers and the general public into a closer relationship with each other. His own designs ranged from highly decorated neo-baroque pieces of furniture covered with Fornasetti prints to simple, formally self-conscious industrial designs. Ponti's sewing-machine for Visetta in 1949, flatware for Krupp in 1951, and sanitary equipment for Ideal Standard in 1954 all displayed the familiar curved lines of 'the new taste'.

Marco Zanuso also played an important role in the evolution of Italian design in this period. Born in 1916, Zanuso was responsible for many design innovations, including the use of foam-rubber in seating. He

Hard comfort and soft silliness: organic sculpture and the idea of 'sculpting' influenced Italian design in the 1960s. A lavatory designed by Gio Ponti **(above)** and seating for B&B Italia by Gaetano Pesce **(left)**.

was the artistic director of the firm Arflex from 1950 onwards, and participated in the arrangements for the 1954 Triennale and the discussions that arose from it. In 1956 he won the Rinascente Compasso d'Oro award for his design for the Borletti sewing-machine, and he was particularly noted for his television and radio designs for Brionvega. All Zanuso's designs conformed to his principles of simplification of form which were inspired by the process of production itself.

In the field of transport design, Pinin Farina was the most inventive Italian designer of the period. Born in Turin in 1895, he set up his own workshop at an early age and visited Detroit in 1919. In 1947 he designed the 'Cisitalia' which became the prime example of the 'Continental look', depending upon sleek simplicity rather than exaggerated streamlining.

### THE COMPANIES

Many new companies were formed in the 1950s to fulfil the needs of the new consumer market, which had become aware of the American notion of 'the ideal home'. Arflex, Tecno, Azucena, Gavina, Cassina, Artemide and others produced furniture which conformed to the new technology and style; Flos and Arteluce produced lights, and Kartell, Brionvega and others manufactured a multitude of highly styled and highly coloured plastic and electrical items for the home, office and public areas.

Two other firms had a longer history of design awareness: Pirelli's was reflected in its publicity policies, and Olivetti's in its total design policy. The latter had been instigated by the founder, Camillo Olivetti, and passed down through his son Adriano, who led the company from 1938 until his death in 1960. The Olivetti factory and surrounding community buildings in Ivrea were designed by the rationalists Figini and Pollini in 1940. They provided an integrated environment for the corporate personality that the company developed in its advertising, typography, furniture and product design. Humanism lay at the heart of Olivetti's attitude towards its workers, expressed in a strong welfare programme, and towards its designs. These included the 'elegant and cheerful machines' designed by Marcello Nizzoli—the Summa 14 adding machine of 1947, the Lexicon 80 typewriter of 1948, and the Lettera 22 portable typewriter of 1950 among others. Nizzoli's work consisted of 'sculpting' expressive shells for engineered mechanisms, and he achieved his results by constant refinement. Ettore Sottsass Junior was responsible for Olivetti's electronic computer, the Elea 9003, in 1958. He replaced Nizzoli, working for the firm from that year onwards.

Writing in a book entitled *Italy: The New Domestic Landscape*, which accompanied an exhibition of Italian design at the Museum of Modern Art in New York in 1970, Emilio Ambasz claimed that: 'Design in Italy does not present a consistent body of ideas, either in form or ideology.'

A television designed by Marco Zanuso and Richard Sapper in 1962. The design challenge was to make the bulk of the cathode tube 'disappear'.

While the forms varied, there was, nonetheless, up until the mid-1960s, a consistency of style, or rather taste. Although the ideological premises changed, many consistent themes ran throughout the post-war period— humanism; a commitment to expressive form; a belief in tradition, and innovation springing from it; an interest in new materials; above all, a strong faith in the ability of design to influence, rather than merely reflect, the social and cultural context.

# Germany: technique and analysis

Germany had a stronger pre-war foothold in industrial design than most countries. The *Deutscher Werkbund* had brought designers and industrialists together and encouraged them to cooperate in the first part of the century, while the Bauhaus was an early experiment in radical education towards the role of the 'designer' and the form of the industrial object. Together they showed the extent to which the German nation was committed to industrial design. The design theory which accompanied them focused upon the aesthetic, economic and philosophical implications of functionalism, again reflecting the strength of the industrial commitment.

As it had already demonstrated early in century with its sudden rise to power, the German nation measured its strength by its level of production and industrial organization. After the defeat of National Socialism, the Germans sought to eradicate all shameful associations with the immediate past. They looked further back, to the more democratic aspects of the early 1930s and this implied a reappraisal of the Bauhaus, and a total rejection of the 'retrospectrive romantic fantasy' of the Nazi regime.

Several pre-war firms had already developed policies of production which emphasized the aesthetic simplicity of the mass-produced object, and the anonymous and unobtrusive nature of utility goods. Glass and ceramic manufacturers—among them Arzberg, Rosenthal, Schoenwald and the Lausitz and Jenaer glassworks—employed designers to work specifically with mass-produced items. This aesthetic was to characterize German production in the post-war years. The plain white ceramic ware by Hermann Gretsch and Heinrich Löffelhardt for Arzberg, for example, reflected a concern with extreme simplicity, and subordination of the object to its functional dictates.

The war years saw the eclipse of the Werkbund as its ideals clashed with the policies of the Nazi regime. Its efforts to bring about cooperation between designers and industry, initiated in 1907, were thus temporarily halted. With the defeat of National Socialism, the Werkbund was resuscitated. A number of architects, including Otto Bartnung in Baden and Scharoun, Max Taut and Lily Reich in Berlin, put forward a suggestion for a new Werkbund which would develop 'a new form for the object' and a new *Lebensform* (life-style). This perpetuated the idea of an essential link between design and political and cultural regeneration. The Werkbund was formally reconstituted in 1947, and held its first post-war exhibition in Cologne in 1949.

One of the first projects it undertook was the establishment in 1951 of

the *Rat für Formgebung*. This was a Council of Industrial Design, which set out its criteria for *gute Form* and judged objects according to them. Among its neo-functionalist specifications for good design was the idea that, 'the object as a whole must have no expressive feature which is not in accordance with the purposes for which the object is intended', a demand that encouraged an emphasis upon simple formalism.

The Werkbund helped to select German goods for the 1954 Triennale, choosing many items from the technical end of the design spectrum, pieces of laboratory equipment among them. Werkbund architects were also responsible for the buildings of the Berlin Interbau of 1957, and the German contribution to the Brussels World Fair in 1958.

Several designers took a leading role in both of the high periods of twentieth-century German design—the 1920s and the 1950s. Walter Gropius continued his architectural practice into the post-war years,

German designers such as Dieter Rams turned design austerity into a mannerism that, in turn, became associated with 'quality' and 'expense'. A heater (**above**) and film projector (**right**) by Rams. Cut glass design by Wilhelm Wagenfeld (**left**).

although on a more international basis; Otto Lindig, the Bauhaus ceramicist, taught at Hamburg from 1948 onwards and Wilhelm Wagenfeld contributed ideas and designs until the end of the 1950s. Wagenfeld's consistent attitude towards design was reflected in the lamps he made in the Bauhaus metal workshop under Moholy-Nagy; in his glass for the Jenaer workshops in the 1930s; in his cutlery for the WMF in the 1940s and '50s; and, to complete the circle, in the lamps he made for Lindner in the 1950s. As an editor of *Form* from 1957 onwards, Wagenfeld repeated his ideas about form, stating that: 'All utilitarian things should be unobtrusive . . . each piece must be a harmonious entity.' Yet he was careful to explain that form was not a surface consideration or an artistic idea, but the result of technical, economic and practical factors deriving from the industrial process.

This link in twentieth-century German design theory between function—the practicalities of producing the industrial object—and form, provided a philosophical base for German designers. On one hand, it led to a concern with form as a symbol of a technological culture; on the other, to an attempt to involve design directly in industry thereby circumventing the problem of the right style. The two different approaches were developed by the firm of Braun and in the educational philosophy of the *Hochschule für Gestaltung* at Ulm respectively.

## BRAUN

The products of the electrical firm of Braun, left by Max Braun to his sons Erwin and Artur in 1951, epitomized a concern with form and style as symbolic factors. Technical equipment, rather than furniture or interior design, was the medium through which German design communicated the idealization of technology which lay at the roots of the country's industrial and cultural renaissance. Machines symbolized organization and efficiency, which in their turn meant increased production and strength.

Fritz Eichler, who was design director for Braun from 1951, Dieter Rams, who joined the firm as staff designer in 1955, and Hans Gugelot, who worked for Braun as an outside consultant, aimed at conveying symbolic meaning through form. The first Braun products that received attention were the radio and TV sets exhibited at the Düsseldorf Fair in 1955. They were notable for their clean, simple lines and efficient appearance. Details such as the control knobs all contributed to what came to be known as the 'instrument look'. The mechanical analogy was extended later into other pieces of electrical equipment, for example the 'Kitchen-Machine' of 1957 (a food-mixer designed according to very strict, formal rules) and the 'Multi-press' juicer of 1958. Richard Moss described the Braun products in *Industrial Design* in 1962, showing how

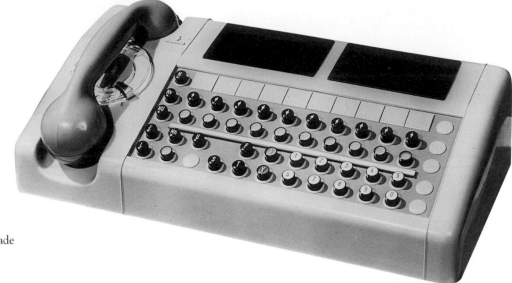

An intercommunication unit made
by Siemens of West Germany in
high-impact polystyrene, 1958.

their aesthetic content of 'order, harmony and simplicity' determined their appeal. Braun won prizes at the Milan Triennale of 1960 and the Compasso d'Oro in 1961, and quickly became internationally well known.

## HOCHSCHULE FÜR GESTALTUNG

The *Hochschule für Gestaltung*, founded in 1951 at Ulm from a fund set up by Inge Aicher-Scholl as a tribute to her brother and sister, who were killed by the Nazis, was an attempt by the German nation to provide an educational base for their new commitment to functional design. Under the original directorship of the Swiss Max Bill, it was intended as 'a continuation of the Bauhaus', but when Tomas Maldonado, an Argentinian painter, took over in 1957, he denied the relevance of the Bauhaus' formalism and idealism in a post-industrial society. Maldonado suggested instead a more rigorous, inter-disciplinary framework for design studies: subjects such as sociology, social psychology, anthropology, perception theory, cultural history and other related disciplines would be included in the training of a designer. Maldonado wrote in *New Perspectives on Design Education* in 1959: 'The only certain thing is that aesthetic considerations have ceased to be a solid conceptual base for industrial design.' His approach was relativist, and he mistrusted the idealistic romanticism of much pre-war thinking. He put forward a radical redefinition of the concept of industrial

design—'scientific operationalism', which held that design was part of the production process, determined by its laws alone. The lack of involvement with the finished product *per se* fuelled the objections of those critics who maintained that Ulm products simply perpetuated 'the neater look' or 'the compact style'. Sadly, the fate of Ulm resembled that of the Bauhaus, as its international disputes led to press criticism and accusations of wasting tax-payers' money. Maldonado left in 1967, and the school was closed the following year.

German post-war design was characterized by intellectual rigour and by the severe, neo-functionalist style of its technical goods from firms such as Braun, Siemens, AEG-Telefunken and Bosch. The style was promulgated by the German design press, which developed an appropriate photographic style of direct, geometrically exact images, devoid of background interest, which completed the effect of dehumanized mechanical efficiency. This neo-classical, rational aesthetic was to become a strong international design idiom in the late 1950s and 1960s, replacing the more expressive forms of American streamlining. It symbolized the aspirations of countries such as Germany and Japan, for whom increased productivity and scientific exactitude meant increased power, affluence and successful progress into the technological future.

Wherever an active design policy was developed in the post-war period, the objects produced became part of that country's ideological super-structure, conveying and often moulding the aspirations and values of the nation.

Among the countries where this was particularly evident was Japan, where the post-war policy of rapid industrialization, which was carefully linked with their design traditions, was visible in the products. Motor vehicles, optical instruments, acoustic instruments and domestic electrical appliances all symbolized technical sophistication, efficiency and innovation. Other European countries—Holland, Austria and Switzerland among them—were forced to compete and develop industrial policies of their own. Their policies often owed as much to contemporary industrial exigencies and to the German model, as to their own pre-war theories and traditions, strong though these had been.

The idea of 'good design' obsessed all these countries and was defined by many different criteria—formal, technical, social and ethical. The watering down of Modernist ideals into a number of national stylistic alternatives led to the international crisis in design values that occurred in the late 1950s and the 1960s, when different brands of 'alternative' design were put forward as a means of redefining man's relationship with his environment.

The obsession with making things look designed resulted in some strange fantasies – some, like the Bosch hand drills, obviously echo macho weapons, but the sprightly 1959 Braun television looks like an affable space bug.

# CHAPTER NINE

# DESIGN AFTER MODERNISM

> **"THE GREAT ENEMY OF ART IS GOOD TASTE"**
>
> *MARCEL DUCHAMP, QUOTED IN R. LEBEL, MARCEL DUCHAMP (1959)*

By the late 1950s, the term 'design' had gained international currency as a concept which was less superficial than 'styling', and more anonymous than 'craft'. It was synonymous with good taste, consumer appeal and high exports on the world market. The old terms—the decorative and the applied arts—were subsumed by this new, abstract concept which was crucial to the expanding economies of the post-war powers.

By this time, international trends in design development had largely taken over from national innovations. The new international spirit was expressed in events such as the Milan Triennale, the Aspen Conference (an annual design event which took place in Colorado from 1951 onwards), and the establishment of the ICSID (the International Congress of the Societies of Industrial Design) which began its activities in 1962. Such events encouraged the development of what has been called 'the transatlantic mainstream modern look'—a style based upon a neo-Bauhaus attitude towards form while taking features from many national variants. By the late 1950s, this had become an international design language spanning the entire spectrum of consumer goods, from the 'neat rectangularity' of furniture to the equally regular 'instrument look' of mechanical goods.

As a reaction to this bland formalism—a second-generation Modernism which espoused the values of advanced capitalism and lacked the intellectual base of the original movement—a range of 'anti'—or post-Modern—design manifestations emerged between 1965 and 1985. They were a response to the changing socio-economic and intellectual climate of these years as well—a response to the 'post-Modern condition' which has been so hotly debated by philosophers, economists and artists over the last twenty years.

The condition has been characterized by French philosophers such as Jean-François Lyotard as the end of the 'Enlightenment'—the age dominated by reason, science and progress—and the beginning of a more relativistic age without absolute values. Mass culture, within post-Modernism, challenged the avant-garde, and aesthetic judgments were exchanged for notions of popular taste or tastes. Other discussions focused on the notion of the 'post-industrial' society and the way in which mass communications and automation, brought about by advances in electronics, changed man's relationship with the production system, as well as with the environment as a whole. Regionalism replaced the earlier emphasis upon the megalopolis and the cultural emphasis moved away from homogeneity towards variation. Within mass production, theories of standardization—the base-line of Modernism—began to be replaced by ideas about batch production within which cultural variation was possible. The debate stressed the multi-disciplinary nature of the new culture and moved freely across a range of subjects such as philosophy, economics, anthropology, sociology and women's studies. Literature, theatre, television, film, performance art and sculpture, as well as architecture and design, began, from the mid-1960s onwards, to express the new sensibility. In design, its propositions were radical ones in most areas, although feminism, for all its growing influence at the time, uniquely failed to percolate the reactionary design establishment. Yet soon all the other Modern Movement tenets which the establishment held to, were challenged, one by one.

The post-Modern interior **(opposite)** as designed by Memphis was a mixture of Pop-art, Classicism, art deco – anything that caught the designers' fancy – all done with an arch cleverness. The Sindbad armchairs by Vico Magistretti **(above)** date from 1981.

# Towards Pluralism

By the 1960s, designed artefacts had penetrated to practically every level of the market in the industrialized world, due to increased consumer affluence. It was no longer possible to think in terms of absolute design values, as the market place was made up of different sub-groups, each with its own social, economic and cultural context. The pluralism of the market fed design variation, and Modernism, utterly inadequate in this situation, gave way to a series of design alternatives. Some were reassuring, conveying a sense of cosy nostalgia to the consumer, others more futuristic, suggesting hi-tech efficiency, social status or expressing the latest fashion and fun. The Modern style remained one of the alternatives, selected for its symbolic appropriateness rather than the abstract theories which inspired it.

Another influential factor in the move away from standardization towards 'culturally-determined' products, was the role of electronic automation in industrial manufacture. This technology brought with it increased flexibility, and the ability to batch-produce sets of varied objects. The problem of high investment in production machinery disappeared as soon as automation took over in the factories. This was most marked in Japan, a country that went aggressively in search of world markets after the Second World War. The Japanese not only pioneered the idea of cultural variation in the products they marketed at different countries, they also developed rapid object obsolescence, particularly for technological goods.

Expanding pluralism, therefore, was the framework within which all the discussions of anti- or post-Modernism took place from the 1950s onwards.

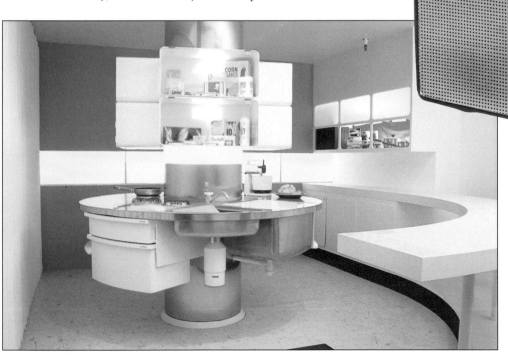

Miniaturization removed bulky innards and the need to disguise an object's guts with 'sculptural' packaging. The Sony TR-55 was the world's first mass-produced transistor radio. Meanwhile kitchens began a further round of slimming: a British kitchen design, 1968 **(left)**. Micro circuitry and vastly improved computing power made industrial robotics a reality in the late 1970s **(right)**.

# The crisis of functionalism

The programme of adaptation to machine production later subsumed into Modernism, which determined early post-war design, received a set-back in the late 1950s. It had failed to take into account the consequences of mass consumption—the emergence of mass culture and mass taste. These factors jeopardized all the national variants of 'good design' which had evolved from élitist Modernist principles. The short-sighted 'over-valuation' of the machine had ignored the fundamental issues of mass production when it took over the mainstream of international design.

A clash between the neo-functionalist aesthetic, which Stephen Spender described as incorporating 'bareness, simplicity, squareness, or roundness, solidity, seriousness and impersonality', and the desire for a reinstallation of human values in design accompanied the crisis of functionalism. The struggle was fought on aesthetic, social, cultural and moral fronts simultaneously, and it led to the development of a series of design alternatives in the 1950s and '60s and, in the late 1970s, to the movement called 'post-Modernism'.

The theories of the leading early twentieth-century architects and designers which were rooted in Sullivan's 'Form follows function' bore the brunt of the criticism in the 1950s. They were accused of failing to take into account the consumer and the laws of consumption. American architectural critics were the first to question the Modern Movement's assumptions, which still provided the backbone of much contemporary architectural theory. They wanted to unravel the paradoxes that they had inherited, and to redefine and update Modernist ideas to allow for human involvement. Louis Mumford explained in 1951 that, 'thanks to advances in biology, sociology and psychology, we begin to understand the whole man', and he advocated the inclusion of a subjective, expressive element in design, such as in the work of Matthew Nowicki. Nowicki had seen the shortcomings of the 'Form follows function' formula in the modern world and had explored the stylistic implications of 'Form follows form' instead. In 1964 Rudolf Arnheim wrote in the same vein stating that 'pure functionalism does not eliminate the need for stylistic choice'.

In England the architectural historian Banham was also looking back to the Modern Movement as a means of sorting out contemporary architectural and design theory. In an article of 1955 entitled *The Machine Aesthetic*, he blamed the early theorists for self-deception in their belief that they were working according to engineering principles.

He developed his argument in his book *Theory and Design in the First Machine Age* (1960), showing that the emphasis upon expression and an acceptance of style in the Modern Movement had been ignored by critics and historians. Banham's criticisms of functionalism provided a base for his proposal of 1955 that 'the aesthetics of consumer goods are those of the popular arts'. The logical way of reinstalling human values in design theory was to look to where those values were naturally exhibited, ie in the popular, or rather mass, arts—the pulp novel, the cinema, advertisements, pop music and the popular end of industrial design.

The most articulate proposals for a serious look at popular culture came from a group of people with varied interest in the visual arts, who met at the Institute of Contemporary Arts in London in the early 1950s.

Instant City, 1969 **(left)**: urban culture, urban beings, urban communication, urban media, the world village, advertising consumerism led to a realization that the complexity of the city defied one person's planning.

In the 1950s design intellectuals found new soil to till: it is almost impossible to reconcile the prescribed social and aesthetic order of Corbusier **(left)** with the creamy, dreamy taste of Main Street **(right)**.

Membership of the group included Banham, the artists Richard Hamilton, Eduardo Paolozzi and John McCale, the critic Lawrence Alloway, the photographer Ian Henderson and the architects Alison and Peter Smithson. The first session was devoted to questions of a technological nature, and the second to popular culture, mainly because they discovered that this was a point of common interest.

The main area of debate was mass-produced urban culture and they set about it with all the seriousness usually bestowed upon fine art. Alloway described their ideal thus: 'The new role for the fine arts is to be one of the many possible forms of communication in an expanding framework that also includes the mass arts.'

The main problem was analysing this new material. Two members of the group went towards a solution. Banham advocated an anthropological definition of culture, which depended upon the examination of symbols and icons in society. McCale wrote two articles in 1959 entitled *The Expendable Icon*, in which he set out to define the essential quality of mass cultural icons, showing how they depended upon change and expendability.

The way in which this new 'both/and' view of culture and the idea of a new relationship between man and the world of objects was put into practice was by critical analysis of mass media products. The prevailing disapproval of American car design on the part of the British design establishment was broken when Banham championed such design as the perfect example of 'design-as-popular-symbolism'. Surface styling and

**WOULD THE MACHINE
STOP?**
In the 1950s the young
dreamed in coffee bars, but in the 1970s optimism
collapsed as the urban environment and the new
consumerism were found to be flawed, and the
mess of the throwaway society was like the dirty
crockery after the 1960s party.

anti-functionalist features were considered by the group to be the means by which the object world symbolized man's desires and aspirations, expressed mainly in terms of power and sex. Hamilton's *Hommage à Chrysler Corps* of 1957, a collage which made use of American car advertising, was a direct result of Banham's studies, as was the Smithsons' *House of the Future*, which exploited Detroit production techniques.

The effect of this critique of functionalism, both as a historical theory and as a contemporary aesthetic, was at first minimal. Yet it implied a new form for objects, and a new relationship between the design establishment and the consumer, based no longer on what the customer was thought to need but on what he wanted. It threatened the concept of 'good taste' which had been synonymous with 'good design', and led to a total redefinition of design, while the problem of expendability meant a radical modification of the purist, neo-Bauhaus mainstream design of the late 1950s.

Criticisms of the functionalist aesthetic continued to appear throughout the following decade, mainly in England, the US and Italy. In 1959, for instance, the poet Stephen Spender wrote an eloquent account of why he considered that 'functionalism is inadequate as an aesthetic creed'. He too saw the solution in terms of design allying itself to the more 'spontaneous aspects of culture', and he wrote: 'Perhaps espresso bars and jazz show an underlying sense that bad taste is nearer to the truest inspiration—which is life—than officialized good taste.' The fear, frequently reiterated, was that design no longer had man at its centre; that the emphasis upon manufacturing rather than the environment had won the day; in Herbert Read's terms, that the 'abstract' had overcome the 'humanistic'. In 1966 the design critic Ken Baynes wrote that: 'The functionalist aesthetic has outrun itself. It is a self-contained system of belief.' In 1968 historian Christopher Cornford added, with feeling: 'Just as cold rice pudding as an exclusive diet would become monotonous because the human palate has richer and more exotic ambitions, so also the Phileban forms of the Bauhaus do not exhaust the potentialities which human inventiveness could appropriately exact from machine processes.'

The critics of functionalism fell into two camps. On the one hand, they cast doubt on its theoretical foundations, and on the other, they found its aesthetic lacking in symbolic and expressive content. These criticisms in turn set off two distinct reactions. A new theoretical approach extended the anthropological idea of seeing design as a cultural symbol which reflected society as a whole, and a new design language developed which took expression, symbolism, ephemerality and fun as its *sine qua non*. The earliest sign of this new language was the movement in art and design known as 'pop'.

**217**

# Pop design

Writing in 1965, Michael Wolff announced: 'It will be a great day when cutlery and furniture designs (to name but two) swing like the Supremes.'

The changing attitudes of theorists and artists towards the 'mass' environment were absorbed by a number of the creators of the environment themselves, and new energy was injected into consumer design in the early 1960s.

In 1967 Paul Reilly, the director of the British Council of Industrial Design, commented ruefully that: 'We may have to learn to enjoy an entirely new palette, for gaudy colours have long been associated with expendable ephemera.' He bemoaned the fact that the taste revolution which had occurred at the beginning of the decade had forced the arbiters of 'good taste' to rethink their purist principles and adapt to the pressures of the market.

This change in Britain in the early 1960s was the result of several factors. They included the fears expressed by the critics of functionalism; the increasing affluence of the 'teenage' population and its growing dissatisfaction with the social and cultural values of its parents; and a general swing in the design profession towards the use of the expressive power of form and colour.

The anti-functional design ideals first took form in the new objects

and life-style accompaniments which the young generation adopted to express its values. The style was welcomed instinctively by the new youth culture in its music, behaviour and clothes, but was deliberately created by a number of designers who saw there the seeds of a design renaissance, and was commercially exploited by a host of entrepreneurs. No one single style characterized the 'movement'. It depended upon the freedom of ephemerality and stylistic variance. The changes occurred first in England and the US, and the American journalist Tom Wolfe captured the spirit of this liberation from the past when he wrote: 'Free form!

The 1960s: Mary Quant (**left**); modelling a space swimsuit in 1969, the year Americans walked on the moon (**right**); and stepping out in London's Kings Road, 1967 (**above**).

The psychedelic 1960s invented the discothèque, decorated with art nouveau-like designs for a Peter Pan generation. Flashing lights and loud music gave kids a temporary high by exciting their senses and obliterating thought.

Marvellous! No hung-up old art history for these guys. America's first unconscious avant-garde. To hell with Mondrian, whoever the hell he is. To hell with Moholy-Nagy, if anybody ever heard of him. Artists for the new age, sculptors for the new style and money for the . . . Yah! "lower orders".'

The new generation of designers consciously employed what came to be called the 'pop' aesthetic in their designs for clothes, furniture, ephemera and, in a few cases, architecture. Their visual sources were derived predominantly from the contemporary fine arts: the American proto-pop painter, Jasper Johns; the work of the third generation of British 'pop' painters at the Royal College of Art, who had picked up much of the mass-culture iconography that the Independent Group had focused upon; and the later 'op' movement in painting which emerged on both sides of the Atlantic. Another source was the visual imagery of the immediate environment, particularly that of the spaceman which had captured the public's imagination. By the mid-1960s, a cluster of images, icons and symbols provided source material for a new school of design, to whom the use of 'arbitrary' surface decoration—anathema to the purists—was welcome. The traditional, twentieth-century introverted relationship between form and function was thus replaced by a more extroverted connection between form and expression.

## POP FASHION

It was in the area of fashion that the new, expendable code of ethics was first expressed. In the early '60s, fashion design succeeded in exploiting the new mass culture based on youth and fun, forming an 'alternative' design profession which rejected the class-ridden aims of its predecessors and aligned itself instead with fine art. The critic Toni del Renzio described its significance: 'Fashion . . . is interesting because, frivolous as it is, it is one of the most successful and fast moving examples of the expendable arts of a technical age.' Clothing provided an immediate means of translating attitude into form, and many designers took this opportunity of evolving a new language of fashion.

Courrèges in France and Mary Quant in Britain were the first of a new wave of designers to realize that the fantasy element in clothing was of equal if not greater importance than the protective function, and to exploit this realization. When Quant opened Bazaar in the King's Road in 1955 she introduced clothing which openly rejected the austere, middle-aged sophistication of French *haute couture*. She stressed instead the 'fun' element of children's 'dressing-up'. Her ready-made identity kits—Christopher Robin, Bank of England and Coal-Heaver among them—proposed a new function for clothing which was classless and ephemeral. As well as liberating clothes from their psychological strait-jackets, Quant also modified the physical nature of clothing. She exaggerated Courrèges' mini-skirt and introduced 'hot-pants' which

**219**

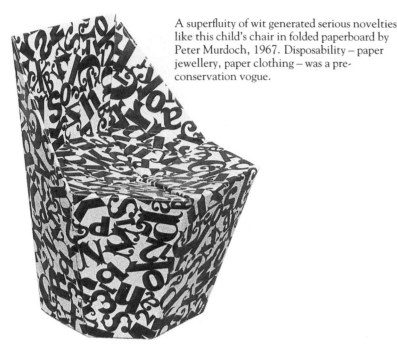

A superfluity of wit generated serious novelties like this child's chair in folded paperboard by Peter Murdoch, 1967. Disposability – paper jewellery, paper clothing – was a pre-conservation vogue.

220

The Italian company Kartell led the way in good design in plastics: these stacking chairs were designed by Jo Columbo in 1965.

increased freedom and movement, literally as well as symbolically. Two Royal College of Art graduates, Marion Foale and Sally Tuffin, were among the fashion designers of the 'boutique' era which developed in England in the early 1960s. The boutiques adopted the innovations of Quant in the area of women's clothing; in menswear, they started with John Stephen, who opened his first shop in Carnaby Street in 1959. Foale and Tuffin were directly influenced by the 'op' paintings of Derek Boshier and Brian Rice, and designed shifts in bright colours with strong geometrical shapes around the waist, neck and armholes—a variation of the 'pop' target which was used first by Jasper Johns in the mid-'50s. They also used the image of the flag, which appealed because of its lack of precise meaning and its high degree of visual impact. Fine art and design often influenced each other in this period, and Boshier was responsible for the flags on the changing-room curtains of a Carnaby Street women's boutique. 'Op' fashion also spread rapidly through the fashion pages of magazines in England and the United States in 1965 and 1966, and the painter Bridget Riley found her black and white 'op' images applied to fabric (in fact she strongly disapproved). The robot-like image which Courrèges created with his severe geometrical clothing forms led directly into his 'spaceman' look, developed through the use of synthetic materials, particularly plastics, in clothing.

## POP FURNITURE

There were also signs of change in the more functional areas of furniture and interior design at this time. Flexibility and expendability were embodied in the 'knock-down' furniture which appeared around 1965 and Peter Murdoch's 'throwaway' paper chairs repudiated once and for all the universality of Modernist forms. He defined furniture as flexible structures rather than sculptural monuments.

A further experiment with transient form was the inflatable furniture which was developed in Italy by Zanotta, Lomazzi, D'Urbino and De Pas; in France by Quasar Khanh; and in England by, among others, a firm called Incadinc. This in turn encouraged numerous sorties into 'free form' in a number of countries in subsequent years. The English architectural group Archigram designed an inflatable interior in 1965, demonstrating how the new interest in flexible structures led to a concern with whole environments. Pop icons including targets, Union flags and abstract patterns were added to items of furniture by Binder, Vaughan and Edwards who produced designs for Gear of Carnaby Street, and Jon Bannenberg designed a 'pop art' room for Mary Quant and her husband in 1965.

It was in Italy that the pop influence produced the most sophisticated, articulate and socially conscious design, particularly interior design. Strongly influenced by the soft sculptures of Claes Oldenburg, the new

**221**

Italian artist/designers rejected the smooth luxury of their elders and produced instead soft, malleable, humorous furniture with indeterminate or ambiguous shapes, often reinforcing its non-functionality by visual reference to other objects. The 'Sacco' of 1969 by Gatti, Paolini and Teodoro, and the playful 'Joe Sofa' of 1970 by Lomazzi, D'Urbino and De Pas led next to the fanciful and idealistic visions of Archizoom, Superstudio, Gruppo 9999, the UFO Group and others at the end of the 1960s.

The Viennese-born Ettore Sottsass, who mixed with the American underground and travelled to India in the early 1960s, saw in pop art 'an ironic attack on the nonsense of consumption'. He systematically applied pop iconography and colours to his designs for furniture and ceramics in order to 'widen the concept of functionalism to the subconscious and unconscious psychic spheres'. Gaetano Pesce also saw pop as a means of inflicting a direct blow to the double-headed giant of consumerism and rationalism. One of the founders of Group N in Padua in 1959, Pesce worked in the field of interior design from 1962, as well as in the visual arts. By removing the explicit function from his chairs and interiors and concentrating on the expression of symbolic themes like death and destruction, Pesce succeeded in eliminating the distinction between the designer and the artist.

Banham wrote in 1963 that: 'The aesthetics of pop depend upon a massive initial impact and small sustaining powers, and are therefore at their poppiest in products whose sole object is to be consumed.' This strong emphasis upon surface appeal meant that the traditional categories of objects became redundant as different consumer products were linked through common surface motifs. The designer Paul Clark, for instance, applied the Union flag and targets to drinking mugs, tiles and clocks, and the same images appeared on carrier bags, clothing, tea-towels and many

Freedom takes different forms in different countries: in America companies like ATC (this is their telephone) fed popular taste with greater licence than in Britain, where the phones required government approval which Mickey did not have.

### ALL MOONIES THEN?
The Cavern Club, Liverpool **(top left)**, led to the allegedly licentious pop festivals held in muddy fields **(far left)**. David Hockney, the charismatic English painter, was able to tease the establishment with his talent, but he later wooed them with his opera stage sets. People were bent on enjoyment, and the youth of the West seemed too distracted to care much that Americans were moon walking.

other suitable surfaces.

The problem that the 'pop' design movement presented to its successors was deciding on its ultimate significance. It was an essentially spontaneous movement and, as such, failed to provide a theory to justify its actions. Nor did it resolve the incompatibility of mass production and the freedom of the individual, nor provide more than a small number of designs which were truly innovatory. Contemporary critics disagreed radically about its importance. Ken Baynes stated optimistically in 1967 that 'one day Carnaby Street could rank with Bauhaus as a descriptive phrase for a design style or legend', whereas Corin Hughes-Stanton maintained a year later that 'red mugs, orange colanders, jolly washing-up cloths, bull's-eye trays and chests of drawers, export reject flowered cups and French peasant casseroles do not add up to a school of design'.

The awareness of an important new set of mass cultural values which questioned earlier ethical and aesthetic assumptions and the attempt to revise design accordingly were important steps forward. Pop involved taking a step back from the mainstream of development, and focusing away from production to consumption. Its effects were widespread, particularly in the fresh attitude towards the use of colour and expressive form in the environment.

Under the umbrella of pop a number of issues were raised which developed on parallel lines in the latter half of the 1960s. These included the central questions of taste and style, which developed into the question of revivalism in design; the role of individualism and expression, which was reconsidered in the context of a craft revival; a questioning of the importance of consumption which led to the 'Design for need' movement; and a thorough revision of Modernism, which led directly to post-Modernism. The rest of the book will consider each of these in turn.

Archigram's 'Instant City' sought to turn the lessons of Pop Art into popular architecture.

# Nostalgia and bad taste

One of the ways in which the pop revolution's desire to restore the psychological value of decoration in design was shown in the stylistic revivals of the 1960s. These followed a chronological sequence through fascination with Victoriana to the art nouveau and art deco style of the 1920s and 1930s. The 1970s witnessed the completion of the cycle with a revived interest in the 1940s and 1950s and, finally, the 1960s themselves. This involvement with the past was yet another rejection of the Modernists' obsession with the 'spirit of the age' and their wish to stand perpetually on the brink of the future. It also extended the concern with style in and for itself. It was the product of a period which lacked a self-contained theory of design, but which saw change in design as a tangible means of cultural reassessment, of reordering man's relationship with his environment. Looking back provided a form of comparison, anchoring what seemed like random thoughts and feelings to a model which was fixed by the flow of time.

The post-war interest in the Victorian age in England was largely a nostalgic quest for the comfort and opulence of Victorian middle-class life, as glimpsed through the extravagantly decorated objects found in attics. Peter Floud, in his exhibition of 1952 entitled *Victorian and Edwardian Arts,* modified this view of Victorian life by showing the work of more forward-thinking designers of the mid-nineteenth century, among them William Morris and members of the Arts and Crafts Movement and the Aesthetic Movement. The exhibition revealed the care of Victorian and Edwardian craftsmanship and the beauty of their floral patterns. These decorative ideas caught the imagination of the public in the 1950s and 1960s, encouraging firms like Sandersons to reprint Morris wallpaper from old blocks, while Liberty and Company, an old Aesthetic Movement shop, reproduced a collection of art nouveau furnishing fabrics. The *fin de siècle* mood, which shared in the 1960's preoccupation with the work of machine production and of the artist, inspired a fashion for anything that contained the familiar whiplash line, surface patterning or rich colours of the earlier period. In 1965 a writer commented: 'Stimulated initially by revivalist art exhibitions, the influence of art nouveau can already be spotted in many different forms—films, advertising, fashion and photography.' In England, then in the US and on the Continent, Morris wallpapers and Tiffany lamps were joined by pine-wood tables, jelly moulds and enamel mugs—the latter supplied in England by shops like Gear in Carnaby Street and Terence Conran's newly formed Habitat. The Portobello Road market

It is difficult to assess whether this London bathroom interior of 1976 is an example of deliberate kitsch; less inventive than psychedelia, and certainly ephemeral, it is a poor pastiche of art nouveau.

supplied Victorian clothing and general bric-à-brac.

The strongest nineteenth-century influence was in the area of graphic design. In America an exhibition of Mucha's work on the West Coast in 1963 inspired a new wave of poster designs which emulated the sinuous curves and complex linear patterns of art nouveau posters. Americans saw in this 'decadent' period of history a resemblance with the values of their new 'underground' society, in which 'mind-expansion' through hallucinogenic drugs became a way of life. The work of Wes Wilson and others, advertising rock concerts, was a reaction against Bauhaus typography and rationalism.

The 1966 Aubrey Beardsley exhibtion at the Victoria & Albert Museum marked the high point of England's contribution to underground graphics. It reinforced the *fin de siècle* idea of a poster as art object rather than mere advertising tool.

Among the artists to develop this new medium were Michael English and Nigel Waymouth, who together formed the company of Hapshash and the Coloured Coat. Their work showed traces of many diverse influences, among them surrealism and more ancient ethnic sources such as Red Indian engravings and illustrations to alchemic texts. It shared

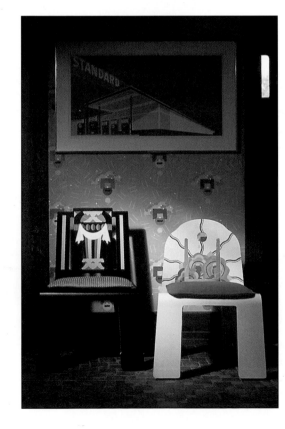

The 1980s saw a *trompe-l'oeil* revival of the 1950s **(right)**. Post-Modernism is both word-ridden and backward looking – irony, literary metaphor, visual puns and art history are seen in force in Robert Venturi's 1984 homage to Chippendale, art deco, Alvar Aalto etc., etc. Mackintosh reproductions **(above)** sold well.

with art nouveau an eclecticism which borrowed freely from the motifs of primitive cultures. The 'underground's' extension into the general environment via posters, illustrations and light-shows recalled the late-nineteenth-century interest in multi-media events like the dances of Loie Fuller. It shared the same preoccupation with sensation above rationality, with visual effect as opposed to function. In 1968 Christopher Cornford diagnosed the obsessive revival of art nouveau as, 'by no means only a fad, rather the search for a vitamin', showing how deeply its roots were embedded in social unrest.

Bevis Hillier commented in his *Art Deco of the '20s and '30s* that 'by the autumn of 1967 the force of art nouveau as a popular movement was practically spent'. It had been replaced by a move away from the sensuous floral style to the more geometric forms of the inter-war years, again inspired by an exhibition. This time it was the commemorative exhibition in Paris entitled *Les Années '25*, which took as its focus objects from the International Exhibition of Decorative Arts which had been held in Paris in 1925. The wide spectrum of 1925 was reflected in the variety it inspired—from the revival of purist Bauhaus furniture by Zeev Aram in England, Cassina in Italy and Knoll International in the US, to the kitsch interest in the extravagances and glamour of Hollywood. Like the late nineteenth century, the 1925 period of consolidation of machine production contained an essential dualism which was common to the 1960s—an interest in both élitist and mass taste. Bevis Hillier was the first chronicler of the popular end of this 'last of the total styles', and Martin Battersby added a history of its more purist aspects, creating a body of visual sources which were to move beyond design proper to music and film.

Aestheticization was a strong element in the continuation of stylistic revivals. It shifted the relationship between man and his environment one remove back from functional needs. The deliberate involvement with products as life-style signs led to a concern with taste, and particularly bad taste. 'Kitsch' was the term used to describe the new category of mass-produced ephemera to which the design world found it difficult to respond. Gillo Dorfles edited a book in 1968 entitled *Kitsch* which contained a number of papers on the subject, and Abraham Moles took a critical line in his book of 1970, in which he described Kitsch as 'the negation of the authentic'.

## CLAMOURING FOR THE REAL

The 1960s had been a lovely romp, as Carnaby Street boutiques retailed fun imitations of art nouveau jewellery (Mucha poster, **left**). But people woke up to find that even their bread had been transmuted by mega-manufacturers into something most horrible. Thus 'real' bread shops emerged, while the Campaign For Real Ale fought to bring back 'real' beer. CAMRA was so successful in its campaign that other consumer pressure groups have taken heart and now battle for reality in a plethora of consumerables.

# Craft and individualism

By the 1960s the Scandinavians' pioneering ideas about craft production had become submerged by their increasing involvement with industry and technique. But in Britain, where the nineteenth-century Arts and Crafts Movement had laid the foundations for a belief in craft as redemption from the machine, a renewed interest in the subject developed. By the 1970s, both Britain and the United States showed an interest in the ethical and aesthetic implications of hand-production in a highly industrialized society. A sense of nostalgia, for traditional methods of production rather than for decorative styles from the past, led to a search for new forms which fulfilled the craftsman's criteria of 'quality and variety'. The machine, with its commitment to expendability and standardization, had considerably undermined such qualities.

The ethical ideas about design and society put forward by the members of the Arts and Crafts Movement remained a characteristic of British design throughout the twentieth century, from the presence of Gordon Russell and Ambrose Heal in the Design and Industries Association, through the work of the studio potter Bernard Leach and his disciples in the 1920s, to the foundation in 1948 of the government-sponsored Crafts Centre, headed by John Farleigh. Within this apparently consistent tradition, however, disparate threads disentangled themselves. By the 1960s, the boundaries between 'artist-craftsman', 'artisan-craftsman' and 'designer-craftsman' had become indistinct and problematic. The ambiguous line between the fine and the industrial arts was exemplified in the work of some designers, among them the toy-maker Sam Smith, who saw their position as separate from that of the industrial designer, but who were nonetheless convinced that only hand-made products could 'help to raise industrial standards'. Others, including the silversmiths David Mellor and Robert Welch and the weaver Peter Collingwood, believed in a direct connecting line between the studio and the factory. Faith in such a collaboration characterized developments in British craft in the 1960s and Sir Gordon Russell, by 1965 the chairman of the Crafts Council, did all he could to encourage it, reinforcing his beliefs in an exhibition of craft at the Design Centre in the same year.

Yet ambiguity lingered, and by the end of the decade the pendulum had swung once more away from design and back to art. In 1973 an exhibition was sponsored by the newly formed Crafts Advisory Council which served 'to promote Britain's artist-craftsmen' at the Victoria & Albert Museum. Entitled 'The Craftsman's Art', it reflected a move away from the 'functional' aesthetic of the mid-'60s to a more 'romantic' use of hand-made form, in which material was subordinated to the artist's

Achille Castiglione's table for
Zanotta – 1958.

Craft had already been reinvented by potters like Bernard Leach in the 1920s to mean quasi-art or quasi-design. It grew strong in the 1970s in response to a demand for perceived quality, another aspect of the real bread phenomenon.

expressive intentions. In the words of James Noel White, 'painting is becoming sculpture, is becoming ceramic, is becoming three-dimensional weaving, is becoming jewellery'. This breakdown of the barriers between art and craft resulted in a new role for the artist-craftsman which minimized his relationship with industry. Familiar names like those of the studio potters Hans Coper and Ruth Duckworth were joined by a new generation which interpreted freely the expressive possibilities of both traditional and new craft materials. The work of the Crafts Council through the 1970s and 1980s helped develop in England a crafts revival, in which the artist-craftsman was the most favoured individual.

The American faith in making by hand was part of an indigenous transcendentalist tradition expounded in the writings of Thoreau and Whitman, but it was also rooted in the same nineteenth-century Arts and Crafts background. Twentieth-century pioneering craftsmen like the ceramicist Charles Binns worked alongside immigrant Scandinavians and Germans in the 1920s and 1930s. The Cranbrook Academy directed its attentions to craft education for 'a new life-style of self worth'. Interest in craft and studio work accelerated after the war, sponsored by the universities and by the establishment of the Museum of Contemporary Crafts in 1956. The intellectual attachment to the process of making by

232

Virtuosity once more in the making, but not by design – a yew stool by John Makepeace, 1973.

hand encouraged a sophisticated approach, and from the late 1950s craft was firmly allied to avant-garde fine art, from abstract expressionism to pop and funk in the 1960s and '70s. Peter Voulkos working with clay, Lenore Tawney the weaver, and Wharton Esherick with his work in wood, were responsible for initiating this exchange. Robert Arneson's satirical clay pieces reinforced a remark in the catalogue of the 1976 contemporary Craft exhibition, *Objects USA*, that: 'One of the most heartening developments in the arts in recent years has been a revision of attitudes regarding the crafts.'

The rejection of the technical and industrial model and the realignment with fine art made design, in the Crafts Revival movement, into its own critic. Like minimal and conceptual art, it was continually refining and analysing its own meaning, and denying its primary 'use' function. It was partly as a reaction against this intellectual distancing of design from its practical purpose, and partly in direct response to the moral question of consumer-design that the movement towards 'design for need' emerged in the late 1970s.

### RIGHTS ON
Kennedy was never blamed for getting America into Vietnam, the war which fuelled protest groups across America and Europe. But Bob Dylan did well with his peace lyrics. Women, recognizing that the liberal 1960s had done nothing for them, began to be politicized. Then Victor Papanek published **Design For The Real World**, upbraiding designers for not listening to people's needs. Influential among lecturers and students, it was soon superseded by technological advances that Papanek could not have imagined – such as the microchip.

# Design for need

The fear that design was losing its early missionary zeal was expressed in a pamphlet heralding a Society of Industrial Artists and Designers conference in 1973, 'Design for Quality in Life'. It was a growing preoccupation among designers and members of the public in the late 1960s. They saw design becoming a pawn in the game of conspicuous consumption, used for the refinement of 'toys for adults', rather than as a tool for improving the general conditions of life. The crisis of conscience precipitated a return to grass roots, in terms of the meaning and function of design. Many designers, architects and writers re-examined the ways in which design could provide answers to the problems which beset those who lacked the basic requirements of life—the poor, the homeless, the handicapped, the Third World. They also turned their attention to worldwide ecological problems such as pollution, shortage of resources and waste—to all of which industrial design had contributed. As early as 1954 the American architect Richard Neutra, in his book *Survival through Design*, had envisaged the possibility that 'man may perish by his own explosive and insidious inventions'. He maintained that this fate could be avoided if design turned from its commercial ends to meet psychological needs, and if the notion of 'general and integrated design on a world-wide scale' could be adopted. This resembled Richard Buckminster Fuller's concept of 'Comprehensive, Anticipatory, Design-Science Exploration'. After the death of his daughter in 1917, Fuller devoted his life to discovering ways of solving design problems in order 'to better man's effective survival chances'. He was concerned with the development of designs which would improve life directly, rather than merely make money to buy living-means. His vision embraced a new, worldwide, non-political industry, as well as objects of transport and shelter.

Fuller's influence in the post-war period derived from his theoretical statements, which became ever more relevant in a world of accelerating consumption, and from his designs for living structures, which were based upon his ideas of 'synergetic and energetic geometry'. Dome structures based on Fuller's designs appeared in many different

Peter Cook's Arcadian city, 1976: the twentieth-century urban architect returned to the garden city idea to fulfil the need for more trees, less concrete.

Capsule kitchen designed in 1968 by Allied
Ironfounders – it was functional and designed for
its space-saving purpose.

corners of the globe from 1952 onwards, wherever there was a need for
light, prefabricated shelters. In 1963 Fuller began his World Resources
Inventory at Southern Illinois University, consolidating his commitment to 'the era of survival'.

The use of technology as a basic resource was a fundamental premise
of 'design for need', and distinguished it from the pre-industrial stance of
the craft revival. The movement identified itself in the 1960s with the
idea of an 'alternative technology' which had grown out of a feeling of
disillusion with the effects of the prevailing economic system controlling
technology and its products. Industrial design, as it had developed in the
last thirty years, was seen as an ideological support to this system,
furthering its ends and impotent to look outside them or change them in
any way.

In his 1973 book *Design for the Real World*, Victor Papanek put
forward a definitive account of this situation, showing where and how
changes could be made. His analysis of contemporary design was
expressed in the emotive statement, 'today industrial design has put
murder on a mass-production basis', and he considered that until
designers took a morally and socially responsible attitude towards their
work, instead of simply perpetuating design's position as 'a marketing tool
of big business', it would be better if design activities ceased altogether.
Papanek advocated 'a return from form to content', showing how
designing for people's needs rather than for their wants was the only
meaningful direction for design. He suggested that all designers should

spend a percentage of their time on such problems. Such a view was idealistic and Papanek admitted that achieving his Utopia would require a revolution in design theory and education, as well as in economic organization. His book filled a gap in design theory, moving beyond a concern with production and form, towards a view of design in use. It allied the designer to the sociologist and the anthropologist, and put forward the idea of 'total design', which would bring together the architect, the industrial designer, the graphic designer, and the regional and city planner. Papanek confronted head-on the forging of a new relationship between man and his environment, exploring all the avenues of theoretical possibilities.

**237**

Many other examples of 'alternative design' appeared in the late 1960s and early 1970s in America and Europe. The American *Whole Earth Catalog*, edited by Stewart Brand from 1968, was a stocklist of design which fulfilled needs rather than wants, and became a hand-book for all those who allied themselves to the causes of conservation and 'real design'. In England the Royal College of Art developed its researches into the design of hospital and medical equipment through the 1960s and '70s. In April 1976 it organized an exhibition and symposium entitled *Design for Need*, at which Papanek's analysis was repeated in this statement: 'Changes of attitude towards the consumer society, combined with the growing awareness of the need for resource-conservation, the dangers of pollution and the threat of a growth economy to the quality of life, have brought into question the functions and purposes of industrial design, as they have done also with certain applications of advanced technology.'

'Survival through Design' developed, in the 1970s, into a popular interest in 'autonomous' services like those provided by methane gas and solar heating, and in 'Do-it-Yourself', encouraged by a spate of publications which included Papanek and Hennessey's *Nomadic Furniture* of 1973-4, the mail-order *Survival Scrapbooks*, which circulated widely on the west coast of America, and B. and R. Vale's *The Autonomous House* of 1975. Design took on a strong environmental concern, but there was little evidence of this threatening its traditional role as part of the industrial complex. The new definition of design existed alongside its other manifestations, as one element of the pluralism which characterized the early 1970s.

**AND THE WORLD SHRANK**
In the 1970s everyone discovered their rights – including OPEC's Sheikh Yamani (far left), who scared western economies into energy conservation with price increases. Conservation went from being cranky to being serious politics as everyone got everyone else's pollution, and handy television told people that their world was dying.

# Post-Modernism

The movement covered by the umbrella term 'post-Modern' rejected the absolutist approach of the Modern Movement. Post-Modernism described a general cultural mood, expressed in such diverse disciplines as literature, philosophy, political theory, critical theory, politics, architecture and design.

The roots of post-Modern architecture lay in the US in the early post-war period. In 1966 the American architect Robert Venturi published his seminal book, *Complexity and Contradiction in Architecture*, giving the movement a manifesto. Venturi proposed an architecture which was all the things Modernism was not—messy, complex, ambiguous, eclectic, symbolic, historical—and he quickly turned into a spokesman for 'post-Modern' architecture.

The architecture Venturi produced in the 1960s had close affinities with the contemporary 'pop' painting movement, and he sought his imagery within mass culture and the mass environment. Later American architects who clustered around the 'post-Modern' label included Michael Graves, Robert Stern, Richard Meier and, a little later, the ex-pupil and follower of Mies van der Rohe, Philip Johnson. These architects moved away from mass culture, making sophisticated refer-

Post-Modernism: Terry Farrell's Water Treatment Plant, Reading **(left)**, and a house by a leading American architect, Michael Graves **(above)**. Charles Jencks, American architectural critic, popularized the term 'post-Modernism', which refers to an eclectic movement, taking images from all kinds of art and architecture. Most architects, embarrassed by the stylistic confusion that has resulted, exclaim they neither use nor understand the term. It mostly means 'anti-Bauhaus'.

A house by Ricardo Bofill, the leading exponent
of concrete neo-classicism. He prefabricates in
concrete buildings that have a strange tendency
to look like stage sets.

### THUGGERY AND PROTEST
Britain: the Carnaby
Street Union Jack was usurped by proto fascists,
the youth of the Nazi-styled National Front, who
terrified anyone who was weak, especially Asian
immigrants. The predicted social backlash by the
disaffected unemployed spent itself in marches,
but no one predicted the establishment of the
all-women Peace Camp at Greenham Common.

242

ences to past architectural styles, in particular Classicism. Like Modernism before it, post-Modernism in the US became recognizable in the late 1970s and '80s by its use of historical motifs, its pastel colours and its shared irony.

It was Charles Jencks' book *Post-Modern Architecture*, first published in the late 1970s, which gave this previously open-ended movement a name and an identity. Aiming to provide a 'semiotic' analysis of the rhetoric of modern architecture which sidestepped Modernist reductivism, Jencks gathered together illustrations of much international architecture, all of which shared an emphasis on content over form, symbolism over rationality and multiple meanings over single meanings. The book served to crystallize an international mood and to articulate what had until then been unspoken, intuitive reactions and intentions. In some ways too, the book signalled the death of the movement by making explicit some qualities of the new architecture which worked

Post-Modern design was anything you could get away with, although frequently it collapsed out of irony into whimsy: wit was a prerequisite for success. A Memphis vase by Marco Zanini, 1982 **(above)** indicates that the style works better as small ornament than as large furnishings **(right)**.

### PRIVATE LIVES

The post-Modern world places a huge value on entertainment and privacy. The Sony Walkman allows the individual to live in a private reality where the world unfolds to a 'film' score of his or her own choosing. The home – with its hi-fi, videos and television – is the centre of private fantasy. In Britain, where every person's home is his (or her) castle, sales of video recorders, like this one by Sony, have boomed.

James Dyson's vacuum cleaner, 1983, was seized upon as an example of the new wave in industrial design but **(below)** Bauhaus modern also enjoyed a revival.

more effectively on a subliminal level.

Whether post-Modernism amounted to a movement or simply to a set of shared responses to the post-pop cultural situation remains to be seen. Its proposals were, however, powerful for a generation disillusioned with bland tower-blocks.

The strongest and most publicized examples of post-Modernism in the world of design emerged from Italy. This was the country which, along with Britain, had engendered the most articulate responses to the pop movement in the 1960s in a desire to rid architecture and design of their associations with Fascism in the inter-war years. Italian architects and designers had mounted a full-scale anti-Modern campaign from the 1950s onwards, seeking allegiance with the more expressive qualities manifested in contemporary fine art instead.

The work of Ettore Sottsass and others in the mid-'60s took inspiration first from 'pop' art 'op' art and minimal sculpture and, later in the decade, from conceptualism. By the early '70s anti-Modernism in Italy had developed a number of sophisticated alternative strategies and, at the end of that decade, had found an opportunity to develop them into a fully fledged movement which had much in common with international post-Modernism.

Two forms of sanitized radicalism: tidy fake decay
by the SITE architects for a chain of American
supermarkets; and the new Modernism of the
Hong Kong and Shanghai Bank by Foster
Associates.

The appropriately visceral imagery of Aachen
Hospital, West Germany.

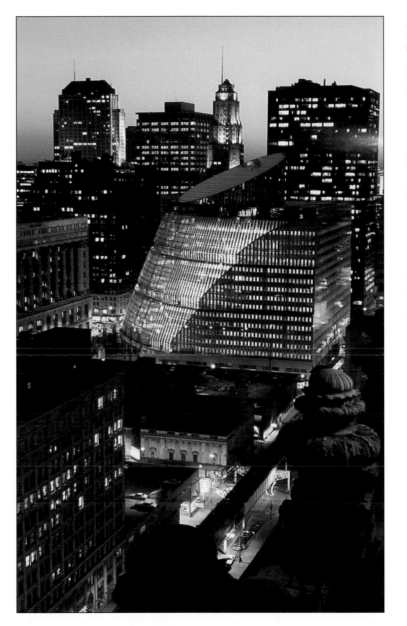

The 1980s saw not only pluralism but the rise once again of the mega building: the State of Illinois Center **(above)**, designed by Murphy Jahn.

The work of individuals such as Sottsass, Andrea Branzi, Michele de Lucchi and others openly espoused eclecticism, stylistic revivalism, decoration, irony and fun. They were associated first with Studio Alchymia, a gallery in Milan, and, from 1981, with Sottsass' group of radical furniture designers, Memphis. Their pieces stood as open threats to the black leather and chrome neo-Modernism of the Italian design establishment and opened a debate about taste which is still going on in Italy and elsewhere. The popular welcome for this new aesthetic, and its immediate translation into a range of mass-produced ephemeral goods, from graphics to fashion, guaranteed it an enormous audience worldwide. Its success lay in this consumer appeal, its acceptance of expendability, and its emphasis on image over form.

Whether the Italian movement will achieve historical significance or whether it will be documented as simply one of the many transient, fashionable styles of the uncertain 1980s remains to be seen. It played an important part in the replacement of Modernism by a set of alternatives and it was an object lesson in how the mass media appropriate and disseminate design innovation.

Post-Modernism, as a term for all those 'messy' design manifestations which resisted categorization, has had a wide influence, emerging in a number of countries, particularly Japan, the US and Italy in both avant-garde and commercial contexts. Through its acceptance of 'mass culture' it has succeeded to some extent in bridging the gap between the two ends of the cultural spectrum, going some way towards fulfilling the symbolic needs of today's pluralistic society.

247

# CONCLUSION

In the 1980s the term 'design' has been appropriated by the mass media and the advertising industry as *the* way of claiming 'added desirability' in products, if not actually putting it there. Style-consciousness has became a *sine qua non* not just of the young, but of the whole spectrum of consumers, and ever more sophisticated product differentiation has meant there are style-choices available for every social sub-group, whether determined by sex, age, class or income.

The democratization of design has, by the '80s, become a reality affecting nearly every consumption choice. The acceleration of stylistic redundancy has the designer increasingly in demand, needed to provide a constant flow of styles which replace each other in the market-place. With advances in micro-processing, manufacturing industry has begun to organize its production methods so as to allow greater stylistic variation. The old, Fordist system, which equated mass production with standardization, is defunct, as is the Modernist equation of mechanization and universality.

Yet Modernism still lingers on. Its values still determine much design, particularly within the areas of education and design reform. Although part and parcel of mass production and mass consumption, some design still resists the implication of this alliance, preferring to take its values from the more exclusive area of craft production.

The story of modern design from the eighteenth century onwards is the story of this resistance, of the tension between the relentless rule of commerce and the idealism of countless individuals who refused to accept the demise of craftsmanship and the values engendered. In the mid-1980s, the phrases 'truth to materials' and 'fitness to purpose' still echo in our ears, in spite of their seeming inappropriateness for objects such as microwave ovens and jug-kettles. The sprig of corn on the side of the toaster is a reminder of rural life, even though it is no threat to the dominance of the all-white kitchen—itself a relic of the days when rationalism ruled.

The main lesson to be learnt from this account is that cultural change takes place at a much slower rate than changes in the organization of production and consumption. While the beginnings of mass consumption, the rule of fashion and the link between the possession of certain objects and social status were realities as early as the eighteenth century in England, in the mid-1980s we have still not fully learnt to come to terms with these forces.

# INDEX

Page numbers in *italic* refer to the illustrations and captions

**251**

# SELECTIVE BIBLIOGRAPHY

## CHAPTER 1 DESIGN AND COMMERCE IN THE EIGHTEENTH CENTURY

M. Berg, *The Age of Manufactures 1700-1820,* London, 1985

H.W. Dickenson, *Matthew Boulton,* Cambridge, 1936

B. Hillier, *Pottery and Porcelain 1700-1914,* London, 1968

J. Kenworthy-Browne, *Chippendale and his Contemporaries,* London, 1975

P. Mathias, *The Transformation of England,* London, 1979

N. McKendrick, J. Brewer and J.H. Plumb, *The Birth of a Consumer Society: The Commercialization of Eighteenth Century England,* London, 1983

## CHAPTER 2 MECHANIZATION AND DESIGN 1830-1914

S. Giedion, *Mechanization takes Command,* New York, 1969

H.J. Habakkuk, *American and British Technology in the Nineteenth Century,* Cambridge, 1962

D. Hounshell, *From the American System to Mass Production,* Baltimore, 1985

L. Mumford, *Technics and Civilization,* London 1934

T. Veblen, *Theory of the Leisure Class,* New York, 1899

## CHAPTER 3 DESIGN REFORM 1830-1914

E. Aslin, *The Aesthetic Movement,* London, 1969

A. Boe, *From Gothic Revival to Functional Form,* Cambridge, 1957

W. Hamish Fraser, *The Coming of the Mass Market,* London, 1981

S.T. Madsen, *Art Nouveau,* London, 1967

G. Naylor, *The Arts and Crafts Movement,* London, 1971

M.J. Weiner, *English Culture and the Decline of the Industrial Spirit,* Cambridge, 1981

## CHAPTER 4 POLITICS, SOCIETY AND DESIGN

S. Bann, *The Tradition of Constructivism,* London, 1974

C. Gray, *The Great Experiment: Russian Art 1863-1922,* London, 1982

H. Jaffé, *De Stijl,* London, 1970

B.M. Lane, *Architecture and Politics in Germany 1918-1945,* Massachusetts, 1968

R. Cowan Schwartz, *More Work for Mother: The Ironies of Household Technology from the Open Hearth to the Microwave,* New York, 1983

## CHAPTER 5 INDUSTRY, TECHNOLOGY AND DESIGN

J. Dubois, *Plastics History USA,* Massachusetts, 1972

A. Forty, *Objects of Desire,* London, 1986

R.W. Fox and T.J. Jackson, *The Culture of Consumption,* New York, 1983

J. Meikle, *Twentieth-Century Limited: Industrial Design in America 1925-1939,* Philadelphia, 1979

L. Mumford, *Art and Technics,* London, 1953

A. Pulos, *The American Design Ethic,* Massachusetts, 1982

## CHAPTER 6 THEORY AND DESIGN

R. Banham, *Theory and Design in the First Machine Age,* London, 1960

M. Berman, *All that is Solid Melts into Air: The Experience of Modernity,* New York, 1982

P. Collins, *Changing Ideals in Modern Architecture,* London, 1969

V. Conrads, *Programmes and Manifestos on Twentieth Century Architecture,* London, 1970

C. Jencks, *Le Corbusier and the Tragic View of Architecture,* Great Britain, 1973

G. Naylor, *The Bauhaus Reassessed,* London, 1986

## CHAPTER 7 POPULAR STYLE IN THE 1930s

D. Bush, *The Streamlined Decade,* New York, 1975

M. Grief, *Depression Modern: The Thirties Style in America,* New York, 1975

B. Hillier, *Art Deco,* London, 1968

P. Sparke, *Consultant Design,* London, 1981

G. Veronesi, *Style and Design 1909-1929,* New York, 1968

## CHAPTER 8 RECONSTRUCTION AND DESIGN

J.K. Galbraith, *The Affluent Society,* Harmondsworth, 1962

K.B. Heisinger (ed), *Design since 1945,* London, 1983

T. Hine, *Populuxe,* New York, 1986

F. MacCarthy, *A History of British Design 1830-1970,* London, 1979

D. McFadden (ed), *Scandinavian Modern Design 1880-1981,* New York, 1982

V. Packard, *The Hidden Persuaders,* Harmondsworth, 1960

P. Sparke, *Ettore Sottsass,* London, 1981

## CHAPTER 9 DESIGN AFTER MODERNISM

H. Foster, *The Anti-Aesthetic: Essays on Post-Modern Culture,* Washington, 1983

W.F. Haug, *Critique of Commodity Aesthetics,* London, 1986

D. Hebdidge, *Subculture – The Meaning of Style,* London, 1979

C. Jencks, *The Language of Post-Modern Architecture,* London, 1979

V. Papanek, *Design for the Real World,* London, 1972

P. Sparke (ed), *Reyner Banham: Design By Choice,* London, 1981

# ACKNOWLEDGEMENTS

The pictures are reproduced by permission of the following sources. (Abbreviations: *t* top; *l* left; *r* right; *b* bottom; *c* centre; *f* far; *m* middle)

p12 Angelo Hornak; p13 E T Archive; p14-15 Bridgeman Art Library; p15 *t* Bridgeman Art Library, *b* E T Archive; p16 *l* Bridgeman Art Library, *r* Angelo Hornak; p17 *t* E T Archive, *bl* BPCC/ Aldus Archive, *br* Angelo Hornak; p18 *tl, cr* Bridgeman Art Library, *cl, b* E T Archive; p19 *bl, br* E T Archive; p20 Bridgeman Art Library; p21 *cr* Victoria and Albert Museum, *b* Bridgeman Art Library; p22 *l, tr, b* Bridgeman Art Library; p23 *c, b* E T Archive; p25 *tl* Mansell Collection, *tr* Wedgwood, *bl* Royal College of Surgeons; p26 *br* E T Archive, *tl, br* Bridgeman Art Library, *tr, bl* BPCC/Aldus Archive; p27 *l, r* E T Archive; p28 Wedgwood; p29, 32 Victoria and Albert Museum/photo Eileen Tweedy; p31 Mansell Collection; p33 Bridgeman Art Library; p34 *l, r*, p35 Victoria and Albert Museum; p36, 37 Western Americana; p38 *l, r* Victoria and Albert Museum, *c* Science Museum; p39 Science Museum; p40 *t* E T Archive, *b* Mansell Collection; p41 *t* E T Archive, *c, r* Bridgeman Art Library; p42 Peter Roberts; p43 BPCC/Aldus Archive; p44 *tl, b* Western Americana; 45 *l, r* BPCC/Aldus Archive; p46 *l, r* p47, 48 *l, r* Western Americana; p49 Bridgeman Art Library; p50 *l* BPCC/Aldus Archive; p50-1 Peter Roberts; p52 *l* Bridgeman Art Library; p52-3 E T Archive; p53 *tr, c* BPCC/Aldus Archive; p53 *b*, p54 Western Americana; p55, 56 *l* Bridgeman Art Library, *r* Angelo Hornak; p59 *t* Victoria and Albert Museum, *b* E T Archive; p60 *t, b* Bridgeman Art Library; p61, 62 BPCC/Aldus Archive; p63, 64 *l* E T Archive; p64-5 E T Archive; p65 *b, r*, p66, 67 National Portrait Gallery; p68 E T Archive; p68-9 *b* BPCC/Aldus Archive; p69 Angelo Hornak; p71 E T Archive; p72 *t* BPCC/Aldus Archive, *bl, br* E T Archive; p72-3 Fine Art Photographic Library; p73 *r* E T Archive; p75, 76 *l, r*, 77 *tl, bl* Bridgeman Art Library; p77 *bc, b* Angelo Hornak; p78 *tl, tr* E T Archive, *b* BPCC/Aldus Archive; p79 *t* Fine Art Photographic Library, *b* Angelo Hornak; p80 *l* Bridgeman Art Library, *r*, p81 *t, c, b* Angelo Hornak; p82 *t* BPCC/Aldus Archive; p83 *tl* Angelo Hornak, *tr* Bridgeman Art Library, *b, t* Architectural Association; p84 *b* Bridgeman Art Library; p85 *tl, b* BPCC/Aldus Archive, *tc* Western Americana, *tr* E T Archive; p86 *tl* Angelo Hornak, *bl* David King, *br* BPCC/Aldus Archive; p88 David King; p89 Design Council; p90 Imperial War Museum; p91 *t* BBC Hulton, *b* David King; p92 David King; p93 *tl* E T Archive, *tr* Bridgeman Art Library, *bl* David King; p94-5, 96 *tl, tr, b* David King; p98 *l* Architectural Association, *r* RIBA/photo Jeremy Butler; p99 *l* E T Archive, *r* RIBA/ photo Jeremy Butler; p100 *t* BBC Hulton, *b* Ullstein Bilderdienst; p101 *l* Western Americana, *r* Peter Roberts; p102 *t* Western Americana, *bl* David King, *br* E T Archive; p103, 104 *l, r* Western Americana; p106 *t* BBC Hulton, *b* Western Americana; p107 *t* BPCC/Aldus Archive, *b* Western Americana; p108 Victoria and Albert Museum; p109 Western Americana; p110-111 Peter Roberts, p111 Western Americana; p112 Design Council; p113 *t* Peter Roberts, *b* Angelo Hornak; p114 Rasmujssens Snedkerier; p115 *t*, p116 *b* A.B. Gustavsberg, *l* Svensk Tenn, *r* Design Council; p117 *l, r*, p118 Design Council; p119 *l* BBC Hulton; p120 *t* Design Council, *b* E T Archive; p121 *l, r* Design Council; p122 Victoria and Albert Museum; p123 *l, r* Design Council; p124 *l* BPCC/Aldus Archive; p125 *t* Design Council; p126 Bauhaus Archiv; p127 *cr* E T Archive; p128 *tr* Bauhaus Archiv, *br* E T Archive; p129 Bridgeman Art Library; p.131 *br* Bauhaus Archiv, *tl* BBC Hulton; p133 *br* BPCC/Aldus Archive; p139 E T Archive; p140 *tr, b*, p141 *l, tr*, p142 *tl* Deidi von Schaewen; p142 *bl*, p144 *bl* Bauhaus Archiv; p145 *tl* Ullstein Bilderdienst, *bl* Bauhaus Archiv; p146, 147 *t, br* Design Council; p148 BPCC/Aldus Archive; p150 *l* Western Americana; p151 *cl* Architectural Association, *br* Popperfoto; p152 Ullstein Bilderdienst; p153 *tl* BPCC/Aldus Archive; p154 Angelo Hornak; p155 Western Americana; p157 Musée des Arts Decoratifs, Paris; p158 *l* BPCC/ Aldus Archive, *t, r*, p159 *r* Angelo Hornak; p160 *l* Metropolitan Museum of Art, New York, *br* Museum of Modern Art, New York, *tc* BPCC/Aldus Archive; p162 *l, c*, p163 Angelo Hornak; p164 *r* BPCC/Aldus Archive; p165 *tr* Bettman Archive, NY/BBC Hulton; p166 E T Archive; p167 *l* Angelo Hornak; *r* Design Council; p168 *l* Design Council, *c*, p169 *r* Western Americana, *c* Peter Roberts; p170 *r*, p171, 172 *r* Bettman Archive, NY/ BBC Hulton; p173 *t* Design Council; p174, 175 *br* Svensk Tenn; p175 *tr* Design Council; p176 *tl* Massachusetts Institute of Technology; p177 Nordiska Kompaniet; p178 *tl* Daily Telegraph Colour Library, *bl* Fritz Hansens eft, *br* Herman Miller Inc, USA; p179 Peter Roberts; p180 Herman Miller Inc, USA; p181 Zanotta spa; p182, 183 *l* Svensk Tenn; p183 *tr*, 184 *tl*, 185 *b* Design Council; p186 *l*, 187 *b* Fritz Hansens eft; p186 Louis Poulson & Co; p188 *t* Wartsila; p189 Design Council; p190 *tr* Chevrolet, *cr* Design Council; p191 BPCC/Aldus Archive; p192 Popperfoto; 193 *br, r* Design Council, *bl* Western Americana; p194, 195 *tl, bl* Popperfoto; p195 *tr* BPCC/Aldus Archive; p196 *tr*, 197 *tl* Design Council; p198 *tl* Peter Roberts, *tr* Western Americana, *b* Popperfoto; p199 Popperfoto; p200 *tr* BBC Hulton, *br* Design Council; p201 *l* Tate Gallery/E T Archive, *tr* Design Council; p202 *b* BPCC/Aldus Archive, *tr* Olivetti; p203 Ettore Sottsass; p204 Gaetano Pesce, *tr* Design Council; p205 Brionvega Spa; p206-9 Design Council; p210 Deidi von Schaewen; p211 Cassina; p212 *bl* Design Council, *cr* Sony; p213 *Daily Telegraph* Colour Library; p214 Deidi von Schaewen; p215 *t* Architectural Association, *cr* Peter Roberts, p216 *tl* Popperfoto, *bl* BPCC/ Aldus Archive; p217 BBC Hulton; p218 *bl, cr* Popperfoto, *r* BBC Hulton; p219 *Daily Telegraph* Colour Library; p220 Design Council; 221 BPCC/Aldus Archive; p223 *bl* *Daily Telegraph* Colour Library, *tl* Popperfoto; p224 Architectural Association; p225 BBC Hulton; p228 Bridgeman Art Library; p229 *b* BBC Hulton, *tl* BPCC/Aldus Archive; p231 *bl, cr* Design Council, p232 *tl* John Makepeace; p233 *tr* BBC Hulton; p234 Architectural Association; p235 Design Council; p236 BBC Hulton, *r* Sony; p237 BBC Hulton; p238 Architectural Association; p239 Deidi von Schaewen; p240 *Daily Telegraph* Colour Library; p241 Popperfoto; p242 *tl* Design Council, *br* Deidi von Schaewen, *bl*, p243 Sony; p244 *tl* Design Council, *r* Deidi von Schaewen; p245 E T Archive; p246, 247 Deidi von Schaewen.

Quarto Publishing plc would like to thank Michelle Stamp and Alun Jones of Crucial Books.